instructional design for special education

instructional design for special education

David Baine

University of Alberta
Edmonton, Alberta
Canada

Educational Technology Publications
Englewood Cliffs, New Jersey 07632

Library of Congress Cataloging in Publication Data

Baine, David.
  Instructional design for special education.

  Bibliography: p.
  Includes index.
  1. Instructional systems. 2. Resource programs
(Education) 3. Handicapped children--Education.
I. Title
LB1028.35.B34   371.9   81-9693
ISBN 0-87778-179-6   AACR2

Printed in the United States of America.

Library of Congress Catalog Card Number:
81-9693.

International Standard Book Number:
0-87778-179-6.

First Printing: January, 1982.

Acknowledgments

THANKS to: My wife Karen for advice, assistance, and love
my family: Elsie and Grace
my helpers: Judy, Carla, Linda, and Nancy; and
Holly at the Fidalgo School
Siegfried Engelmann, Wesley Becker, and Douglas
Carnine whose work in the area of instructional
design and special education has influenced me
significantly

THANKS also for sabbaticals, Guemes, Triste, Alice, and Mrs.
Benny

Preface

This book is designed for senior undergraduate and graduate students in courses on instructional design. The material is suitable for regular education students in general, and special education students in particular. No previous training or instruction is required; thus, the material is introductory. Because the text provides an in-depth study of each topic, and because many research questions are raised, the content is also suitable for advanced students.

As the techniques described are appropriate for the instruction of both young children and low functioning children and youth, the material is applicable to preservice and inservice personnel in regular and special education. All of the examples used in the text have been taken from special education. The techniques described may be used for the instruction of motor, preacademic, academic, prevocational, vocational, language, self-help, and personal-social development. The methods fill the gap between theory and practice for instructional personnel attempting to implement the policies of *zero exclusion, normalization, accountability,* and *individual educational programming* (IEP) in special education.

The text has a dual purpose. First, the material is designed to provide teachers and allied personnel with an understanding of the nature and the rationale of highly structured, prepackaged instructional programs. The reader is shown how to select, adapt, implement, and validate these materials in the classroom. The book also reviews a number of practical educational techniques that may be directly adopted by classroom teachers. The second and major purpose of the text is to provide a complete step-by-step guide to instructional design for students being trained to develop and evaluate prepackaged instructional programs; the book discusses what to do, why it should be done, and when and how to do it.

The methods described in the book incorporate systems analysis, applied behavior analysis, and direct instruction techniques. Systems analysis involves a systematic sequence of steps and decisions made in the development, evaluation, and revision of instructional programs. The approach employs the use of behavioral objectives, task analysis, criterion-referenced testing, and formative and summative evaluation. The systems approach is usually represented by flowcharts depicting the sequences of steps, decisions, and options involved.

The behavioral approach focuses upon the systematic modification of observable, measurable behavior. Cognitive, perceptual, and affective goals of instruction are operationally defined in objective terms. The approach employs techniques such as shaping, chaining, prompting, fading, and reinforcement. Applied behavior analysis is an empirical, data-based approach in which instructional decisions regarding when, what, and how to teach are founded upon a continuous evaluation of individual learner responses. The direct instruction model involves preanalyzed instruction, sequenced into graduated steps coordinating scripted teacher instruction, evaluation, correction, reinforcement, and management strategies, and instructional materials. The approach employs placement tests, homogeneous instructional grouping, and a structured teaching model including readiness signals, focusing and response prompts, continuous evaluation, feedback, correction, and reinforcement procedures.

A number of instructional techniques are employed in the text. Brief advance organizers at the beginning of each chapter describe the content that follows. Each chapter reviews and incorporates material discussed in preceding chapters. All technical terminology is introduced in *italic type* and is clearly defined in the context of the discussion. Numerous practical examples are used throughout. Flowcharts and checklists are used to provide abbreviated summaries of the sequences of steps and decisions involved in developing and evaluating various aspects of instruction. Each topic area concludes with a review of the major concepts and procedures presented.

The methods discussed in the text have a theoretical and/or

empirical basis. Many of the techniques have been repeatedly tested in well controlled experimental studies with a variety of learners. Some of the methods, however, have been evaluated under very restricted conditions with limited numbers and types of subjects and tasks. Because of the variety, complexity, and changing relationship between learners, teachers, learning tasks, and instructional methods, materials, and contexts, instructional design is an extremely complex area of study. As a result, it is difficult to establish the general validity of any technique used singly or in combination with other procedures. Thus, the reader is urged to thoroughly study the chapter on formative and summative evaluation before employing the methods discussed in the text.

D.B.
June, 1981

Table of Contents

instructional design
for special education

Chapter 1

Behavioral Objectives

Contents

Behavioral Objectives: Introduction

Terminal behavioral objectives describe the observable, measurable behaviors that a learner should be able to perform at the end of an instructional unit or program. *Enabling* instructional objectives describe the *skills* that a learner must acquire to progress from his/her *entry* (initial) level of achievement to a terminal behavioral objective.

Terminal objectives, found at the end of an instructional module, are usually quite detailed and make an explicit statement about a *learner's performance,* the *conditions* under which s/he will perform, and the *standards* of performance that must be achieved. The following is an example of a terminal behavioral objective.

> *Given* two objects of different heights, the learner will point to the tallest object. During 20 trials, the pairs of objects will be randomly placed in an upright position, one inch to 12 inches

3

apart. The objects will differ 1/2 inch to three inches in height
and will be different in color, shape, and design. The learner must
respond correctly on the first try within three seconds on 17/20
trials. No error should be committed where the difference in
height between the objects is greater than one inch or where the
objects are placed less than eight inches apart.

This terminal objective describes the *conditions* that the learner
will be *given* (20 pairs of objects differing in position, height,
color, shape, and design), the observable, measurable behavior
performed by the *learner* (point to the tallest object), and the
standards of performance that s/he must achieve (the number of
correct responses, time limits, and an error tolerance).

   Enabling objectives are found *within* an instructional module.
During the early stages of program development, enabling objectives
are not described in as much detail as are terminal objectives. As a
program is tested with various learners, some enabling objectives
may be expanded, revised, or deleted, and new objectives may be
added. An example of an *enabling* behavioral objective follows:

Given an underlined, single syllable word followed by three single
syllable words, one of which rhymes with the sample word, the
learner will underline the rhyming word.

After several applications with a variety of learners, this objective
may be refined in the following manner:

Given an underlined, single syllable word followed by three single
syllable words, one of which rhymes with the sample word, the
learner will underline the rhyming word. Only the following
phonograms will be used: ap, at, ed, em, et, ig, im, in, ip, it, ob,
od, og, om, op, ot, ub, ud, ug, un, up, and ut; each of which the
child has previously sounded out. The nonrhyming words will
have the same letters as the sample word in their initial and
medial, or initial and final positions. The learner will underline
the word having the same medial and final letters as the sample
word. When each phonogram is used randomly three times in a
sample word, during a two-week period, the learner should obtain
2/3 correct for each phonogram and no less than 59/66 correct
for all phonograms.

   Behavioral (instructional or educational) objectives are used to
describe the knowledge and skills taught in a curriculum, program,
lesson, or module. Objectives are also used to describe the
knowledge or skills tested in criterion-referenced tests. Figure 1.1

Figure 1.1

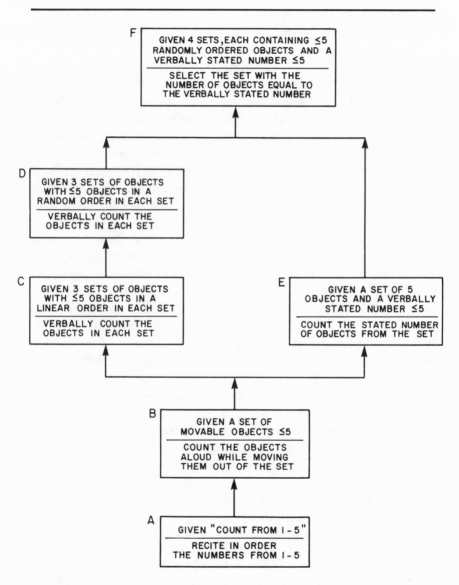

F

GIVEN 4 SETS, EACH CONTAINING ≤5
RANDOMLY ORDERED OBJECTS AND A
VERBALLY STATED NUMBER ≤5

SELECT THE SET WITH THE
NUMBER OF OBJECTS EQUAL TO
THE VERBALLY STATED NUMBER

D

GIVEN 3 SETS OF OBJECTS
WITH ≤5 OBJECTS IN A
RANDOM ORDER IN EACH SET

VERBALLY COUNT THE
OBJECTS IN EACH SET

C

GIVEN 3 SETS OF OBJECTS
WITH ≤5 OBJECTS IN A
LINEAR ORDER IN EACH SET

VERBALLY COUNT THE
OBJECTS IN EACH SET

E

GIVEN A SET OF 5
OBJECTS AND A VERBALLY
STATED NUMBER ≤5

COUNT THE STATED NUMBER
OF OBJECTS FROM THE SET

B

GIVEN A SET OF
MOVABLE OBJECTS ≤5

COUNT THE OBJECTS
ALOUD WHILE MOVING
THEM OUT OF THE SET

A

GIVEN "COUNT FROM I - 5"

RECITE IN ORDER
THE NUMBERS FROM I - 5

Figure 1.1. Terminal and enabling objectives and entry level skills (adapted from Wang, 1973).

shows the relationship between terminal and enabling objectives in a *module* of instruction. Although there are various definitions, in this context, a module is considered to be a self-contained unit of instruction having an integrated theme and providing students with information needed to acquire specified knowledge and skills. A module serves as one component of a total curriculum (Dick and Carey, 1978). Objective F is the terminal behavioral objective for the module. The objectives are stated in an abbreviated form. Conditions are written above the horizontal line in each box, performance is written below, and no standards are specified. Objectives B to E are enabling behavioral objectives describing the skills the learner must acquire to progress from his/her entry level to the terminal objective. Objective A describes the entry level skills already in the learner's repertoire before instruction begins.

Advantages of Behavioral Objectives

Behavioral objectives are the basis of instructional design. Objectives provide explicit statements interpreting the *goals** of education. Instruction provides a means of achieving those objectives. Of course, there are many different routes to each objective. Explicitly stated behavioral objectives, however, increase the likelihood that each of the various routes of instruction will provide the learner with, at least, the minimum essential skills to reach the objective.

Instructional design begins with the *task analysis* of one or more behavioral objectives to determine the prerequisite skills required to *enable* a learner to reach the objective(s). These enabling skills are described in terms of enabling objectives. Terminal and enabling behavioral objectives facilitate the selection of appropriate teaching materials, activities, and methods. These advantages, while leading to consistency of interpretation among various teachers, do not prevent the exercising of creative innovation or enrichment beyond the acquisition of essential skills. Neither do

*Educational goals are broad, general statements about the aims or purposes of education, e.g., "to develop intellectual curiosity and a desire for lifelong learning." The broadness of the statement promotes its adoption by all teachers, for all students, in all subject areas.

behavioral objectives stifle spontaneity. In fact, having a clearly defined behavioral objective permits a teacher to detour scheduled instruction to take advantage of chance events and then to return to instruction without losing continuity.

Behavioral objectives facilitate communication between and among teachers, learners, parents, administrators, and program evaluators. When a teacher describes a learner's achievement in terms of behavioral objectives, s/he provides a clear and concise statement of exactly what the student can and cannot do, the material with which the learner was tested, and the standards against which the student was judged. This information indicates where and how to begin testing and teaching to avoid redundancy or omission. With mature students, objectives can be made available as *advance organizers* before instruction begins. By reading the objective to find out what is expected, the learner may prepare for the instruction that follows. Objectives may also be made available as *post-organizers* upon completion of instruction. Used in this manner, objectives assist the learner to review and evaluate his/her understanding of the material covered.

In the development of individual educational programs (IEP), objectives provide clear statements of individually suitable goals of instruction. Objectives also provide well defined structural parts of a curriculum; these parts can be systematically modified to facilitate diagnostic testing and teaching. For example, during testing, various aspects of either the conditions, performance, and/or standards of an objective may be independently and temporarily modified until the learner is able to perform a task. These adjustments indicate where to begin instruction and which variables to modify to promote learner growth.

The construction of behavioral objectives can be an elucidating experience. Otherwise vague, implicit, trivial, irrelevant, or value-laden goals can be made explicit, evaluated, and modified, or be replaced with objectives describing essential skills and knowledge.

Problems Associated with Some Behavioral Objectives

Not all behavioral objectives are well written. In fact, many so-called behavioral objectives in commercially available instructional programs and criterion-referenced tests are poorly written. The following objective is typical of these commonly found "behavioral objectives." Study the example carefully. What problems are inherent? If two or more teachers were independently given this objective, would they teach and test the same knowledge and skills?

> The learner will discriminate similar objects (e.g., different chairs and tables, etc.).

The verb "to discriminate" is ambiguous and the process of discrimination is *covert*. There are many different ways that a learner could *overtly* demonstrate the results of a covert discrimination. These demonstrations could range from having the learner simply *point* to tables and/or chairs, to having him/her *write* a description of the distinguishing and non-distinguishing characteristics of the members of each category. There is an obvious difference between the level of difficulty of these tasks.

The stimulus material is not adequately described in the objective. Of course, there is a "difference" *between* tables and chairs, but does the objective imply that there is also a difference *among* some of the tables, and *among* some of the chairs? If so, how similar are the chairs to each other, and how different are they from the tables? Obviously, the number and magnitude of identical, similar, and different characteristics among and between categories will significantly influence the difficulty of the task.

In addition, as is often the case, the objective does not describe any standards of performance that the learner must achieve before advancing to the next level of instruction. Thus, the learner's achievement cannot be evaluated consistently.

What skills did the author of this objective intend to be taught? What skills should be taught, to what level of competence, to insure that the learner has acquired the minimum essential prerequisites for successive instruction? Although behavioral objectives may be tedious and time-consuming to write, there is an obvious advantage to the removal of ambiguity and subjectivity in interpretation.

Behavioral Objectives: Their Characteristics and Construction
The following section describes how to write behavioral

objectives. The discussion is summarized in a checklist at the end of the chapter. Although many aspects of objectives are discussed, an important point to note is that behavioral objectives should be AS SIMPLE AS POSSIBLE AND AS DETAILED AS NECESSARY. A behavioral objective is sufficiently explicit when two or more competent teachers, independently using the same objective, would teach and test essentially the same knowledge and skills as intended by the author of the objective.

Performance. The *performance* described in a behavioral objective is stated in a verb, verb + complement, or verb + adverb construction specifying the *observable, measurable behavior* that the learner is expected to perform upon completion of an instructional unit, module, or program. The following examples are taken from objectives discussed earlier in the chapter: "The learner will *point* (to the tallest object); "The learner will *underline* (the rhyming word)." Since learning can be inferred only from a change in student behavior, the performance does *not* describe the teacher's behavior, but *does* describe the learner's observable, measurable behaviors that can be assessed pre- and post-instruction.

When the goals of instruction describe *covert cognitive, affective,* or *perceptual* processes or states that cannot be directly observed, a behavioral objective must be written to translate the verb into an *overt,* measurable form. For example, verbs such as: to *know, understand, recall, recognize,* or *appreciate* must be rewritten as observable, measurable behaviors. Of course, each teacher reading an objective could interpret how his/her students should demonstrate their "understanding" or "appreciation." However, the various methods of demonstration selected might require skills that differ in number, type, and difficulty. As a result, various teachers might teach and test quite different knowledge and skills. This situation is not desirable when the purpose of an objective is to describe the *minimum, essential* skills prerequisite to the next level of instruction. These difficulties are avoided through exclusive use in behavioral objectives of verbs that describe *observable, measurable* behaviors.

The method of performance described in an objective should be the simplest method available to fulfill the demands of the most difficult, commonly found conditions. Frequently, the manner in which tasks are usually performed is not the *simplest* method. Before assuming that a commonly used method is the simplest or best way to perform a task, one should study the behavior of both adequate and inadequate performers and experiment with various procedures under the most difficult, commonly found conditions. The study of a variety of performers may reveal a number of techniques to either avoid or develop.

There are several additional considerations to be made in selecting a suitable method of performance. Whenever possible, methods should be chosen that are congruent with the learner's existing skills. That is, the method that the learner will be taught should:

    (a) employ the skills s/he already possesses;

    (b) require acquisition of the least number of new skills; and

    (c) avoid the need to revise existing skills or habits.

Methods should also be selected that will facilitate performance in other areas at the same time or at a later date. For example, learning does not occur in isolation, and the manner in which a student learns to perform in one area may facilitate or impede the learning of skills in other areas. Finally, and of particular importance to special education, an attempt should be made to select a method of performance that will facilitate independent, normative functioning in the greatest number of areas.

Conditions. Behavioral objectives also describe the conditions under which the learner will perform. The description may delineate: (a) objects or events, present or absent, that may assist or hinder performance; (b) instructional materials; (c) social and/or physical circumstances; (d) instructions, verbal and/or written; as well as (e) the stimulus and response formats used. The description should be concise, and yet, sufficiently detailed to avoid misinterpretation among various teachers.

A terminal instructional objective should also describe the most difficult, commonly found conditions in which the learner would be required to perform. Selection of conditions of this nature is particularly important in the field of special education, where learners are often taught to perform under simplified conditions that are rarely, if ever, found in the general environment. For example, a learner taught to tell the time from a clock face with 12 numbers or with one green hand and one red hand may not have been given adequate skills to meet the demands usually found in the general environment. Objectives should also describe the typical range of conditions in the general environment. Once again, if a learner is not taught to perform under the usual range of conditions, s/he will not be prepared to cope with typical demands.

Standards. Many behavioral objectives describe only performance and conditions and do not specify the standards of performance. As a result, there is no way to judge consistently the adequacy of the performance. However, since testing is an integral part of effective teaching, behavioral objectives should specify the minimum essential standards of performance. That is, to avoid attempting to teach the learner what s/he already knows and to ensure teaching all that one is required to know, a teacher should assess which objectives have been achieved and what remains to be taught.

The fact that objectives describe the *minimum* essential standards does not mean that all learners should be equated to the least able learner; in fact, each student should be given the opportunity to demonstrate his/her highest level of capability. In the area of special education, it is particularly important that the minimum *essential* level of performance for each objective be clearly specified. One of the goals of special education is to assist slow learners to "catch-up" to their chronological age peers. Economy and efficiency of instruction are required to achieve this goal. Thus, it is advantageous to determine, as soon as possible, when a learner has achieved the minimum essential skills and thus, when s/he is ready to progress to the next level of instruction.

Frequently, the standards described in an objective require the performance of some relatively arbitrary number or percentage of correct responses. A more effective way to assess a learner's competence is in terms of the percentage of *consecutive* correct trials performed. When only the number or percentage of correct responses is specified, the learner may meet the requirements when his/her performance is punctuated by an increasing number of error responses. This situation is not uncommon as newly acquired skills frequently are not well established and may alternate between periods of adequate and inadequate performance. The requirement of a percentage of consecutive correct trials insures that the response can be made in a consistently acceptable manner while still allowing for an acceptable margin of error.

One very important consideration in special education, where learners sometimes experience difficulty in maintaining newly acquired skills, is to specify that successful trials be distributed over several days or weeks. For example, a terminal behavioral objective might specify that ten consecutive correct trials (CCT) be performed at the end of instruction followed by ten CCT the next day, and on the fourth, sixth, tenth, fifteenth, twentieth, and thirtieth days. In addition, behavioral objectives may also require an assessment of the generalization of a newly learned skill in various contexts and with various people in the learner's life space. Training and assessing for generalization is discussed in Chapter Five.

Because of the nature of some tasks, successful performance must be completed within a limited period of time, thus, the standards may limit the time allotted for task completion. Also, as the *rate* or speed of performance may deteriorate after the completion of instruction, it may be desirable to compensate for this slowing down. During instruction, the learner may be required to perform in a shorter period of time or at a higher rate than would usually be required following instruction. On many tasks, it may *not* be necessary to complete performance within a limited duration; some people, however, feel that *rapid* and accurate performance indicates the strength and durability of a newly acquired skill. For this reason, it may be desirable to specify a time limit for performance that is estimated to indicate sufficient habit strength.

When behavioral objectives designed for handicapped performers do not require 100 percent accuracy of performance, the standards may specify an acceptable margin of performance error.

The standards may also require that errors should not be of a certain type or exceed a particular magnitude. For example, in an objective discussed earlier in this chapter, where the learner was being taught to point to the tallest object, the objective stated that, "No error should be committed where the difference in height between the objects is greater than one inch or where the objects are placed less than eight inches apart." A specification of this nature may be made where a behavioral objective, designed for a heterogeneous group of learners, tests achievement that exceeds the minimum requirements. An objective of this type specifies the minimum requirements that all learners must achieve while presenting a task that will accommodate a range of learners capable of exceeding the minimum standards.

The standards of accuracy required are often determined by the eventual application of the skill and the consequences of subsequent errors. Errors of a certain number and type may be acceptable in some circumstances, but other errors, even of infrequent occurrence, may be generally unacceptable. Therefore, when performance standards are being established and 100 percent accuracy is unnecessary, care must be taken, not only to specify the correct responses required, but also to discriminate acceptable from unacceptable types of errors. An acceptable rate or type of error should not impede learner progress to successive stages of instruction. Unacceptable errors should not be tolerated and must be prevented from occurring; or, if performed, they should be corrected immediately to prevent them from being strengthened through repeated practice.

An additional reason for discriminating acceptable from unacceptable errors is that in special education one of the goals of instruction is to teach the learner to perform independently in a normative, nonstigmatizing manner in as broad a context as possible. Unfortunately, it is not uncommon to find successful graduates of vocational training programs for the mentally handicapped who are unemployable. They may be able to perform a variety of acceptable behaviors at a high rate of response, but small, infrequent, and unacceptable behaviors may prevent them from gaining or holding employment.

Preliminary Stages of Instructional Design

Several stages of information gathering actually precede the writing of a behavioral objective. First, a *learner evaluation* is conducted in various areas of performance to determine: (a) what skills the learner has acquired, (b) what skills remain to be learned in each performance area, and (c) how the learner responds to various instructional conditions. Second, the foregoing information is used to *select* and *priorize* instructional goals for a particular learner or population of learners. The tasks described in the instructional goals are subjected to further study. A *literature review* is performed to reveal the methods by which these tasks have previously been taught. This review provides information about: (a) the behavioral objectives used in existing programs, (b) the instructional methods and materials employed, and (c) the types and sequences of skills taught in the programs reviewed. Next, a number of novice and accomplished individuals are observed performing the tasks described in the instructional goals. During the performance, *conditions* and *performance analyses* are conducted. A conditions analysis is used to ascertain the variety of conditions that occur and that influence the performance of the task under study. A performance analysis, administered in conjunction with a conditions analysis, is employed to determine the number, type, and sequence of steps taken when the task is performed under the variety of conditions that occur. Each of the above analyses is discussed more fully in the following paragraphs. The information derived from these analyses is used to develop a suitable behavioral objective. This information also forms the basis of the ensuing instructional development and is referred to repeatedly as the instructional program evolves.

Learner evaluation. The first step in assessing a handicapped learner involves a criterion-referenced assessment of his/her achievements in the self-help, social-personal, sensory, physical, academic, communication, and vocational areas of performance. An assessment of this type indicates, in terms of behavioral objectives, what the learner can and cannot do, under what conditions s/he can perform, and what standards of performance have been attained.

An assessment is also made of the student's *learning style*. The following list describes some of the behaviors that should be repeatedly evaluated in the instructional environment (classroom or workshop, as applicable) under normal and experimentally controlled variations in the conditions. The object of the assessment is to establish the learner's characteristic mode of response to typical changes in conditions and his/her sustained "optimum" response to experimentally modified conditions.

1. Determine which, if any, student behaviors interfere with learning (e.g., "attention span" or "hyperactivity"). How are these responses defined in terms of observable, measurable behaviors? What is the frequency or duration of these behaviors; under what conditions do they occur? How do instructional personnel and other students or trainees respond to these behaviors, and what is the effect of the response?

2. Evaluate the learner's response to various instructional strategies: verbal instructions, models, prompts, and correction procedures.

3. Determine what (instructional and motivational) techniques best facilitate acquisition, generalization, and maintenance of skills. What amount and type of repetition and massed and distributed practice are required?

4. Assess the student's response to individual and group instruction in terms of behavior management, and rate and style of learning.

5. Record the learner's response to various management strategies, such as reinforcement, extinction, and time-out.

6. Examine the learner's physical, sensory, and communication skills. What type of stimulus and response format can s/he respond to adequately? What is the level of his/her receptive and expressive communication?

7. Describe the learner's problem solving skills. For example, how does the learner characteristically analyze discriminative features of stimuli, define and choose appropriate response alternatives, apply rules and procedures to achieve a solution to novel problems, and check the accuracy of the problem solving procedures?

Selecting and priorizing goals. When the learner's achievement within each of the areas of performance has been determined, new goals of instruction must be established with priorities assigned within and between areas. The relative importance of the skills within each area can be evaluated in terms of the following considerations.

1. Evaluate the short-term and long-term functional values of the various skills that might be taught. That is, determine how many new tasks acquisition of the skills will assist the learner to perform?

2. Establish which skills can be immediately and frequently used, reinforced, and maintained in the individual's daily life.

3. Decide which skills best facilitate independent, normative functioning in the greatest number of environmental contexts.

4. Consider how the various skills that might be taught may facilitate or hinder the learning of other skills taught at the same time or at a later date.

5. Decide whether any of the skills being considered are prerequisite or corequisite to learning other skills.

6. Review the literature to determine if a "developmental priority" has been assigned to particular skills.

7. Evaluate the possibilities of simultaneously teaching skills from different areas of performance to enhance generalization and maintenance.

8. Ascertain whether necessary instructional personnel, materials, and time will be available often enough and long enough to ensure acquisition, maintenance, and generalization of the skills.

9. Decide if the skills can be taught in an individual and/or group format.

Literature review. The literature review involves a thorough review of the research and theoretical literature, textbooks, instructional programs, curriculum guides, teaching strategies, and materials. This review provides information about the behavioral objectives used in existing programs, the instructional methods and materials employed, and the types and sequences of skills taught.

When reviewing the literature for information about task analysis, some cautions should be exercised. Williams and Gotts (1977) warn against generalizing observations or conclusions about normal development to the development of handicapped individuals. They claim that a student's handicapping condition(s) may alter the sequence in which certain skills are learned and/or prevent the learning of some skills. For example, blind infants may learn motor skills in a different sequence than sighted infants (Adelson and Fraiberg, 1974). Also, children, adolescents, and adults may learn the same skills in a different manner. Furthermore, the literature on "normal development" describes the *average* rate and sequence of development of children receiving an *average* type and amount of stimulation. However, exceptional individuals by definition, are not average, and the purpose of special education is to modify the learner's experience and alter his/her rate and course of development. How much the rate, style, and sequence of development can be altered among various groups of exceptional learners is an empirical question that remains to be answered. Nevertheless, the account of normal development provides a richly detailed framework that can be used as a starting point for comparison and experimentation.

Conditions analysis. A conditions analysis is conducted in conjunction with a performance analysis. During the writing of a behavioral objective, a conditions analysis consists of an analysis of the conditions surrounding and influencing performance of a task. The purpose of the analysis is to ascertain the number, type, and variation of conditions that occur so that a terminal behavioral objective can be written describing the most difficult, commonly found conditions. As discussed earlier, the learner is required to perform under these conditions to insure that s/he will be able to meet common environmental demands.

The conditions and performance analyses also form the early stages of the task analysis. To this extent the conditions analysis is designed not merely to determine the most difficult, commonly found conditions, but also to identify: (a) changes in conditions that alter the number, type, and sequence of subtasks performed; (b) all variations in conditions that should be introduced into instruction; (c) any existing or potential *prosthetic* adaptation of conditions that could be made to accommodate various handicaps; and (d) the simplest conditions under which instruction of the task could begin with a particular population of learners.

Prosthetics. Prosthetics involve the replacement of an absent part of the body with an artificial substitute, or the improvement of a dysfunctional part with an artificial addition. Prosthetics may be of several different types, for example, visual: sound-tactile reading machines for the blind; auditory: amplified telephones for the hearing impaired; communication: Bliss Symbols for cerebral palsied persons who are unable to speak or sign; motor: artificial limbs and wheelchairs; cognitive: electronic calculators to improve computational skills; physiological: an ostomy to compensate for loss of bladder control; and social: the use of tinted glasses to conceal an unusual facial appearance. Smith and Neisworth (1975) and Bigge and O'Donnell (1976) provide comprehensive reviews of prosthetic devices for a variety of handicapping conditions. Prosthetic devices improve or make possible an act that a handicapped individual otherwise would not be able to perform. There are two disadvantages to prosthetic devices. Their visibility tends to call attention to the user's functional inadequacies, and the devices may establish an unnecessary dependence when they compensate for a handicap that the individual could overcome by natural means. For these reasons, prosthetic devices should be introduced only where necessary—where immediate training cannot rectify a problem—and wherever feasible, their use should be temporary. The use of such devices should be faded as rapidly as possible. For example, physically handicapped individuals may be trained to go from the use of a walker, to the use of canes, and finally to independent walking. A conditions analysis includes a study of any existing or potential prosthetic adaptations that could be made on a temporary or permanent basis. The abbreviated results of a conditions analysis of "utensil use in eating" are presented below.

Conditions Analysis   **Common Variations and Prosthetic Adaptations**

1. Utensils:

    a. general

—size: adult or child; oversized handles.
—prompted: color-coded spots on fingers and utensils indicating proper finger placement.

    b. fork

—standard size and shape with four tines.
—with enlarged cutting edge on one tine.

    c. fork and spoon

—with palm-grip having a dorsal brace extending to back of hand.
—with palm-loop holder strap.
—with feeding splint attached to arm and utensil extending from back of hand.

    d. spoon

—fist-gripped swivel spoon.
—laterally curved handle.
—deep or shallow bowl.
—soup or dessert size.

    e. knife

—dull or sharp.
—serrated edge.
—"rocking knife" with curved blade for easy cutting.

2. Food vessels:

    a. plates or bowls

—deep or shallow.
—edge turned inward or outward.
—with suction cup on bottom to stabilize.
—on swivel.
—on non-slip mat.

3. Food:

    a. form

—liquid: soup.
—pureed or semi-solid: ice cream, applesauce, thin custard.
—mashed: potatoes, squash.
—chopped or cubed: carrots, beets, beef.
—rolling stock: peas, beans.
—semi-solid: potatoes, cheese.
—solid: steak.

b. consistency   —soft: banana, canned fruit.
                            —medium: meatloaf, macaroni.
                            —hard: raw carrots, steak.

c. preparation   —precut, whole, mashed, chopped.

d. preferred foods   —ice cream, custard, fruit, jello.

4. Conditions surrounding seating and positioning accommodations for severely and profoundly handicapped individuals with difficulty sucking, swallowing, and chewing are reviewed in Stainback, Healy, Stainback, and Healy (1976).

Obviously, these and other conditions derived from the conditions analysis will influence the performance of handicapped individuals in an independent feeding program. This information is used to develop a behavioral objective, and as discussed in Chapter Two, is employed in the process of task analysis.

Performance analysis. A performance analysis is also used to develop a behavioral objective. The analysis involves a detailed breakdown of the number, type, and sequence of steps taken in the performance of a task by a variety of *novice* and *accomplished* performers. The steps involved in a performance analysis are summarized below.

1. The information derived from the survey of the literature and existing instructional materials is reviewed to determine what number, type, and sequence of skills have been taught in the past.
2. The results of the learner evaluation are assessed to establish what skills the learner currently possesses and which "special skills," if any, the learner will be required to learn because of his/her unique handicapping condition or learning style.
3. The programmer "thinks-through" and, if possible, actually performs the task.
4. Performance of the task by novice and accomplished performers is assessed under a variety of conditions.
5. In steps 3 and 4, the programmer observes what the performer does, what s/he does with it, what s/he does to it, and why s/he does it (Davies, 1973).

The information derived from the performance analysis is used to develop a behavioral objective describing the simplest manner of performing a task under the most difficult, commonly found conditions. The information obtained also forms part of a task analysis discussed in Chapter Two.

The flowchart in Figure 1.2 displays the preliminary stages of instructional design and the development of a terminal behavioral objective. The checklist that follows summarizes the major considerations to be made in writing and evaluating behavioral objectives. When reviewing the checklist, an important point to recall is that objectives should be as simple as possible and as detailed as necessary. A behavioral objective is sufficiently explicit when two or more competent teachers, independently using the same objective, would teach and test essentially the same knowledge and skills as intended by the author of the objective.

Checklist for Writing and Evaluating Behavioral Objectives

	Completed	*N/A*
1. Review the research and theoretical literature, textbooks, instructional programs, curriculum guides, and teaching strategies and materials.		
2. Perform a conditions analysis: a. analyze the number, type, and range of conditions that occur and their usual variations;		
b. record changes in conditions that alter the number, type, and sequence of subtasks performed;		
c. determine the most difficult, commonly found conditions.		
3. Do a performance analysis of the number,		

	Specified	N/A
type, and sequence of subtasks required to perform a task: a. review information derived from the evaluation of the learner population and the review of the literature and instructional materials;		
b. "think-through," or, if possible, actually perform the task;		
c. assess the task being performed by novice and accomplished performers under various conditions;		
d. in (b) and (c) above, observe and record what the learner does, how s/he does it, what s/he does to it, and why s/he does it.		
Conditions The conditions specify: 4. What is given or absent that may facilitate or impede performance.	*Specified*	*N/A*
5. What instructional materials are required.		
6. The social and/or physical circumstances.		
7. The instructions provided (verbal and/or written).		
8. The presentation and response format.		

	Specified	N/A
9. The most difficult, commonly found conditions.		
10. The common range of variations among normative conditions.		
Performance The performance specifies: 1. The observable, measurable behavior *not* covert knowledge, understanding, or appreciation.		
2. The simplest method of fulfilling the most difficult, commonly found conditions.		
3. A method of performance that requires the least amount of learning or relearning.		
4. A method of performance that will facilitate learning in other areas of instruction.		
5. A method of performance that is most normative and least stigmatizing.		
Standards The standards specify: 1. The minimum essential level of performance.		
2. The number of consecutive trials to be correctly performed.		

	Specified	N/A
3. The least number of trials required to sample each condition.		
4. Sufficient trials to ensure that each type of performance *reliably* exceeds what would be expected by chance alone.		
5. Time or rate of response requirements: a. to insure a strong and durable habit;		
b. to link behaviors smoothly together into a chain;		
c. to compensate for rate loss after instruction ends.		
6. An acceptable margin of error.		
7. Where less than 100 percent accuracy is specified; a description of the number and type of acceptable and unacceptable errors.		
8. The distribution of successful performance over time to ensure maintenance of the skill (e.g., performance on the first, second, fourth, sixth, tenth, fifteenth, twentieth, and thirtieth days).		
9. Environmental conditions under which generalization of the performance should be assessed: changes in physical context, language, physical and social cues, people and materials (see Chapter Five).		

The practice exercises at the end of the following chapters do not simply review materials discussed in the chapter, but also provide additional information in the context of solving practical problems.

Practice Exercises
Problems
Answers to each of the following exercises are found at the end of this section.

1. Briefly list the problems associated with each of the following "behavioral objectives."
   (a) The child will recognize and repeat familiar nursery rhymes.

   (b) The learner will demonstrate understanding of the words "in" and "on" by selecting appropriate pictures.

   (c) The student will be able to write a given repeated addition problem as a multiplication problem and compute the answer.

2. Improve the following behavioral objectives while trying to retain the same general type of task as that described by the author.
   (a) Given a toothbrush, toothpaste, and water, the child will be able to brush his/her teeth without dropping the brush and without getting toothpaste on face or clothing.

   (b) Given a kitchen broom, a dustpan, and a wastebasket, the learner (a trainable, mentally retarded adolescent in a vocational training program) will sweep the floor of all debris and deposit the sweepings in the wastebasket.

   (c) Given an uncontrolled intersection of two busy streets, the learner will cross the street safely without assistance on five occasions.

Figure 1.2

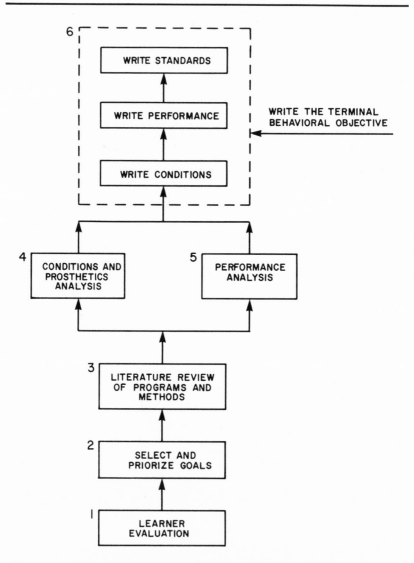

Figure 1.2. Preliminary stages of instructional design, and development of a terminal behavioral objective.

3. Write behavioral objectives for the following goals.

   (a) To teach a grade one child to use scissors properly.

   (b) To teach an educable mentally retarded teenager to tell the time.

* * *

Answers

1 (a). The first objective, *"The child will recognize and repeat familiar nursery rhymes,"* presents many problems. The verb "will recognize" describes a *covert* activity that could be expressed overtly in many different ways. *Subjectivity* is required to *interpret* how recognition should be demonstrated. Different expressions of recognition may require various prerequisite skills that may vary markedly in their levels of difficulty. If the author of the objective wanted the child to express his/her recognition merely by repeating the nursery rhyme, the words "will recognize and" should be deleted from the objective.

The verb "will repeat" familiar nursery rhymes is ambiguous in this context. The reader is uncertain if the child is to *repeat* a nursery rhyme directly after it has been read to him/her, or if the rhyme is to be *recited* by the child some time after s/he has heard or read it. The ambiguity occurs, in part, because the conditions surrounding the task have not been described adequately.

No standards are specified for judging the adequacy of the recitation. Is 100 percent accuracy in all respects required? Are small mispronunciations acceptable? Is rhythm of reading or emphasis upon particular words important? Are self-corrections of errors acceptable? How many trials are given?

What does the word "familiar" mean in reference to "familiar nursery rhymes"? The child cannot recite a rhyme that s/he has not previously heard or read. If "familiar" means simply that the child has heard or read the rhyme before, then the word should be deleted. If "familiar" means something else, then that meaning should be specified. In general, the word "familiar" should be avoided unless its meaning is clearly described.

Finally, what is a nursery rhyme? Nursery rhymes may vary in their length, vocabulary, syntax, rhyme, rhythm, and theme. Each of these variables will influence the difficulty of the recitation. The type of nursery rhyme to be recited should be defined and/or titles of suitable rhymes should be provided.

1 (b). The objective, *"The learner will demonstrate understanding of the words 'in' and 'on' by selecting appropriate pictures,"* is analyzed in the following manner. The use of the word 'understanding' is acceptable in this objective because the author has described how understanding will be demonstrated in terms of observable, measurable behaviors. Unfortunately, the descriptions of the stimulus conditions presented to the learner are inadequate. How many pictures will be presented to the learner at any one time? Will a multiple-choice format be used in which the learner selects one or more pictures depicting "on"? How will "on" be represented? If a table and a toy car are used, will the car be placed at various locations on the table? Will one-half of the car be shown extending off the table? Will a sloping table be used? Will other objects and surfaces be employed? How will "not on" be depicted? These variations and a number of others will influence the difficulty of the task.

The objective does not describe how the learner will *select* appropriate pictures. For example, s/he might *point* to one or more pictures of "on" presented in a multiple-choice format; s/he might say "on" or "not on" when presented with individual pictures; or s/he might physically sort a number of pictures into categories. These tasks may vary considerably in their difficulty. No standards of performance are described. Probably a separate objective should be written to describe the stimulus conditions depicting "in" and "on."

1 (c). The objective, *"The student will be able to write a given repeated addition problem as a multiplication problem and compute the answer,"* is analyzed as follows. Use of the phrase 'will be *able*' to write is unnecessary. The student's *ability* to write an answer can be verified only if s/he *does* write the answer. The objective should be revised to read, "The student will write . . . ."

The repeated addition problem that is 'given' is not

adequately described. A problem of this nature could involve numbers less than or equal to ten, for example, $5 + 5 + 5 + 5 = 4 \times 5$ or numbers of a higher value, such as $93 + 93 + 93$ in which carrying may or may not be involved. The addition problem could be presented in numerical form or as sets of objects.

The process of "computing" an answer is covert, and a suitable overt demonstration of the computation must be described. For example, the student will either write or state the correct answer, or select the answer from among several choices in which particular types of errors are represented.

A small but significant point concerns the format in which the repeated addition problem is presented. If a sentence form is used, such as $67,539 + 67,539 + 67,539$, the student is also likely to use the sentence form, $67,539 \times 3$, which may increase the frequency of multiplication errors beyond those that would occur if a vertical format had been used.

Once again, this objective does not specify the minimum essential standards of performance that a learner must achieve with this type of task before progressing to the next level of instruction. In special education, description of the minimum standards of performance is particularly important. Some so-called "learning disabled children," for example, may not have minimal cerebral dysfunction or maturational lag. They may simply have been promoted prematurely to higher levels of instruction without having achieved the minimum essential level of competence on prerequisite skills.

2 (a). *Toothbrushing.* Given a toothbrush, toothpaste, and water, the learner will brush his/her teeth after a meal. The learner must use between 3/8 to 3/4 of an inch of toothpaste and after brushing, wash any residual toothpaste from his/her mouth and face. No toothpaste must be spilled on clothing or other parts of the environment.

To verify cleanliness of the teeth after each brushing:

    (a) a dentist or dental hygienist must clean the teeth of all hardened plaque before the toothbrushing program begins;

    (b) a disclosing dye that temporarily discolors plaque and food deposits should be used before each brushing;

(c) *all* disclosing dye should be removed from the teeth following brushing;

(d) a second application of the dye following the brushing will disclose any remaining plaque;

(e) steps c and d should be repeated until no plaque is revealed in step d;

(f) the program is complete when no plaque is disclosed in the first application of step d on five consecutive trials.

The behavioral objective for toothbrushing should not describe the chain of behaviors involved in toothbrushing: uncapping the toothpaste tube, putting toothpaste and water on the brush, returning the cap to the tube, and brushing teeth in an up and down motion. These steps of the task are the result of a task analysis. Writing a behavioral objective requires only that the conditions, performance, and standards be specified.

The emphasis in this objective is upon the standards. In other objectives, the emphasis may shift to the conditions or performance. In the next objective, the conditions are written with considerable detail.

2 (b). *Sweeping.* For this objective, one might assume that a vocational program instructing trainable, mentally retarded adolescents to sweep floors might be part of a larger training program for building maintenance skills. The most difficult, commonly found situation a janitor is likely to face would be to sweep a large, roughly surfaced floor area covered with "hard-to-remove" material. The task would require the moving and replacement of several pieces of furniture; some breakable items would be involved. The following instructional objective incorporates these problems.

> Given a kitchen broom, a dustpan, and a wastebasket, the learner will sweep a floor with uneven tiles covering approximately 75 square meters. The area will include: three movable office desks and chairs, three stationary filing cabinets, three wastepaper baskets, and a movable table on which there is a variety of equipment including two high vases with narrow bottoms. One kilogram of sand and one hectogram of confetti have been evenly distributed over the entire floor area, except under the filing cabinets. The learner will sweep the floor and deposit at least eight hectograms of sand and confetti in the wastebasket s/he was given. Up to five pieces of confetti may be left on the floor in

unobvious places. The legs of all desks and tables, and the wastebaskets should be relocated within one inch of their original positions. Chairs belonging to desks should be inserted under the respective desks. Nothing should drop to the floor or break during the sweeping.

2 (c). *Crossing the Street.* Given: (a) the intersection of a four lane through-street (with approximately x-vehicles per minute) and a secondary street (with approximately y-vehicles per minute), (b) stop signs on the secondary street, (c) no stop sign or light on the through-street, (d) no crosswalks on either street, (e) situations with and without pedestrians, and (f) a speed limit of 60 km/h or less, the learner will walk across the through-street to the nearest opposite corner. The learner will take one step from the curb when there is no moving traffic within m-meters in the first, left lane and cross the first lane and each successive lane when there is no moving traffic within m-meters in the lane to be crossed. Where there is a moving vehicle within m-meters in a lane to be crossed, the learner will either wait on the curb or wait just behind the line of the lane to be crossed. Running or changing direction of travel is not permitted. The learner will demonstrate this behavior without assistance and in the presence or absence of other pedestrians who may or may not conform to the same procedures. The behavior must be exhibited and unobtrusively evaluated at four different street corners on six consecutive occasions randomly distributed over a three-week period.

In this objective, the conditions, performance, and standards are all described in considerable detail. It is obvious from the amount of detail in the objective that classroom teachers do not have enough time to write detailed behavioral objectives for all of the skills that they have to teach. To design a complete training program, however, all of these details must be considered. Frequently, handicapped children cannot fill in gaps in instruction when vital skills are not taught. The problem of not having enough time to write objectives can be rectified by providing all teachers with curriculum guides that are described in the form of behavioral objectives rather than merely in terms of statements such as "teach pedestrian skills."

3 (a). *Scissors.* Given a pair of sharp, adult size scissors (left- or

right-handed as appropriate) and a piece of 8-1/2 by 11 inch bond paper on the left side of which the capital letter E has been printed, with the capital letter S on the right side. These letters in block type offer concave and convex curves and 90 degree angles to the left and right. Both letters are six inches high and each stroke of the letters is one-inch thick. The learner will cut the letters from the paper, within five minutes, while staying within ± 1/8 inch on either side of the line on three consecutive trials randomly distributed over two weeks.

3 (b). *Time.* Given a wrist watch with four Arabic numbers: 12, 3, 6, and 9 and two hands differentiated only in terms of length; given three trials under each of the following conditions: (a) where the minute hand is on 12, (b) where both hands are on 12, (c) where the hands overlap, (d) where the minute hand is either to the right or to the left of six, and (e) where the hour hand comes before or after the minute hand. The learner will verbally state the time in the form 3:25, 3:45, 4:00, or 12:00 to within five minutes accuracy. Under each set of conditions, the learner must obtain 2/3 trials correct with no less than 18/21 trials correct for all conditions. All numbers must be counted silently, and no number must be touched during the counting.

Chapter 2

Task Analysis

Contents
1. A brief description and demonstration exercise in writing a behavioral objective and conducting a performance analysis.
2. A comprehensive, in-depth review of the methods of task analysis:
   (a) summarizing the results of conditions and performance analyses in a flowchart;
   (b) constructing a lattice of subskills;
   (c) performing a hierarchic learning analysis to determine what enabling skills are required;
   (d) hierarchically sequencing enabling skills in a lattice; and
   (e) performing a cross-check of the lattice to validate the task analysis.
3. Definitions and examples of levels of a learning hierarchy.
4. A checklist summary of the major steps involved in performing a task analysis.
5. Practice exercises: Problems and answers.

Performance Analysis: An Example
As was discussed in Chapter One, following the selection of an instructional goal, several preliminary steps of instructional design are completed. The information derived from the literature review, the conditions and prosthetics analyses, and the performance analysis is used to develop a terminal behavioral objective. This information also forms the basis of a task analysis. An example of a conditions analysis is described in Chapter One. The following exercise demonstrates the writing of a behavioral objective and the

results of a performance analysis. A performance analysis involves establishing and listing in sequence the steps involved in performing a task.

Note that although the conditions and performance analyses form the basis of a terminal behavioral objective, a performance analysis cannot be conducted unless a terminal behavioral objective has already been established. In other words, a task cannot be analyzed unless there is an explicit definition of the nature of the task. Alternatively, a terminal behavioral objective cannot be developed before the conditions and performance involved in the task have been analyzed. As a result, rather than one step following the other, conducting the conditions and performance analyses, and writing the terminal behavioral objective are concurrent and complementary activities.

The process develops in the following manner. Given an instructional goal, one has only a very general description. of a task. To obtain a more explicit definition, a programmer must develop a behavioral objective that describes in detail the conditions and performance characteristics of the task. To obtain this information, s/he must conduct conditions and performance analyses on the task as it is initially described. Given the information obtained from these analyses, the programmer may refine the description of the task. As a detailed terminal objective is developed, the programmer will modify the conditions and performance analyses so that the task being analyzed is identical to that defined in the behavioral objective.

In each of the following exercises, use paper and pencil in attempting to solve the problems before looking at the solutions provided.

Problem 1. Given the goal, "To teach the learner to dial telephone numbers," construct a terminal behavioral objective.

Solution 1. Of course, there are a variety of behavioral objectives that could be written to interpret this goal. Because of the possibility of these different interpretations, it is imperative that various teachers responsible for teaching telephone skills work together to develop one or more behavioral objectives explicitly describing the task(s) involved. One solution to the problem is as follows:

Given: (1) a standard desk or wall telephone with a dial mounted on the body of the phone; (2) ten, unfamiliar, seven-digit telephone numbers printed separately on cards; (3) a familar name to ask for (name of family, siblings, or friends); (4) a cooperating person to answer the telephone at each number; (5) three of each of the following situations (randomly presented over several days): either (a) the party line is using the telephone for three to ten minutes; (b) the number dialed is busy for three to ten minutes; (c) there is no answer at the number dialed; or (d) the cooperating person answers the telephone; *the learner will* dial the correct number 9/10 calls without error, without dialing over the party line, without listening to the conversation on the party line for more than three seconds, gently replacing the receiver in the cradle after a call, waiting from three to seven minutes before attempting a call when the other line is busy, and repeating a call if a wrong number is dialed.

Problem 2. Again, before looking at the solution, use paper and pencil to carry out a performance analysis on the above objective. List in sequence the steps or subtasks a learner would be required to perform to complete the task described in the behavioral objective.

Solution 2: Result of the performance analysis.

1. Lift receiver with non-dominant hand.
2. Hold receiver to ear on non-dominant side with speaker to mouth.
3. Listen to receiver for three seconds.
   a. If party line is busy, hang up gently, wait five to ten minutes, and repeat steps 1 to 3.
   b. If dial tone is heard, proceed with step 4.
4. Locate the first number in the seven-digit telephone number provided.
5. Locate the same digit on the telephone dial.
6. Insert index finger of the dominant hand into the hole closest to the number.
7. Using index finger, rotate the dial in a clockwise direction to the finger stopper.
8. Remove the finger and let dial return to original position.
9. Select second digit in seven-digit number and repeat steps 5 to 8.

10. Repeat the sequence of steps for the remaining five numbers in order.
11. Listen:
    a. If busy signal is heard, hang up, wait five to ten minutes, and repeat steps 1 to 11.
    b. If phone rings five times without answer, hang up, wait one-half to one full hour, and repeat steps 1 to 11.
    c. When person at number called says, "Hello," ask for name given.
    d. If wrong number is reached, say, "I'm sorry, I have the wrong number," hang up, and repeat steps 1 to 11.

These telephone dialing subtasks represent a response *chain* in which each step must be performed in sequence to successfully complete the task. Many tasks do not have a fixed sequence of steps and the subtasks may be completed in various orders. The sequence of some subtasks varies depending upon changes that occur in the conditions surrounding the performance.

The number, type, and sequence of telephone dialing subtasks described above represent *one* way to analyze the task; many tasks can be analyzed into different sequences of subtasks. For example, there are several different ways to lace and tie shoe laces; each procedure has a unique set and sequence of subtasks.

Task Analysis: The Process

Task analysis involves the process of analyzing the task described in a terminal behavioral objective to determine the essential *skills* that *enable* a learner to proceed from his/her current level of performance (his/her entry level) to the terminal objective. Although some authors consider the ordering of *enabling skills* into an instructional sequence to be a part of task analysis, in the present context, task analysis and instructional sequencing are considered to be independent activities. Instructional sequencing is discussed in Chapter Three.

Several steps are included in a task analysis. The first steps, already discussed, are those of conducting conditions and performance analyses. The results of these analyses indicate the range of conditions that occur during performance of a task, and the corresponding steps or *subtasks* involved in the performance. This information is summarized in a flowchart showing the relationship between the conditions and the various sequences of subtasks. The subtasks are then put into a *lattice* where a *hierarchic learning analysis* is performed to determine what skills, *enabling skills,* a learner would require to perform each subtask. The enabling skills are then *hierarchically sequenced* in the lattice and a *cross-check* is made to validate the accuracy of the task analysis. Each of these steps is discussed in the following section.

Flowcharts. A flowchart summarizes the results of the performance and conditions analyses. It provides a graphic representation of the sequence(s) of subtasks required to complete the task described in a terminal behavioral objective. A flowchart may display a single, *linear* sequence of subtasks or a number of *branching* sequences arising from changes that may occur in the conditions surrounding the performance of each subtask. One or more flowcharts may be used to illustrate various methods of performing a single task.

The subtasks in the flowchart are derived and sequenced according to the information provided in the literature, from "thinking-through" and actually performing a task, from observing its completion by novice and accomplished performers, and by recording various methods of performance and variations in performance resulting from natural and prosthetic changes in conditions. The flowchart in Figure 2.1 displays the sequence of subtasks involved in completing the task of "multiplying with a single-digit number." A sample problem is provided at the right side of the figure.

The start and stop points in the flowchart are indicated by circles; decision points (indicating that various conditions may occur at particular junctions in the performance) are represented by diamonds, and rectangles are used to indicate subtasks. Alternative sequences or *branches* of subtasks are followed by a performer depending upon the presence or absence of various conditions occurring at the decision points. Where only one set of conditions exists, the flowchart would not include decision points, and a *linear* sequence of subtasks would be shown. The arrow

Figure 2.1

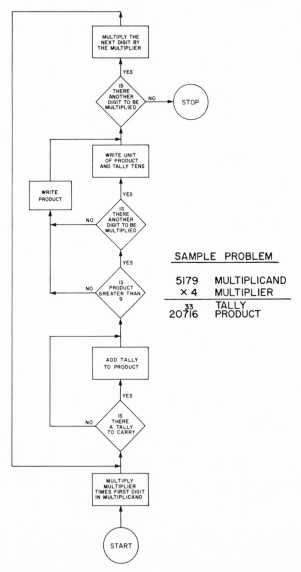

Figure 2.1.   Flowchart of multiplication with a single-digit number.

from the last subtask back to the first subtask is called a *loop*. A loop indicates that a learner may repeatedly perform the same series of subtasks until the terminal behavioral objective is reached.

Several benefits arise from the use of flowcharts. First, a flowchart provides a concise, graphic summary of the number, type, and sequence(s) of subtasks involved in performing a complex task under a variety of conditions. Second, with the aid of a flowchart, the sequence of subtasks can be repeatedly retraced in "slow motion" to verify the completeness of the performance analysis. Third, the relative efficiency of various sequences of performance can be evaluated in terms of the number and type of subtasks involved in each. Fourth, the information provided by flowcharts assists the development of an instructional program designed to teach the simplest, most effective method of performing a task under the most difficult, commonly found conditions. Finally, after the skills required to complete a task have been taught during an instructional program, the flowchart provides a guide for resequencing the skills into the order in which they must be performed.

Following the construction and evaluation of a flowchart, the subtasks in the various branches of the chart are collapsed into a linear sequence forming the ridgeline of a lattice. A hierarchic learning analysis of each subtask is then made to determine the enabling skills required to perform each subtask.

Lattices. A lattice displays the results of a hierarchic learning analysis of the enabling skills required to perform each of the subtasks in a flowchart. The display shows the sequential relationship between the terminal behavioral objective, the subtasks, the enabling skills, and the entry level skills. A lattice does not represent an instructional sequence. The type of lattice described below is an adaptation of one discussed by Smith, Smith, and Edgar (1976).

Figure 2.2 shows the manner in which lattices are constructed. First, the terminal behavioral objective is placed in the upper right corner. The subtasks I, II, . . . in the flowchart are sequenced from left to right along the ridgeline of the lattice in the order in which

Figure 2.2

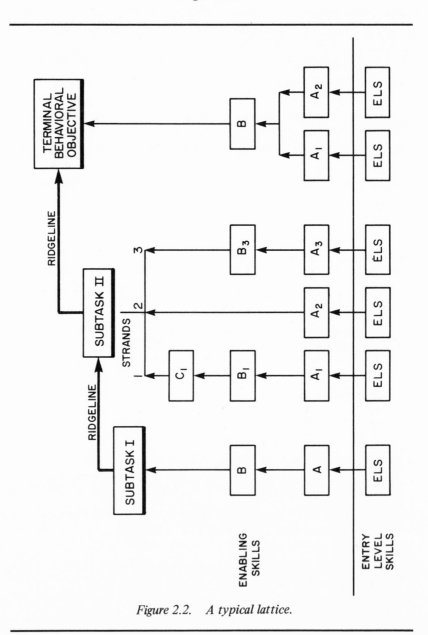

Figure 2.2.   *A typical lattice.*

they are performed. The enabling skills for each subtask identified in the hierarchic learning analysis are listed in the order A, B, C, . . . N. The order of the enabling skills beneath each subskill illustrates either: (a) a *procedural* relationship where A is performed before B, or (b) a *hierarchic* relationship where A is a prerequisite or a component of B. Each subtask is analyzed down to the entry level skills of the lowest performer in the population for which an instructional program is being designed. The organization of enabling skills into strands 1, 2, 3 under subtask II indicates that the enabling skills within each strand are independent from those in the other strands and that the skills learned within each strand are joined together in the performance of subtask II. Figure 2.3 shows a *flowchart* for bicycle riding. This flowchart is simpler than the flowchart of multiplication subtasks. The bicycle riding flowchart shows a series of subtasks listed in a simple, *linear* sequence where there are no decision points or branches. A flowchart of this nature readily forms the ridgeline of a lattice.

Figure 2.4 shows a *lattice* produced from the hierarchic learning analysis of the bicycle riding flowchart. Because of the limitations of space, the entry level skills are not shown. The hierarchic learning analysis reveals the enabling skills required to perform each subtask. The enabling skills are sequenced in the order of their performance. The subtasks and enabling skills may be taught in a different order than that in which they are performed. For example, the enabling skills involved in mounting and dismounting a bicycle may be taught together. Sequencing enabling skills for instruction is discussed in Chapter Three.

Constructing a lattice ridgeline. When a flowchart is in the form of a simple, linear sequence (as in the case of bicycle riding), the ridgeline of the lattice may be readily constructed by listing the subtasks from the starting point to the stop point in the flowchart in a left to right sequence along the ridgeline of the lattice. However, when more complex flowcharts having one or more branches are involved, sequencing skills along the ridgeline becomes more difficult. The sequence of subtasks in the ridgeline may be retained, as much as possible, by using the following procedures.

Figure 2.3

Figure 2.3.   A flowchart for bicycle riding.

Figure 2.4

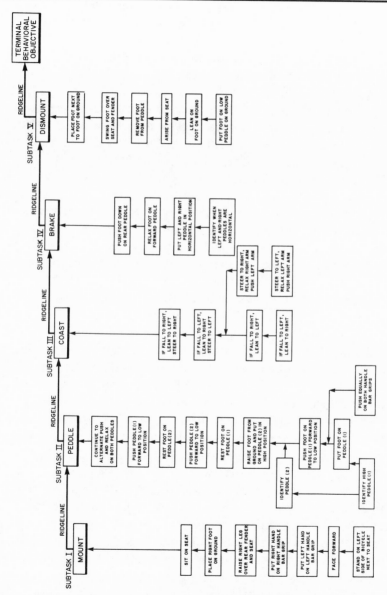

Figure 2.4.   A lattice for bicycle riding.

(1) The subtasks in the flowchart are consecutively numbered from the starting point to the stop point following
the longest branching pathway through the flowchart.

(2) The flowchart is again retraced in the same order as
above, and any subtask not included in the numerical
sequence is alphabetically labeled in the order in which it
is performed in the flowchart.

(3) The alphabetically labeled subtasks, in order of their
performance, are then merged in a linear sequence with
the numerical subtasks. The alphabetical subtasks are
listed along the ridgeline directly following the numbered
tasks that precede them in the flowchart.

The procedure is illustrated in Figure 2.5. The subtasks in the
flowchart are sequenced from left to right along the ridgeline in
the order 1, 2, 3, A, B, 4, C, D, 5, 6, 7, 8, 9, 10. Preserving the
order of the subtasks in this manner may assist: (1) later
comparisons where two or more lattices describe the same task
performed in different manners, and (2) cross-checking a task
analysis to determine if the sum of its subtasks and enabling skills
equals the terminal behavioral objective.

Hierarchic learning analysis. After the subtasks in a flowchart
have been sequenced along the ridgeline of a lattice, a hierarchic
learning analysis of each subtask is performed to ascertain the
enabling skills required to perform the subtask. There are several
different types of hierarchies. The hierarchy depicted in Figure 2.6
is a vertical classification system in which members of higher levels
of the hierarchy are analyzed into smaller, less complex components at successively lower levels of the hierarchy. For example, a
book may be analyzed into various types of chapters, paragraphs,
sentences, and words. Conversely, lower members of the hierarchy, such as words, may be joined together to form successively
higher, more complex members, such as sentences, paragraphs, and
chapters. Thus, a hierarchy of this type provides a vertical
classification system of each of its members. For example, various
types of paragraphs are classified at level three. The hierarchy also
shows how to analyze a member, such as a paragraph, into
successively smaller components: sentences (types a-e) and words

Figure 2.5

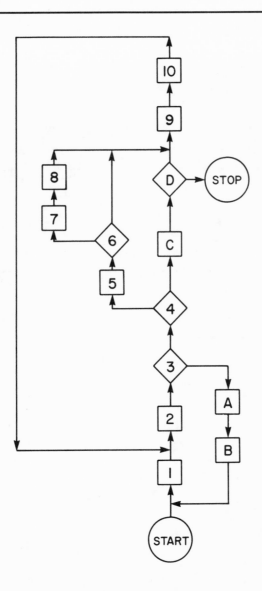

Figure 2.5.   *The order of listing flowchart subtasks in a lattice.*

Figure 2.6

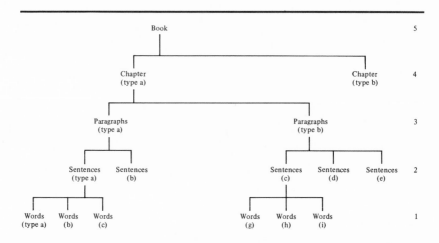

Figure 2.6.   Abbreviated hierarchic learning analysis of a book.

Figure 2.7

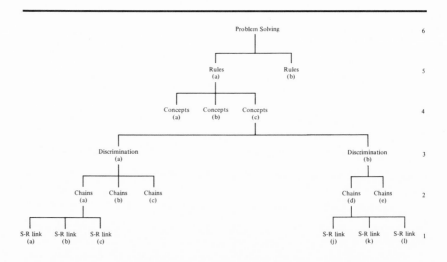

Figure 2.7.   Abbreviated hierarchic learning analysis of learning tasks.

(types a-i). In addition, the hierarchy shows how lower level members, such as words (types g, h, and i) are joined together into higher, more complex members, such as type c sentences.

Figure 2.7 depicts a similar type of hierarchy for the classification and analysis of learning tasks. The simplest task is a stimulus-response link (S-R link); these links are joined together to form various chains of responses. For example, S-R links (j, k, and l) are joined to form chain (d). Problem solving is the highest, most complex task in the hierarchy.

Several hierarchies similar to that in Figure 2.7 have been proposed for the classification and analysis of learning tasks. These hierarchies can be used to analyze subtasks to deduce the enabling skills prerequisite to performing each subtask. Bloom, Engelhart, Furst, Hill, and Krathwohl (1956) developed a theoretically based, hierarchic classification of cognitive or educational knowledge and skills. This system classifies performance into six levels: knowledge, comprehension, application, analysis, synthesis, and evaluation (the highest level). Krathwohl, Bloom, and Masia (1964) developed a taxonomy of affective performance. Harrow (1972) published a taxonomy of psychomotor skills. In the present context, a system based upon a hierarchy developed by Gagné (1977) appears to be the most useful means of classifying and analyzing learning tasks. Six levels of the hierarchy are described below. Note that although the hierarchy is based primarily on Gagné's taxonomy, some modifications have been made to the scheme; these changes are discussed following the definitions and examples.

Definitions and examples of each level of the learning hierarchy.

Stimulus-response links. A stimulus-response link involves a *single* link between *a* stimulus and *a* response. The occurrence of a *simple* stimulus (S) and response (R) link such as S = "light on" and R = "lever press," is rare. *Compound sets* of stimuli and responses joined by a *single* link are more common, for example, S_1 the teacher presents S_2 a spoon and says S_3 "point to spoon," and the learner R_1 raises his/her arm, R_2 extends his/her finger, and R_3 points to the spoon. Compound stimuli and responses that are joined by a single link and that can be taught or performed as

one continuous act with undifferentiated parts are defined as
stimulus-response links.

Chains. A chain is comprised of a set of verbal and/or motor
stimulus-response links (a series of alternating discriminative
stimuli and responses) performed in a fixed order. For example,
the chain: 1. picking up a spoon, 2. scooping food, and 3. putting
the food in one's mouth, involves three stimulus-response links.
The presence of the spoon and food is a stimulus for response 1,
picking up the spoon; the spoon in the hand is a stimulus for
response 2, scooping food, and the food on the spoon is a stimulus
for response 3, putting the food in one's mouth. A chain consists
of a number of responses that initially must be individually taught
before being linked together into a continuous chain.

Discriminations. Simple discriminations involve the distinguishing of one or more identical objects (e.g., the letter "n") from one
or more objects (e.g., the other letters of the alphabet). The
objects (letters) from which "n" is discriminated may be: 1.
identical to each other (e.g., s, s, & s), or 2. different from each
other (e.g., s, g, & a); as well as 3. similar to "n" (e.g., r, m, u, & h)
or dissimilar (e.g., s, d, & e). *Multiple* discriminations involve the
distinguishing of two or more objects (e.g., the letters n & a) from
one or more other objects (letters). One consistent S-R link or
chain such as either pointing, labeling, or selecting is made to
indicate each type of discrimination. Discriminations involve
learning the *discriminative features* or *essential characteristics* of
stimulus objects such as color, shape, texture, loudness, brightness,
and/or orientation.

Concepts. The learning of *concrete* concepts involves the
classification of (by pointing to, or naming) one or more familiar
and unfamiliar objects that are within the same class. Objects
within the same class are similar (have the same *discriminative*
characteristics), but they are not identical (have different *nondiscriminative* or *irrelevant* characteristics). Classification involves
discrimination of objects within a class from objects outside of the
class, and *generalization* of a response (classification) to similar,
previously unencountered members within the class. For example,
concept learning involves the classification of (e.g., by selectively

pointing to) a variety of different dogs, some previously unencountered (involves generalization), among several objects similar to dogs (involves discrimination). A learner who indicates that s/he can *discriminate* the features of a fox terrier, chihuahua, and wolfhound by selectively pointing only to these animals, indicates that s/he has learned the "concept of dog" by *generalizing* his/her selective pointing response to previously unencountered members of the class such as whippet, German shephard, and pekingese.

Rules. Rules are statements about the relationship between two or more concepts. A learner is considered to have acquired a rule when s/he has *demonstrated* its *application*. Simple recitation of a rule provides evidence of having learned a verbal chain rather than rule application. For example, the rule, "keys open locks," is a statement describing the relationship between three concepts: keys, open, and locks. To fully demonstrate application of this rule, a learner must: (1) *identify* (select) a variety of keys from among a number of objects that are not keys; (2) *identify* a variety of locks from among a number of objects that are not locks; (3) match keys to locks; (4) identify open and closed locks; and (5) orient, insert, and turn the keys to open the locks.

Problem Solving. Problem solving is demonstrated when a learner discovers a combination of two or more previously learned rules to solve an unfamiliar problem. The solution to the problem is discovered or invented, and the combination of rules produces a *higher-order* rule or problem solving strategy that subsequently can be used to obtain the solution to similar problems. An example of problem solving is demonstrated when an individual discovers that two rules: (1) keys open locks; and (2) striking an object may dislodge it from a fixed position, can be combined to solve the previously unencountered problem of a lock with a jammed bolt. Neither rule in isolation will solve the problem.

In the foregoing discussion of each level of the learning hierarchy, the major changes from Gagné's description of the hierarchy occur in the definition of S-R links and chains. As Gagné and Briggs (1974) define them, "often the distinction between a motor chain and a single connection S-R link is difficult to draw" (p. 38). "It is difficult indeed to find an example of human learning that might represent stimulus-response learning [an S-R link] in relatively pure form. Many instances that seem at first glance to be suitable examples turn out on closer inspection to represent somewhat more complex forms of chaining" (Gagné, 1977, p. 83). "Finding examples of this type of learning in adults is a practically impossible task" (Gagné, 1977, p. 88).

Should the following three behaviors be classified as S-R links or chains: pointing to an object, drawing a square, or saying "dog"? In the operant literature, each of these acts typically would be referred to as *a* response. The same literature, however, has also described speech training programs for handicapped children where sounds such as "d-o-g" were individually shaped and linked together into a chain. Similarly, programs have been developed to train the drawing of horizontal, vertical, and parallel lines as separate skills to be chained together in the drawing of squares. What about "pointing"? Is it a response or a chain? Consider the difficulty of teaching cerebral palsied children to point. The task involves: (a) raising an arm, (b) straightening the arm, (c) orienting the arm, and (d) extending the forefinger. These four separate responses are linked together in a chain. Part of the confusion between S-R links and chains appears to arise from the difficulty of defining a unitary response; even the smallest behavior can usually be analyzed into a number of subresponses that are linked together. Vargas (1977) defines a response as "a *unit* of behavior with a clear beginning and end . . . . How much behavior constitutes 'a response' is largely arbitrary. We can talk about the response of saying one word or of giving a whole lecture" (p. 311, italics added). In this definition, "a response" may include *one* response or several responses linked together. In the present context where the concern is with instruction, a response may be classified as either an S-R link or a chain depending upon the manner in which the response must be taught. If a response can be taught as one unified action, it is classified as an S-R link. Alternatively, if the components of a response must be taught separately before being linked together, the response is classified as a chain. For example, if a child must be taught each of the sounds in the word elephant as a separate component:

e-l-e-ph-a-n-t, the response is classified as a chain and each of the sounds is categorized as an S-R link. When S-R links and chains are defined in this manner, examples of both categories of behavior may be identified frequently and easily in both children and adults.

A hierarchic learning analysis of the subtasks on the ridgeline of a lattice indicates the enabling skills that are prerequisite to performance of the subtasks. For example, a subtask may be hierarchically classified as a concept; the concept is then analyzed into its enabling skills: discriminations, chains, and S-R links at successively lower levels of the hierarchy. The analysis of each successive level continues until a level in the hierarchy is reached where the enabling skills identified are already in the repertoire of the lowest learner in the target population. Those enabling skills already in the learner's repertoire are called entry level skills.

Since a lattice is constructed by analyzing subtasks into their enabling skills, a cross-check of the analysis can be performed by adding the enabling skills and the subtasks to verify that their sum equals the terminal behavioral objective. During the cross-check, redundant or non-essential skills are eliminated, omissions are filled in, and improperly sequenced enabling skills and subtasks may be adjusted.

Figure 2.8 shows a hierarchic learning analysis of the rule, "round things roll." This analysis was developed from ideas expressed by Gagné (1977, p. 137). Note that each of the enabling skills is hierarchically sequenced beneath the subtask.

Where more than one method of performing a task has been identified, a lattice may be prepared for each method. In principle, the simplest method of performance will require the fewest subtasks and enabling skills, and the fewest enabling skills at the upper levels of the hierarchy. The actual degree of simplicity of any method must be experimentally validated on the target population. In fact, since the entire procedure of a task analysis is based upon observation, logic, expert opinion, existing curricula, the principles of child development, and a theoretical learning hierarchy, each of the products of an analysis must be validated on the population for which the program is designed.

Figure 2.8

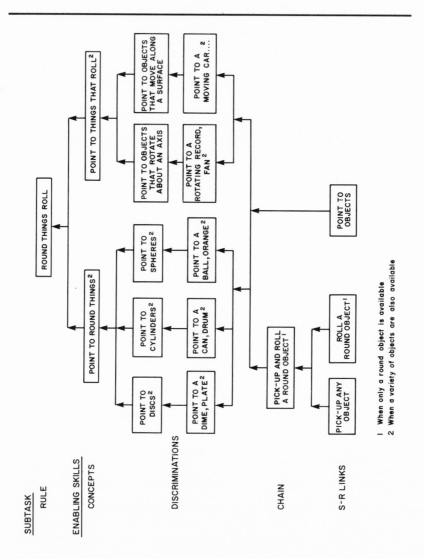

Figure 2.8. Hierarchic learning analysis of a rule.
        Note: 1. When only a round object is available.
        Note: 2. When a variety of objects is available.

The following checklist and Figure 2.9 summarize the major steps involved in performing and evaluating a task analysis.

Checklist for Performing and Evaluating a Task Analysis

	Completed	*N/A*
1. Review the research and theoretical literature, textbooks, instructional programs, curriculum guides, and teaching strategies and materials.		
2. Perform a conditions analysis: a. analyze the number, type, and range of conditions that occur and their usual variations;		
b. record changes in conditions that alter the number, type, and sequence of subtasks performed;		
c. determine the most difficult, commonly found conditions;		
d. determine simplest conditions under which instruction could begin;		
e. evaluate existing or potential prosthetic adaptations.		
3. Do a performance analysis of the number, type, and sequence of subtasks required to perform a task: a. review information derived from the evaluation of the learner population and the review of the literature and instructional materials;		

	Completed	N/A
b. "think-through," or, if possible, actually perform the task;		
c. assess task being performed by novice and accomplished performers under various conditions;		
d. in (b) and (c) above, observe and record what the learner does, how s/he does it, what s/he does to it, and why s/he does it.		
4. Construct a flowchart. Summarize the information derived from the conditions and performance analyses in a flowchart showing the sequence(s) of subtasks involved in performing the task under various conditions.		
5. Construct a lattice. Collapse the branching sequences of performance in a flowchart into the linear sequence on the ridgeline of a lattice.		
6. Perform a hierarchic learning analysis on the subtasks on the ridgeline to determine what enabling skills are required to perform each subtask: 　　　—S-R links 　　　—Chains 　　　—Discriminations 　　　—Concepts 　　　—Rules 　　　—Problem Solving a. hierarchically or procedurally sequence each of the enabling skills beneath the subskill for which it is a prerequisite;		

	Completed	N/A
b. record entry level skills.		
7. Cross-check the task analysis by adding the subtasks and enabling skills to see if their sum equals the terminal objective. a. edit the lattice and eliminate redundant or non-essential skills; fill in omissions.		
8. Compare lattices and select the simplest method of performance: fewest subtasks and enabling skills; fewest enabling skills at highest level of hierarchy.		

Practice Exercises

Problems

Answers to each of the following exercises are found at the end of this section.

1. Construct a flowchart showing the subtasks involved in crossing street corners that have either: (a) pedestrian lights, (b) traffic lights, or (c) no traffic or pedestrian control.

2. Construct a flowchart for the subtasks involved in adjusting the vertical hold knob on a TV set.

3. After exercise (2) has been completed, collapse the flowchart in Figure 2.11 into a lattice.

4. In a lattice describing dressing skills, the subtask of putting on a belt has been identified; analyze this chain into *all* of the S-R links, also sequence the links in the order in which they are performed.

5. The task of adjusting the vertical hold knob involves application of a *rule*: "Turn vertical hold knob left to the end, then turn to

Figure 2.9

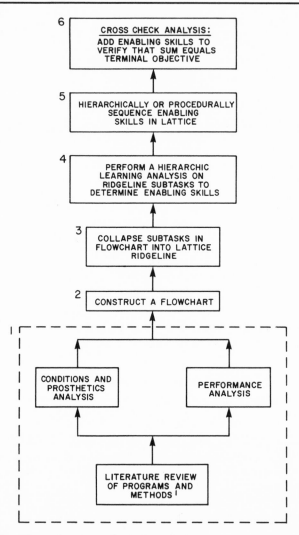

Figure 2.9.   *The major steps of a task analysis.*
          Note: 1. Step number one forms part of the preliminary stage
                    of instructional design and development of a terminal
                    behavioral objective, and also forms the basis of a task
                    analysis.

the right." Identify the concepts and S-R links in this rule. The manner in which concepts are analyzed into discriminations will be discussed in a later chapter.

6. Given a flowchart in which one of the subtasks is "the medial 'i' in consonant-vowel-consonant (CVC) words is short," perform a hierarchic learning analysis and sequence the enabling skills.

* * *

Answers

1. The flowchart in Figure 2.10 shows the operations and decisions involved in crossing street corners that have either: (a) pedestrian lights, (b) traffic lights, or (c) no traffic or pedestrian control. Figure 2.10 is a modification of a flowchart developed by Page, Iwata, and Neef (1976).
2. The flowchart in Figure 2.11 shows the subtasks involved in adjusting the vertical hold knob on a TV set.
3. The flowchart in Figure 2.12 illustrates the manner in which the subtasks in the vertical hold adjustment flowchart would be numbered and alphabetized in preparation for constructing a lattice. The skills would be sequenced in a lattice from left to right in the order: 1-5, A-B, 6-9, C-D, 10-12.
4. The S-R links involved in the chain of putting on a belt are listed in order of performance in Table 2.1. Test the validity of the sequence by following each of the steps as described.
5. The rule: "Turn vertical hold knob left to the end, then turn to the right," involves the following concepts (if a *general* rule is being taught): (a) vertical hold knob, (b) left, (c) to the end, (d) then, (e) to the right. The S-R links involve (a) turn to the left, and (b) turn to the right. If only one television set is involved (a general rule is not being taught), the vertical hold knob and "the end" would be discriminations rather than concepts. For example, the learner would have to identify only one vertical hold knob that would be identical from trial to trial; no generalization would be involved. "The end" would also always be the same from trial to trial; however, if more than one TV

set is involved, there may be several different types of ends: (a) silent or clicking, (b) solid or soft, or (c) will or will not continue to turn with increased effort applied. A turn to the left or a turn to the right are concepts whether or not a general rule is being taught as not all turns will be identical. Turns may vary in direction, speed, or distance turned. The learner must discriminate and generalize the relevant characteristic "direction of turn" while discriminating the irrelevant characteristics of speed and distance. Note that it is not necessary to learn the concepts of left and right or clockwise and counterclockwise to perform the task. The rule may be simplified by substituting "simpler concepts" (an empirical question) in the following manner: turn vertical hold knob in *one direction* to the end then turn in the *other direction.*

6. Figure 2.13 shows the results of a hierarchic learning analysis of the rule "the medial 'i' in CVC words is short."

Figure 2.10

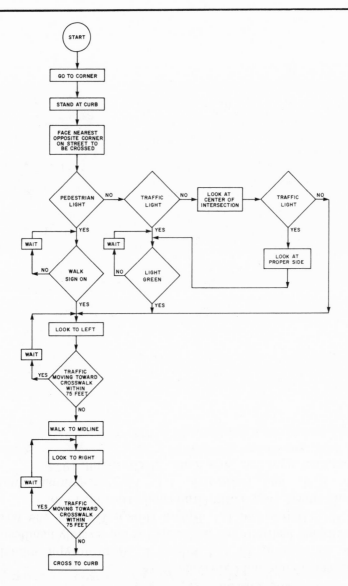

Figure 2.10. Flowchart showing steps involved in crossing a street.

Figure 2.11

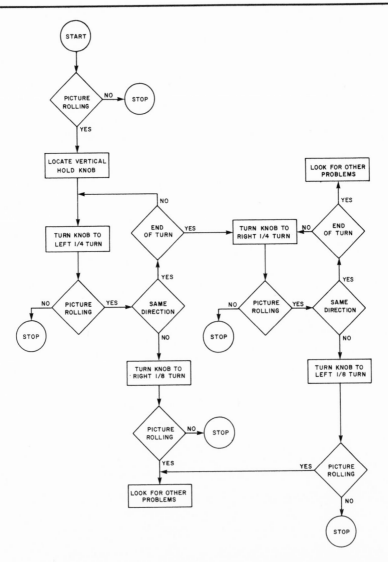

Figure 2.11. Flowchart shows steps involved in adjusting a vertical hold knob.

Figure 2.12

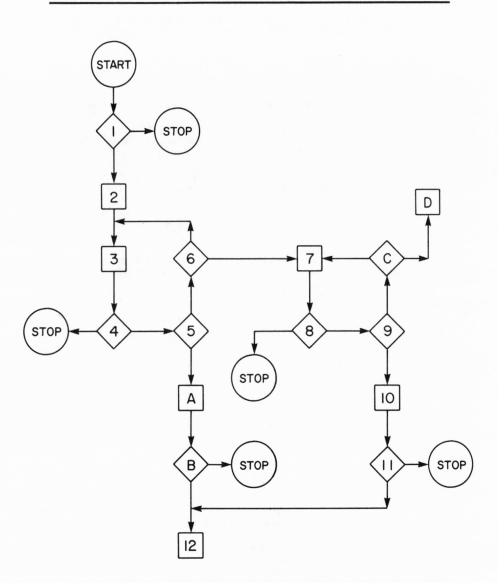

Figure 2.12. Numbering and lettering the vertical hold adjustment flowchart in preparation for constructing a lattice.

Table 2.1

---

1. Grasp tongue of belt with *right* hand and outside surface of belt towards palm and tongue in line with thumb.

2. Push tongue from right through the first loop to the left of the fly.

3. Pull belt through loop with left hand.

4. Repeat Step 1 and push tongue from right through the next loop to the left.

5. Repeat Step 4 on next loops in succession until next loop is even with or one loop beyond left shoulder.

6. Grasp tongue of belt with left hand and outside surface of belt away from palm and tongue in line with thumb—push tongue through next loop.

7. Move *right* hand from front, left side of body to rear, left side and pull belt through loop.

8. Repeat Step 6 on next loops in succession while pulling belt through each loop with right hand until next loop is just behind right shoulder.

9. Grasp tongue of belt with *right* hand as in Step 1.

10. Push tongue from right through each successive loop until just to the right of fly while pulling belt through each loop with left hand.

11. Grasp buckle in left hand.

12. Grasp tongue of belt with *right* hand.

13. Insert tongue of belt through rear of buckle.

14. Grasp tongue with left hand and pull until snug.

15. Transfer tongue to right hand.

16. Pull tongue away from body until snug.

17. Grasp tongue of *buckle* with left hand.

18. Insert tongue of *buckle* through eye in belt closest to buckle.

19. Grasp tongue of *belt* in right hand.

20. Push tongue of belt through retaining loop on belt.

Table 2.1. S-R links in belt buckling.

Figure 2.13

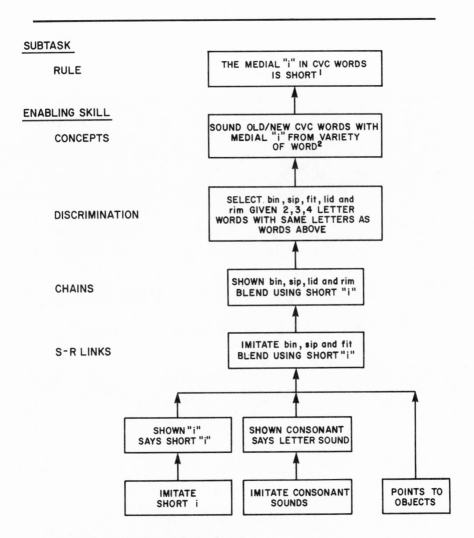

Figure 2.13. Hierarchic analysis of a rule.
> *Note: 1. Clymer (1963) claims that the rule, "The vowel in CVC words is short," applies in only 62% of the cases.*
> *Note: 2. Non-CVC words used may or may not have a medial "i" and may be in the form of: CCV, VVC or VCV, etc.*

Chapter 3

Instructional Sequencing

Contents

Instructional Sequencing: Introduction

Task analysis involves the analysis of a terminal behavioral objective to determine the subtasks and enabling skills required for a learner to proceed from his/her entry level to the terminal behavioral objective. The results of a task analysis are summarized in a lattice. Enabling skills in a lattice are hierarchically or procedurally sequenced into one or more strands beneath each subtask on the ridgeline. This organization of subtasks and skills provides an initial guideline for developing instructional sequences. Instructional sequencing involves the organization of subtasks and enabling skills into the order in which they will be taught. Generally speaking, the skills within a lattice are taught hierarchically. S-R links are taught first and then are combined into chains; discriminations are then taught as the bases for concepts that are later incorporated into rules and, subsequently, into problem solving strategies. Subtasks and enabling skills *may* be taught in the same sequence as they are performed in the terminal behavioral objective.

Beyond these general considerations, this chapter discusses three types of sequencing problems: how to sequence for instruction (a) S-R links and chains within a single strand of a lattice; (b) skills from two or more strands in one or more lattices; and (c) several skills within a single lesson. The discussion focuses primarily on the sequencing of S-R links and chains. Reference is made to the sequencing of discriminations and concepts; however, since the sequencing of these higher level skills involves a number of special considerations, the topic is more fully reviewed in a later chapter.

Sequencing S-R Links in a Chain

S-R links in a chain may be sequenced for instruction in several different ways. S-R links may be:
  (a) taught successively (one after the other) before being joined into a chain in a reverse order (reverse chaining) or in a forward order (forward chaining);
  (b) taught cumulatively and chained in a forward or reverse sequence. For example, skill A is taught before B; as B is taught, A is practiced while A and B are linked, following which C is taught and linked to A and B.

Two important guidelines for teaching chains regardless of the procedures used are:
  (a) consistently practice the S-R links in the order in which they are performed in the chain;
  (b) during instruction, sequence practice of adjacent S-R links as closely as possible.

Following these guidelines increases the probability that the completion of one S-R link will signal the beginning of the next S-R link in the chain. As S-R links become *discriminative stimuli* for successive links, the likelihood is reduced that any S-R link in a chain will be omitted or performed out of sequence.

In chains where many of the S-R links are difficult to learn and considerable practice is required to reach criterion,* learning the chain may be a long and arduous process. During instruction, there may be considerable time lapse between the performance of each link. As a result, the performance of an S-R link may come to signal the start of a teaching or correction sequence rather than the beginning of the next S-R link in the chain. In this situation, a *successive* teaching procedure may be suitable. Each S-R link would be taught independently and would be brought to criterion before being sequenced into a chain in a forward or reverse order. When a successive teaching technique has been used, it may be advantageous to use *overlearning* procedures. Overlearning requires the learner to continue to practice the entire chain repeatedly, rapidly, and accurately after the chain has reached criterion. Overlearning should increase the association between each link in the chain, providing the repeated practice is rewarding rather than aversive.

Where the S-R links within a chain can be learned relatively quickly with few errors, and where each S-R link can be performed during instruction in relatively close approximation to the next, a cumulative teaching sequence may be appropriate. In a *cumulative*, forward chaining procedure, S-R link 1 is taught and continues to be practiced as S-R link 2 is taught. These links are then chained and continue to be practiced as S-R link 3 is taught. The advantage of cumulative versus successive instruction is that adjoining skills are taught and linked at the same time. During cumulative instruction, the learner receives repeated practice in which adjoining links are performed in rapid succession. Thus, the need for overlearning may be reduced or removed.

Alternatively, where one or two skills within a chain are difficult to learn, a combination of successive and cumulative sequencing may be advantageous. In this case, where it is predicted that an S-R link in a chain will be particularly difficult to learn, the link may be removed temporarily from the chain for

---

*"To reach or achieve criterion" refers to the ability of a learner to perform at a predetermined level of competence, defined in terms of speed and accuracy over a number of trials. The criterion or standard is specified in a behavioral objective.

preteaching. After the task has been mastered during preteaching, it may be reintroduced into the chain for cumulative instruction. Preteaching is also a useful technique when several links in a chain have a common component. For example, Engelmann (1978) suggested that in the task of tying shoe laces, a pincer grip is common to grasping the laces, crossing them over, tying a half-knot, making a loop, wrapping the lace around the loop, and pushing the lace through the eye to make a second loop. If the pincer grip is not well established before the chain begins, it may interfere with the performance of each of these tasks. Thus, it may be beneficial to preteach this skill before beginning to teach the chain.

A precaution should be observed, however, in preteaching S-R links removed from a chain. Removal of a link from the context of the chain may produce a slight change in the conditions surrounding performance and a resulting change in the nature of the response. As a consequence, even though the response reaches criterion during preteaching, it may not fit back into the chain. This situation may be avoided when pretraining conditions and tasks are maintained as closely as possible to those existing within the chain.

Table 3.1 displays the sequence in which five S-R links in a chain are *cumulatively* taught in a forward chaining sequence. In the first *series* of trials, S-R link 1 is taught (T) to criterion. Then as link 2 is taught to criterion during the second series of trials, link 1 is practiced (P). The remaining links in the chain are cumulatively taught in the same manner. In the sixth series of trials, the entire chain is brought to criterion. If required, practice in overlearning the chain is provided in the seventh series of trials.

When a new link in a chain is being taught, each of the previously mastered links may or may not be practiced each time the new link is attempted. For example, if link 3 was being taught, links 1 and 2 could be practiced each time link 3 was attempted, or link 3 could be brought to mastery over several trials before links 1, 2, and 3 were practiced together. Practical experience indicates that where links 1 and 2 can be quickly and easily practiced, they should be performed each time link 3 is attempted.

Table 3.1

		S-R LINKS				
		1	2	3	4	5
	1	T				
SERIES	2	P	T			
OF	3	P	P	T		
TRIALS	4	P	P	P	T	
	5	P	P	P	P	T
MASTERY	6	P	P	P	P	P
OVERLEARNING	7	P	P	P	P	P

Table 3.1. Cumulative forward chaining.

This practice will strengthen links 1 and 2 and their relationship to link 3. However, where: (a) one or more of the earlier links is time-consuming to perform; or (b) the link being taught requires many trials to reach criterion, it may be advisable not to practice all of the previously learned links on each trial. The link being taught could be brought to criterion before being joined to all of the previous links. Alternatively, the previous links could be *intermittently practiced* to maintain the responses at a criterion level.

Perhaps an example will clarify some of these points. The chain of S-R links involved in shoe-tying is listed below.
   (a) grasp left and right laces between thumbs and forefinger of respective hands;
   (b) cross each lace over to the opposite hand;
   (c) pass one lace through the eye of the triangle made by the two laces;

(d) tighten the laces;

(e) form a loop with one lace (x);

(f) pass the other lace (y) one-half way around the base of the loop;

(g) push a segment of lace (y) near the base of loop (x) through the eye made by laces (x) and (y);

(h) pull lace (y) through to make a loop;

(i) pull loops (x) and (y) to tighten.

The following cumulative, forward chaining sequence may be employed to teach each of these S-R links.

(a) Practice step a, above, repeatedly until it is performed quickly and properly three times in succession (criterion).

(b) Practice a and b together until they reach criterion.

(c) Practice a, b, and c together until they reach criterion.

(d) Practice a, b, c, and d together until they reach criterion.

(e) If step e, forming a loop, results in several errors, practice this step repeatedly in isolation before practicing all of the preceding steps. However, if it takes a long time to teach step e, and there is a chance that previous skills will be lost, practice all of the previous steps intermittently while step e is being brought to criterion.

(f) Teach the remaining steps in the same manner.

(g) Whenever a period of time has lapsed between practice sessions, always bring all of the previously taught steps up to criterion before teaching the next step.

In some cases, the S-R links in a chain may be taught in a reverse order. This procedure is called *reverse chaining*. Table 3.2 shows the sequence in which skills are taught (T) and practiced (P). The last link in the chain, link 5, is brought to criterion first, then as link 4 is being taught, link 5 continues to be practiced. Whether to exercise each of the successive skills each time a new skill is practiced is decided in the same manner as it is for forward chaining.

In both forward and reverse chaining, the S-R links are always performed in the order in which they are sequenced in the chain. The major advantage of reverse chaining appears to be that right from the first step, the learner performs the link that completes

Table 3.2

		1	2	3	4	5
						S-R LINKS
	1					T
SERIES	2				T	P
OF	3			T	P	P
TRIALS	4		T	P	P	P
	5	T	P	P	P	P
MASTERY	6	P	P	P	P	P
OVERLEARNING	7	P	P	P	P	P

Table 3.2. *Cumulative reverse chaining.*

the chain being taught. Completion of the chain in this manner may help to increase the sense of achievement, while clearly establishing the purpose of the ensuing instruction. Neither of these advantages is as readily available in forward chaining. A possible disadvantage of reverse chaining is that the learner receives the least amount of practice with the first links in the chain. As a result, in later performances the chain may break down in its early stages as links are either omitted or resequenced. This difficulty may be overcome by increasing the number of overlearning trials. There is insufficient evidence in the research literature to permit a conclusion to be drawn regarding the relative efficacy of forward or reverse chaining, and successive or cumulative instruction. The actual methods used to teach chains of S-R links are discussed in Chapter Five.

Sequencing Skills from Two or More Strands

The foregoing discussion has been concerned with the sequencing of S-R links within a single chain or strand within a lattice. It is also possible to teach concurrently S-R links from different strands in one or more lattices. In addition, various levels of performance, such as S-R links and problem solving, can be taught at the same time. A learner is ready to learn any skill for which s/he has suitable entry level skills. Thus, during a single lesson of instruction, a learner may be *acquiring* new skills, *generalizing* established skills, and practicing or *maintaining* skills learned in previous lessons.

The following discussion describes a method by which skills from two or more strands in one or more lattices are sequenced over several lessons during *concurrent instruction.* Figure 3.1 displays a lattice of the skills required for counting, reading, and writing the numbers one to 100.

Before continuing the discussion on sequencing, some of the characteristics of the lattice will be explained. Look along the ridgeline of the lattice to subtask I; beneath subtask I find strand 1 and enabling skill A. The arrows indicate that the skill of "rote counting by 1^S to a given number ≤ 10" is prerequisite to both enabling skills 1B and 2A. A similar relationship exists among the enabling skills in subtask IV, strand 3.

As previously mentioned, it is possible to teach one strand of this lattice at a time. For example, strand I1, "rote counting by 1^S to 100" could be taught in isolation. Alternatively, strands I1, 2, and 3, all related to rote counting, could be taught concurrently. Also, there may be advantages to teaching counting, reading, and writing skills at the same time. For example, lesson 30 in *DISTAR Arithmetic 1, Second Edition* (Engelmann and Carnine, 1975), includes instruction from the following areas of the lattice: I1A, IIA, IIIA, IVA.

Table 3.3 illustrates the manner in which skills are introduced at the beginning of a program and how successively more skills are added to each lesson as the program progresses. Eventually, a single lesson may involve the instruction of several different skills. For example, in the introductory phases of a program, a single

Figure 3.1

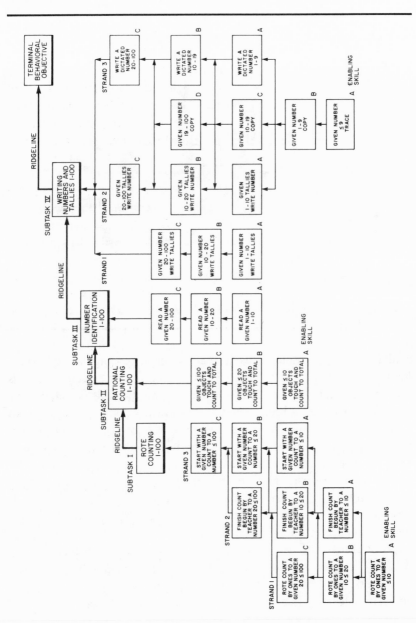

Figure 3.1.   A lattice for counting, reading, and writing numbers of 1-100.

Table 3.3

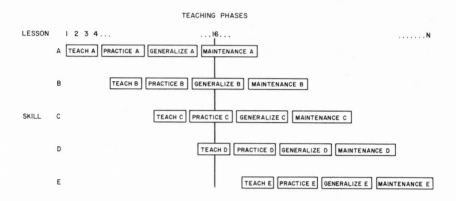

Table 3.3.   Distribution of skills and teaching phases across lessons.

skill (A) may be taught; as it reaches or approximates criterion, instruction in a second skill (B) is begun. As the second skill is taught, the first skill continues to be practiced. Skills (C, D, and E) continue to be added to the program in this manner. In subsequent lessons, for example, in lesson 16, maintenance, generalization, practice, and teaching of various skills (A, B, C, and D) may be included in a single lesson.

The *acquisition* or learning of a skill during the teaching phase of instruction refers to the ability of a learner to perform a skill at criterion level without assistance within a relatively simple instructional context. *Generalization* (or transfer) of a skill refers to the ability of the learner to perform an acquired skill in different contexts, with various control figures (teachers, employers, peers, or parents), and a variety of cues (verbal, physical, or social). A learner has generalized a skill when s/he can perform at criterion without assistance under the most difficult, commonly found conditions and under the usual variations in the conditions. *Maintenance* of a response refers to the ability of a learner to maintain an acceptable rate and style of performance without assistance under the generalization conditions after successively longer periods of time following the termination of instruction. A skill that has been maintained in this manner has been *mastered.* Maintenance trials are generally distributed in a manner somewhat as depicted in Figure 3.2.

After a new response has been taught and generalized, the response is repeatedly rehearsed in a block of trials designated as number one. Following a brief interval, without practice, the response is again rehearsed during a shorter block of trials. As time progresses, the interval between practice sessions increases, while the block of rehearsals decreases. During each practice session, the response is brought to criterion. How many trials to include within each block and how long a period of time to leave between blocks depend upon the nature of the learner and the task. The goal of efficient instruction is to train the learner to function independently, as soon as possible, with the minimum amount of maintenance training. On the other hand, each learner must be provided with a sufficient amount of *distributed practice* to insure maintenance of the response. For example, a learner initially may require several hundred trials per session, morning and afternoon, to maintain a newly acquired response. Another learner may be able to maintain the same response for one week after initially practicing it only four or five times. The nature of the learner and the task determine the number and frequency of trials required to initially teach a response and bring it to criterion before generalization training can begin. The task and learner also influence the schedule of introduction and the number of tasks that can be introduced into a lesson.

Sequencing Instructional Events Within a Single Lesson

The previous discussion describes the manner in which successively more skills from various strands and lattices are introduced into an instructional program until eventually a single lesson may

Figure 3.2

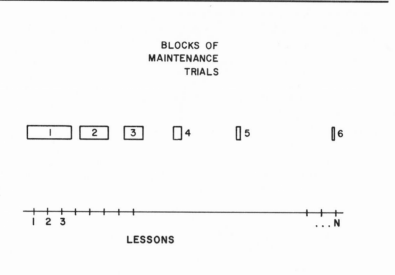

Figure 3.2.   Scheduling of maintenance trials across lessons.

include teaching, practice, generalization, and maintenance of a variety of skills. Table 3.4 displays a generic model for the sequencing of four phases of instruction during a single lesson. Phase One incorporates *rehearsal* and *pretraining* exercises in preparation for the acquisition of new skills. In Phase Two, either new skills are *acquired,* or skills learned in previous lessons are *generalized.* During Phase Three, skills taught in earlier lessons are *maintained* through distributed practice. Newly acquired skills or generalizations are *reviewed* in Phase Four. The rationale for each phase of the model is described below.

Phase one (a): rehearsal. The rehearsal phase provides a review of previously learned skills that are components of, or prerequisites to, the skills to be taught during a later phase of the lesson. Previously learned S-R links may be reviewed in preparation for learning new chains or discriminations. For example, using a

Table 3.4

Phase	Activity	Purpose	Pace	Duration	Rate of Reinforcement
1. (a) Rehearsal and/or	Review of previously learned skills that are components of, or prerequisites to, the next skill to be taught (e.g., review of skills in hierarchy).	• Warm-up: bring skills back to competency level; transition from previous activity (e.g., gym); establish learning set (sitting and attending).	Fast		Intermittent (e.g., VR 3-5) (Verbal)
(b) Pretraining	Pretrain difficult S-R links in the next chain to be taught. Teach new object label for later discrimination.	• Facilitate rapid and smooth sequencing of S-R links in next chain to be learned. Teach first step in a discrimination.	Medium	Total (3-5)	Continuous (Verbal)
2. (a) Acquisition and/or	Teaching a new S-R link, chain, discrimination, or concept. Includes group instruction, and group and individual testing.	• Incorporation of previously learned skills. • Removal of instructional assistance. • Achieve and maintain at least 85 percent accuracy.	Slow		Continuous (Verbal Plus)
(b) Generalization	Introduction of skills learned in previous lessons to variations in context, control figures, and performance cues. Includes group instruction, and group and individual testing.	• Teach learner to perform under most difficult, commonly found conditions. • Teach learner to cope with usual variations of conditions. • Removal of instructional assistance. • Achieve and maintain at least 85 percent accuracy.	Slow	Total (10-12)	Continuous (Verbal Plus)
3. Maintenance	Review one or more skills taught in previous lessons. Use various "game" formats.	Maintain previous learning by review after successively longer periods of time.	Fast	(4-6)	Intermittent Infrequent Verbal Only
4. Review	Review skills and/or generalizations taught earlier in this lesson.	Maintain recent learning and generalization through review.	Slow	(6-8)	Continuous (Verbal and Occasional Plus)
				Total (23-31)	

Table 3.4. Sequence of instructional events within a lesson.

pointing response in matching figures in a match-to-sample format may be rehearsed. Preinstructional rehearsal assists the learner in making the transition to a learning situation from nonacademic activities, such as lunch or gym periods. Appropriate learning readiness skills: sitting, listening to the teacher, attending to stimulus materials, and recalling skills prerequisite to the next task are practiced and reinforced. The rehearsal phase should be as brief as possible. Appropriate study behaviors and prerequisite skills are rapidly reviewed and are brought up to competency level before the next phase of instruction is begun.

The suggested duration of each instructional phase shown in Table 3.4 provides a gross estimate indicating the relative proportion of time to be spent in each activity. The actual amount of time spent in any phase would depend upon the nature of the learner(s) and the task.

Because the skills being reviewed in Phase One are already established, they are only intermittently verbally *reinforced.* Reinforcement, in this context, refers to the provision by a teacher of a rewarding consequence following the performance by a learner of an appropriate response. The reinforcer provides feedback about the correctness of a response and increases the likelihood that it will recur. Reinforcers may be verbal: "good pointing"; or social: smile, pat on the shoulder; or tangible: giving a checkmark; or edible. In token reinforcement, checkmarks or other tallies may be "cashed-in" after the lesson for a variety of rewards. A ratio of approximately one reinforcer for every three to five responses is designed to create a positive atmosphere and motivate the learner to give his/her best effort and to persevere when learning becomes difficult. In later phases of instruction where new skills are being learned, continuous verbal reinforcement (one reward/correct response) is dispensed. The phrase "verbal plus" in Table 3.4 indicates that tangible, or token reinforcers, may also be awarded, as required, on a continuous or intermittent basis.

The *pace* of instruction varies over the four phases. Carnine (1977) defines the pace of instruction in terms of the interval after the learner responds *verbally* and introduction of the next task.

During group instruction using DISTAR materials, fast pace is defined as a delay of one second or less, slow pace is considered to be a delay of five seconds or more. The interval between the point where a response is requested: "What letter is this?" or "Point to the cup," and the manual signal to respond: teacher drops hand or points to child to signal the time to respond, is variable and should give all learners the opportunity to prepare the appropriate answer.

Pace has been shown to be an important variable in instruction. Engelmann and Bruner (1974), using DISTAR Reading I in a group format, studied the effect of increasing the number of questions asked from four per minute to 12 per minute. The percentage of correctly answered questions rose from 30 percent to 80 percent. The percentage of time children were off-task decreased from 70 percent to ten percent. Carnine (1976a) in studies of preschoolers, and first and second graders has found similar results. More material was covered, and there was less disruptive behavior. The authors caution that the results do not necessarily imply that in all cases faster presentations are better. In fact, a rapid pace over a long period may become aversive and disruptive. To establish a suitable pace, it is necessary to monitor the error rate, while using effective reinforcers to shape the rate, duration, and accuracy of responses. In the model presented in Table 3.4, the pace of instruction varies over the four phases in accord with the nature of the task. New skills are taught at a slow pace, while the review of established materials is rapidly paced. No research data are available regarding the appropriate pacing of motor chains. There are physiological limitations on the time required to perform a chain, on the number of times a chain can be performed in succession, and on the time required for *recovery* between trials. Presumably the pacing of motor responses (the period of time between trials) should be slower than that used for verbal responses. Alternatively, to increase variation in stimulation (to increase attention and motivation) and allow sufficient time for recovery following a motor response, the pace of instruction could be maintained at a relatively rapid rate by alternating motor and verbal responses.

Phase one (b): pretraining. Pretraining during Phase One involves advance training of one or more responses in preparation for major skill training in a later part of the lesson. For example, when it is anticipated that some S-R links in a chain will be difficult to learn, they may be pretrained. As discussed earlier, advance training of an S-R link may facilitate its inclusion in a chain and avoid the problems of omission and resequencing. Pretraining may also include the teaching of a new object label for later discrimination training. For example, during pretraining, the learner may be taught the label "cup"; during the acquisition phase s/he may be taught to discriminate cups from other objects. Pretraining warm-up exercises, before discrimination or concept instruction, may include attending to and/or labeling discriminative features of stimuli: colors, shapes, or patterns. Gold and Barclay (1973), in some preliminary studies of moderately and severely handicapped individuals assembling bicycle brakes, found that groups given verbal labels for various parts of the brakes, performed better than groups for whom the parts were not labeled. No pretesting was conducted to find out if the groups understood the labels used. As new skills are being learned during pretraining, the pace of instruction may be slightly slower than the pace used during the rehearsal of established skills.

Phase two (a): acquisition. The acquisition phase involves the learning of new S-R links, chains, discriminations, concepts, rules, and/or problem solving. The actual teaching procedures used during this phase are discussed in the chapters on instructional techniques. During the early part of acquisition training, the learner is prompted (given assistance) while performing to minimize errors and maximize the number of trials in which the correct response is practiced. As the new response becomes better established, the prompts are systematically *faded* (progressively withdrawn) until the learner is able to perform the response without assistance. In programmed instruction, an 85 percent accuracy rate is usually considered to be the minimum criterion required before a learner is permitted to proceed to the next stage of instruction. Some tasks may require higher standards of performance. However, the 85 percent level of competency permits the lowest performer in a group to proceed without holding back his/her progress by demanding higher levels of performance during initial instruction. As the learner proceeds to acquire new skills, s/he is given the opportunity to practice and master previously instructed skills.

Phase two (b): generalization. In the past, the process of generalization of newly acquired skills often has been taken for granted. A child's ability to perform a skill competently in an instructional environment was assumed to *transfer* automatically to other environments in which the response was appropriate. Now, however, it is usually recognized that generalization is not automatic and that procedures to teach generalization must be built into instructional programs. The purpose of generalization training is to teach the learner to use a newly acquired response under conditions that differ in non-essential ways from those in the instructional environment. The learner is taught to make the response in environments in which the people, seating arrangements, and/or manner in which a problem is presented change, but the essential or discriminative characteristics of the situation remain the same. For example, when a teacher presents a hypothetical situation during small-group instruction of proper social conduct, students may correctly describe or demonstrate how they would respond. In this case, generalization training would be concerned with the transfer of the behavior into appropriate action when the hypothetical situation became a reality in the absence of the teacher and in the presence of a different social and physical context. Various means of achieving generalization are discussed in Chapter Five.

Phase three: maintenance. Maintenance training is concerned with the ability of the learner to maintain an acceptable rate and style of response under appropriate conditions following the termination of instruction. Generally, maintenance of a response is trained by requiring the learner to rehearse an appropriate response after successively longer periods of time. Without suitable maintenance training, a learner may be unable to perform a response that s/he had only recently performed to criterion. All newly acquired responses should be put on a maintenance schedule of rehearsal. When a new response is taught, the nature of both the learner and the response should be considered in establishing a suitable schedule for review of the response. During any particular lesson of instruction, however, regardless of the schedule of review, priority should be given to reviewing: (a) troublesome responses with a high error rate; (b) recently learned responses that may not be well established; and (c) skills, discriminations, or concepts not recently reviewed (Carnine, 1979).

Maintenance of a response is also assisted by systematically reducing the amount of reinforcement in the training situation until the frequency, amount, and type of reinforcement approximates that of the general environment. For example, if a learner has acquired a response under highly reinforcing conditions where ample verbal and tangible reinforcement is used, the response may not be maintained in an environment where reinforcement is infrequent, implicit, and rarely in a verbal or tangible form.

If the rate and type of reinforcement in the training situation are changed too abruptly, the response may not be maintained. Reinforcing conditions in the training environment must be progressively changed to approximate those in the general environment. Reinforcement procedures are discussed in Chapter Four.

Phase four: review. During Phase Four, a brief review is provided of skills and generalized responses learned earlier in the lesson. The purpose of the review is to evaluate short-term maintenance and to reinforce recent learning through the use of distributed practice following a brief period in which other skills have been exercised.

Several questions may be raised regarding the efficacy of sequencing four phases of instruction within a single lesson. Are students able to cope with this instructional diversity within such a short period of time? What are the advantages and disadvantages of this type of sequencing? The best evidence in support of this approach comes from the use of the DISTAR programs in the Follow Through Project. DISTAR has been used successfully with a great variety of economically disadvantaged children and with children having IQ's below 80 in kindergarten to grade three (Carnine, 1977). On a much smaller scale, Panyan and Hall (1978) conducted a comparison study of the effects of serial versus concurrent task sequencing on acquisition, maintenance, and generalization with severely retarded females. During serial training, one task was trained to criterion before the other task was introduced. The concurrent method alternated training between two tasks every five minutes during a 15-minute training session. There was no difference in acquisition time or retention between the two methods. Generalization (learning untrained items) favored the concurrent approach. The potential disruption of alternating the tasks was assessed by comparing the results of the last five trials of the first five minutes of each session with the results obtained in the first five trials of the last five-minute session. The results showed that there were twice as many gains as losses during the concurrent training. Concurrent instruction did not produce interference and, in fact, appeared to result in an improvement in the rate of appropriate responses.

Of primary importance in programs using concurrent sequencing of instruction is the nature of the tasks that are alternated. In the Panyan and Hall study, tracing letters (a motor response) was alternated with verbal imitation. If two similar tasks are alternated in quick succession, *inhibition* may occur. In *proactive inhibition,* prior learning influences the remembering of subsequently learned material. In *retroactive inhibition,* learning subsequent to original learning affects recall of the original material. There are many experimental examples of proactive and retroactive inhibition. Underwood (1957) provides a summary of the research on proactive inhibition. Melton and Irwin (1940) performed an outstanding study of retroactive inhibition. To avoid inhibition, closely sequenced tasks should be dissimilar. There are several ways in which tasks may vary; some examples are listed below:

(a) stimulus modality—visual or auditory;
(b) response modality—manual or oral;
(c) stimulus format—match-to-sample, oddity, completion;
(d) response form—manual: cross out, point to, pick-up;
　　　　　—verbal: yes/no, label, explain;
(e) stimulus media—chalkboard, workbook, language master.

Another important feature in the concurrent sequencing of instruction is the amount of organization required by the teacher to rapidly change from task to task to minimize any potential disruption and time loss. The DISTAR programs use "highly engineered material" (McDaniels, 1975); each example within each lesson has been preprogrammed, teacher dialogue and hand signals have been prescripted, and all materials are prepared and packaged in advance.

Considering the problems that are possible, and the steps required to avoid them, what are some of the potential advantages of concurrent instruction?

    (a) The variation in tasks, formats, pacing, and reinforcement between phases may increase interest and motivation among learners with short attention spans who, because of a life-time experience of failure, otherwise may find instruction aversive. "Variations in pacing, rhythm, loudness, and pauses are essential elements in attention holding presentations" (Becker, Engelmann, and Thomas, 1975(b) p. 189).

    (b) The sequencing of various tasks within a single lesson permits massed practice to establish a new response and distributed practice to maintain it. Distributed practice with brief intervening "recovery intervals" is necessary during the acquisition of new motor responses where prolonged exercise may lead to fatigue and an increase in errors.

    (c) Repeated, short, and intense practice sessions may be alternated with slower paced, more interesting material when frequent drill is required to reinforce new responses.

    (d) The inclusion of a review session provides the opportunity to reevaluate a newly acquired response after a brief interval to assess its initial durability and to provide reinforcement as required.

    (e) Repeated practice within a short interval is frequently required to establish new responses and to maintain old responses. With successive sequencing of instruction, both types of responses cannot receive the distribution of practice they require. In successive practice, as a new response is being brought to criterion, old responses may deteriorate from lack of practice.

(f) Having a flexible time interval for each phase of instruction, and requiring that a response be brought to criterion before progressing from one phase to the next permit individualization of instruction. The amount of teaching, practice, and correction required within each phase may be adjusted to individual needs.

Review of Concepts and Procedures Covered in Chapters One to Three

Before proceeding into new material, review the following concepts and procedures discussed in the previous three chapters. Use a paper and pencil as applicable: (1) define or explain; (2) provide a novel example; (3) describe where, when, and how to apply or evaluate; and (4) discuss advantages and disadvantages of each term. As a term is being reviewed, cover all of the other terms to avoid giving yourself clues. If you are unable to recall the information *rapidly* and *accurately*, refer to the listed page number(s) and review the material; page numbers with major references have been underlined. Note troublesome terms and put them into a maintenance schedule for repeated review after successively longer periods of time.

Subject	Page No.

Instructional Methods: One

Contents

Prompting and Fading

Handicapped individuals with a history of learning difficulties may regard instruction as an aversive activity. New instructional exercises may be viewed as new opportunities for failure. Unfortunately, a self-fulfilling prophecy of failure may result. The anticipation of failure may reduce motivation, attention, and effort, resulting in a high error rate and confirmation of the prediction of failure. Noonan and Barry (1967) found that children with a history of failure made stereotyped responses that reflected a lack of effort or involvement; these children appeared willing to accept low rates of success. One of the problems associated with making an incorrect response is that once an error has occurred, it is much more likely to recur (McCandless, 1967; Terrace, 1963). Thus, when introducing new instruction to handicapped learners, it is important to maximize the opportunity for success and reinforce each learner's efforts. *Errorless learning* is a technique employing prompting, fading, and reinforcement procedures to overcome the difficulties described above.

Prompting. A prompt is a supplementary stimulus provided to assist a student to respond in a desired manner. There are two major purposes for which prompts are used. Prompts may be used to aid a learner to perform the mechanics of a difficult or complex motor task. For this purpose, prompts may be provided in the form of verbal, modeling, gestural, and/or physical assistance. Prompts may also be used to assist a learner to select a stimulus in a difficult discrimination task. In this procedure, various techniques may be used to increase the discriminative characteristics of the stimulus that the learner is to select. An increase in the saliency of discriminative characteristics may be achieved by: (a) embellishing the discriminative features, (b) diminishing the intensity of nondiscriminative features, and/or (c) introducing an extra (redundant) stimulus to focus attention on the discriminative features.

Initially, the prompt takes control of the response—assists the response to occur in the presence of the stimulus. Eventually, however, the discriminative features of the stimulus must take control of the response. The transfer of control from the prompt to the discriminative stimulus is achieved through the process of fading.

Fading. Fading involves the systematic and gradual withdrawal of a prompt following repeated performance of a response in the presence of a discriminative stimulus. The purpose of fading is to transfer control of a response from a prompt to a discriminative stimulus. Prompts are faded from use as quickly as possible to avoid overdependence upon them; they are also faded as slowly as is necessary to maintain a high rate of correct responding.

Thus, errorless learning involves the use of prompts to: (a) focus learner attention and assist discrimination learning, and/or (b) facilitate performance of a complex motor response. Errorless learning also involves the use of various fading procedures by which a high rate of correct responding is maintained while control over the response is transferred from the prompt to the discriminative stimulus.

Prompting Motor Responses

Verbal prompts. Verbal prompts involve the use of instructions, rules, or principles to guide the learner's response. Voice inflection may also be used to direct attention to particular parts of a verbal stimulus. When verbal prompts are used, several cautions should be observed: (a) the learner's attention must be secured before proceeding; (b) the vocabulary used must be understood by the learner; (c) the sentence structure employed should be neither too long nor too complex for the learner; (d) it is important to use a consistent vocabulary and sentence structure from trial to trial; (e) the steps of a chain must be described in sequence; (f) the number of statements given at any one time should be limited; and (g) verbal statements should be made slowly, clearly, and with rhythm.

Gestures. Gestural prompts (or primes) involve the use of a gesture to occasion a response. The teacher does not come in direct physical contact with the learner. A gesture may take the form of tapping on the table behind an object to be selected, pointing to or touching an object, or moving one's hand along the path that a movement is to follow. As in the use of verbal prompts, the learner's attention must be obtained before gesturing begins; the gesture should be made slowly, simply, and consistently from trial to trial.

Modeling. Simply stated, modeling (imitative prompting) involves demonstration of an act by a teacher followed by imitation of the act by the learner. There are two general types of modeling that are used, depending upon the length and complexity of the task and the level of functioning of the learner. An act may be performed in its entirety before the student attempts to imitate it, or the task may be performed in segments following each of which the student responds and receives feedback and reinforcement or correction before proceeding. Before modeling begins, it is important to focus the learner's attention on the model, or more specifically, on an object that the model is going to manipulate. Thus, before using modeling, it may be advantageous to teach the learner to orient appropriately to "Look at me," or "Look at this." Bandura (1965) suggested that modeling should be performed in slow motion. Benefit may be derived from exaggerating important parts of the act, and by confirming the learner's observations by having him/her point to critical features. Parton (1976) suggested that if directionality of a response is important, the act should be modeled so that the learner does not have to reverse the direction of the demonstration. In some cases, it may be desirable for the model to stand with his/her back to the learner, to stand beside the learner, or to reach around the learner during the demonstration. When errors occur in the learner's attempt to imitate a model, the modeled response may be repeated in segments (Snell, 1978). Zimmerman and Rosenthal (1974) found that modeling used in conjunction with verbal instruction, which explained the model's behavior, facilitated children's imitation, generalization, and retention. Modeling also has the advantage of permitting group instruction in which both teachers and peers may act as models.

Physical prompting. Physical prompting involves a "hands-on" approach to prompting. There are two levels of physical prompting. In partial physical prompting, the learner is gently touched, pushed, or guided to indicate when and how to respond. In full physical prompting, the teacher fully grasps the learner and "puts him/her through" the task. Foxx and Azrin (1972) described the following graduated-guidance procedure: (a) begin with as much assistance as is necessary; (b) use the minimum amount of pressure for the motion to be completed; and (c) concentrate on the body part that is the locus of action, e.g., in feeding, focus on the hand. To fade a physical prompt: (a) gradually reduce the pressure applied, and (b) move the guidance away from the locus of the action, e.g., in feeding, move assistance from the hand, to the wrist, and then to the elbow. Thomas, Sulzer-Azaroff, Lukeris, and Palmer (1976) successfully used these steps to teach self-care and vocational skills. Striefel and Wetherby (1973) used a similar procedure to teach a profoundly retarded boy to follow instructions. Physical guidance is useful with very low functioning learners and may be used to teach imitation of modeled responses.

Prompts compared. Walls, Ellis, Zane, and Vanderpoel (1979) compared the relative effectiveness of verbal, physical, and modeling prompts as well as a combination of all three. Their subjects were mentally retarded adults (age 18 - 50 years) in a vocational rehabilitation program. The trainees were taught to construct a movie projector, a truck carburetor, a bicycle brake, and a lawn mower engine, each comprised of eight pieces. The results indicated that verbal prompts alone required significantly more time to achieve criterion and produced a higher number of errors. No statistically significant difference was found between the use of physical prompts, modeling prompts, or the use of the combination of physical, verbal, and modeling prompts. On a maintenance test administered two weeks after the termination of instruction, the authors found no significant difference between the retention resulting from the use of each of the four methods of prompting.

These results are comparable to those observed by Levy, Pomerantz, and Gold (1977), who stressed the importance of using physical rather than verbal prompts with retarded populations. However, there may be several advantages to be gained from using verbal prompts with learners having adequate receptive language skills. Verbal prompts offer practice in the use of receptive communication skills; they provide a normative form of instruction and they can be used with a group of learners, whereas physical prompts must be individually administered. Also, verbal prompts may be systematically faded to a simple task command in which the learner is asked to perform an act without prompting.

Hierarchic use of prompts. The various types of prompts may be used individually, as described above, or hierarchically. When

Table 4.1

		Trials				
		1	2	3	4	5
	Task Command	X	X	X	X	X
	a. Verbal	X	X	X	X	
Prompts	b. Gestural			X		
	c. Modeling		X			
	d. Physical	X				

Table 4.1.   The number and types of prompts used on each trial.

used hierarchically, the prompts are arranged from least to most intrusive (Sulzer-Azaroff and Mayer, 1977): (a) verbal, (b) gestural, (c) modeling, and (d) physical. Each successive level of prompting requires increasing teacher involvement. The prompts may be used cumulatively as depicted in Table 4.1.

A task command, e.g., "Make a loop with the lace," is stated on each trial. Trial 1 involves maximum teacher assistance. The task command is used in conjunction with a verbal prompt, "Hold the end of the lace; now pinch the middle . . . ." At the same time, a physical prompt is used. The child is physically assisted to grasp the lace at the appropriate location. On the third trial, the task command is used in conjunction with the verbal and the gestural prompts, e.g., pointing to where the learner should grasp the lace. Finally, on the fifth trial, all prompts have been faded, and the child is able to perform the task without assistance following the task command.

Kysela *et al.* (1976) described a "test-teach" procedure used with moderately to severely handicapped preschoolers. In the test phase, successive levels of prompting: a, b, c, and d in Table 4.1 are introduced cumulatively until a point is reached at which the child is able to perform the task. The object is to occasion the response with the least amount of prompting. Thus, for one child it may be necessary on a particular task to introduce successively and cumulatively verbal, gestural, modeling, and physical prompts before the child is able to perform. Teaching begins at whichever level of prompting the child is initially able to perform. If teaching begins at the point where physical prompting is required, instruction continues at this level until the child is able to perform correctly on three consecutive trials. Instruction would then move to a modeling prompt. In this manner, each level of prompting would be successively "faded" from use until the child was able to perform without prompts following the task command.

Other authors (Alberto and Schofield, 1979) suggest that fading backwards through each successive level of the hierarchy may not be necessary. They recommend that when the desired response has been correctly performed a number of times at a particular level of prompting, e.g., with modeling prompts, the teacher should return to the task command and *probe* the learner's ability to perform without prompts. If the child still requires assistance, each level of prompting is successively reintroduced until the level is found at which the child is able to perform.

Which approach to use, whether to fade backwards through each level of the hierarchy, or to return to the task command after a response has been successfully prompted, depends upon several factors. One must consider: the rate of acquisition, the number and type of errors made, and the amount of maintenance and generalization achieved with particular populations of learners and types of tasks. Similar considerations must be made to determine how many consecutively correct trials should be performed with each type of prompting before fading to a lesser level of prompting or removing all prompts and issuing only a task command.

Prompting Discriminations

The prompting procedures discussed thus far have been concerned with assisting a learner to perform the mechanics of a difficult or complex motor task. Prompts may also be used to assist a learner to make a simple motor response while selecting a stimulus in a difficult discrimination task. Autistic, mentally retarded, and learning disabled children exhibit difficulties selectively attending to the relevant cues available in a learning task (Brown, 1975; Lovaas, Schreibman, Koegel, and Rehm, 1971; Ross, 1975; Wilhelm and Lovaas, 1976). The mentally retarded attend to a limited number of the available dimensions and may respond to those that are not critical for discrimination (Wolfe and Cuvo, 1978; Zeaman and House, 1963). Once the mentally retarded or the learning disabled attend to task relevant dimensions, their performance approximates that of normal subjects (Berlyne, 1970; Ross, 1975; Wolfe and Cuvo, 1978). Two types of prompting have been used to facilitate discrimination learning.

Extra- and within-stimulus prompting. Extra-stimulus prompting (Wolfe and Cuvo, 1978) involves the addition of a stimulus to draw attention to discriminative features of stimuli. The procedure is sometimes called redundant cuing (Snell, 1978) or artificial prompting (Sulzer-Azaroff and Mayer, 1977). Extra-stimulus prompting requires the learner to attend to the prompt as well as to the discriminative feature of the stimulus; in some cases, the learner may be able to make the appropriate discrimination by attending only to the extra stimulus. *Within-stimulus prompting* (Wolfe and Cuvo, 1978) involves direct exaggeration or highlighting of an intrinsic, distinctive quality of a stimulus. To make a discrimination, the learner is required to attend only to the integral and enduring features of the stimulus.

Hull, Barry, and Clark (1976) used extra-stimulus prompting to teach vocational concepts to disadvantaged, learning disabled, and mentally retarded adolescents. In a task teaching discrimination of different types of wood screws, black arrows on a white background were used to point to various features of the screws. For example, arrows pointed to: (a) the extent of the threads, (b) the angle at the base of the shoulder, (c) the screwdriver slot, and

(d) the tip of the threads. A within-stimulus prompt, if used, would have embellished each of these features. For example, the area around the tip, the upper end of the threads, the slot, and the shoulder may have been shaded or colored to focus attention directly on these features.

The DISTAR Reading program (Engelmann and Bruner, 1969, 1974) uses a number of extra-stimulus prompts. Letters sounded together, such as the "th" in "these" and the "sh" in "shore," are joined together in print. Diacritical marks such as the bar over the "ē" are used to prompt the long "e" sound. Arrows are used under sentences to prompt reading from left to right. A small black square is used to cue the end of each word.

Gold (1972) used color redundancy cues to assist mentally retarded individuals to assemble bicycle brakes. Color cues were placed on one side of each part so that when assembled correctly the colored parts faced the worker. These prompts led to significantly faster acquisition and longer retention of the task than did cues provided only by the form or shape of the individual brake parts. Williams and York (1978) taught the discrimination of a brown ball and a potato to severely handicapped individuals by putting the ball on top of a red piece of paper. On successive trials, the paper was gradually reduced in size.

Extra- and within-stimulus prompts compared. Several studies have compared the relative benefits of extra- and within-stimulus prompting. Egeland (1975) studied the effects of these prompts on teaching letters of the alphabet to prekindergarten children. In the extra-stimulus group, selected letters were underlined. In the within-stimulus group, critical features of the same letters were embellished. In both cases, the prompts were faded over ten trials. The group receiving the within-stimulus prompts made fewer errors on the post-tests. Schreibman (1975) compared extra- and within-stimulus prompting with autistic children. Within-stimulus prompting was found to be significantly better than extra-stimulus prompting in both auditory and visual discriminations. Wolfe and Cuvo (1978) compared extra- and within-stimulus prompts in teaching the alphabet to institutionalized, severely mentally retarded individuals. In the extra-stimulus prompting condition, the teacher put his/her finger on the letter to be selected; on successive trials the finger was placed 15 to 30 centimeters above the letter to be chosen. The results showed that letters trained by within-stimulus prompts required significantly fewer trials for acquisition and were recalled significantly better on a two-week follow-up.

Egeland (1975) points out that transfer of stimulus control from a prompt to the discriminative feature of a stimulus is less difficult when within-stimulus prompting is used. Within-stimulus prompts of letters of the alphabet usually involve an expansion, darkening, or coloring of the stroke line at a critical feature of a letter. For example, if discrimination of the letters "u" and "v" were being taught, the angle of the letter "v" would be darkened, colored, or thickened. If a prompt is added to only one of a pair of stimuli, learning will occur more rapidly than if no prompts are used. However, if prompts are added to both stimuli, the learning will occur more rapidly and transfer will be greater than if prompts were added to only one stimulus. For example, if the letter "b" is to be selected from "b and d," the stroke of the loop of the letter "b" could be widened. However, additional benefit would be derived from widening the stroke width of the loop on both letters (Becker, Engelmann, and Thomas, 1975a).

Leading and Signals

Two additional types of prompts, both used in the DISTAR Reading program (Engelmann and Bruner, 1974), are worthy of note. In *leading,* the teacher and students repeatedly and in unison sound out a word or state a rule. Engelmann and Bruner suggest that leading is a more powerful tool than modeling. They cite the example of teaching people to say the alphabet backwards; if the recitation is modeled, learning is slow; if the teacher uses leading, learning is much more rapid. The DISTAR programs also use a number of standardized hand *signals* such as: the teacher drops his/her hand from an elevated position to initiate a choral response, claps hands between words, and points to a letter or word *while* sounding. These signals promote a choral response so that slow responders do not simply imitate the response of other children. The signals also allow the teacher to delay all responding to a new or difficult task until all children have had time to prepare a response. Carnine and Fink (1978) studied the effects of using signals with preschool children. When signals were used, 89 percent of the tasks received full group responses; only 60 percent of the tasks received a group response when signals were not used. Attending to the task also increased from 57 percent to 82 percent with the use of signals.

Fading

In the following discussion, several considerations regarding fading are reviewed. Whenever possible, a prompt is provided after a discriminative stimulus (task command) so that the learner must focus on the discriminative stimulus before the prompt is provided. With this arrangement, fading may take the form of progressive delay procedures where the time between the discriminative stimulus and the prompt is lengthened. After several trials, the learner begins to anticipate the prompt and the reinforcer that follows his/her response, and responds before the presentation of the prompt. Thus, control of the response is transferred from the prompt to the discriminative stimulus. Care must be taken that the delay technique is not used prematurely so that the learner begins to respond impulsively and incorrectly.

Fading to a less intrusive prompt may be achieved through pairing. For example, a physical prompt and a verbal prompt may be repeatedly paired as the physical prompt is progressively faded.

To fade a modeling prompt, over several trials the model becomes less and less complete and may be replaced by gesture and pantomime. Sulzer-Azaroff and Mayer (1977) describe such an example in a demonstration of towel folding where the complete demonstration is replaced by a pantomime of the act.

Snell (1978) described a method for judging when and how to fade a prompt. Evaluation of daily performance in terms of speed, accuracy, and consistency allows one to judge the *stability* (habit strength) of a newly acquired response. This evaluation may also be achieved through periodic inclusion of probes during teaching trials in which all or some of the prompts are withheld. If performance during the probe is maintained, improved, or does not decrease too much, prompts may be withdrawn. If, however, performance significantly deteriorates, fading must be gradual.

One of the criticisms of prompting and fading is the possible lack of frustration tolerance that may develop from a steady diet of errorless learning. To train an "advanced learner" to persist in the presence of difficulty, discontinuous fading procedures may be occasionally introduced where the learner succeeds after successively more errors.

Becker, Engelmann, and Thomas (1975a) recommended that within-stimulus prompts, part of which remains after fading, should be faded slowly while extra-stimulus prompts, none of which remains after fading, should be dropped abruptly.

Just as the within-stimulus prompts of color or shading may be progressively faded *out,* stimuli may be faded *in.* For example, to teach discrimination of the numbers two and seven, the number seven may be introduced initially at a very low intensity—hardly visible. Over successive trials in which the learner is repeatedly asked to select the number two, the intensity of the seven would be increased to equal that of the two. In addition, the most discriminative feature of the seven may be introduced first and the critical features of the two may be prompted from the first trial forward.

If an error occurs following the full or partial removal of a prompt, the prompt may be reintroduced at a more intense level, or the learner may be reminded of the prompt. The latter alternative may be preferable when it reinstates the correct response.

A review has been made of definitions, examples, and techniques for implementing prompting and fading methods for teaching difficult discriminations and complicated motor responses to handicapped individuals. The research evidence describing the effectiveness of various methods of verbal, gestural, modeling, physical, combination, test-teach, and within- and extra-stimulus prompting was discussed. These are the strategies of "errorless learning" designed to increase learner motivation, attention, effort, and success, and decrease the destructive effects of a self-fulfilling prophecy of failure that may be common to handicapped learners.

Motivation and Instruction

Learning is frequently a long, difficult, and sometimes punishing activity, particularly for handicapped learners. The ultimate value of learning some skills is often neither readily apparent, nor easily explained to a student. In addition, completion of the majority of tasks is not intrinsically rewarding and does not automatically produce a pleasurable experience for the performer. As a result, some learners are not willing to expend their best efforts in instructional activities. In fact, some learners "turn off" instruction and accept the anticipated failure, while others rebel against and disrupt instruction.

To overcome these difficulties, instruction must incorporate techniques designed to provide the learner with enough motivation to begin a new task, and a sufficiently positive experience to elicit and maintain his/her best effort. Two methods for increasing motivation are discussed in this section: (a) the use of positive reinforcement, and (b) the selection and variation of program materials and formats.

Positive reinforcement. Positive reinforcement involves the presentation (or occurrence) of any consequence (object or event) following a response that maintains or increases the frequency, intensity, and/or duration of the response. Nothing is reinforcing to all people or to any one person at all times. What is reinforcing at any time is dependent upon the nature of the task performed, the state of deprivation of the performer, the amount of reinforcement dispensed, and the manner in which it is provided. Thus, a reinforcer is defined in terms of its effect upon behavior; these effects may change with time, and the tasks and performers involved. As a result, reinforcers must be carefully selected to suit individual performers, and the continuing effect of the reinforcer must be monitored over time and tasks.

Positive reinforcement may be employed for instructional and behavioral management. Various methods of positive reinforcement may be used to assist the acquisition, generalization, and maintenance of learning. Reinforcement is used to focus a learner's attention and to maximize his/her effort and persistence. In addition, reinforcement can be used to increase behaviors prerequisite to effective instruction. Alternatively, removal of reinforcement is often instrumental in eliminating behaviors incompatible with the process of instruction.

At the same time, reinforcement must not be used in place of well designed instruction. It is important to select instructional materials that are appropriate to the learner's interest, age, sex, functional level, and abilities. The skills taught should be of functional value to the learner and build upon his/her existing skills. The instructional techniques employed should maximize the opportunities for success while minimizing efforts and frustration.

Intrinsic reinforcement. There are several different types of positive reinforcement: (a) intrinsic, (b) social, (c) descriptive verbal praise, (d) activity, (e) token, (f) tangible, and (g) edible. Intrinsic reinforcement is derived from the actual performance or completion of a response. Intrinsic reinforcement is inferred to exist when a response is maintained in the apparent absence of extrinsic reinforcement. The goal of all instruction is to train the learner to derive sufficient intrinsic reinforcement from his/her performance to maintain the behavior in the natural environment. The intrinsic value of a response *may* be taught by teaching the performer:

(1) the functional usefulness of a response; that is, the ability of the response to produce rewarding consequences by changing various aspects of the environment;

(2) to identify the positive sensory, physical, or psychological pleasures derived simply from performing or completing a response;

(3) to identify and evaluate various characteristics of the task on which its qualitative worth can be judged; and

(4) to observe and record his/her ability to maintain or increase the quantitative and qualitative attributes of performance under various conditions.

Accordingly, as training progresses, reinforcement may shift to being available only when the learner can also identify, evaluate, and record quantitative and qualitative aspects of his/her performance in a variety of functional applications. Also, as the performer is taught to focus more on intrinsic sources of reinforcement, extrinsic reinforcement may be dispensed on a more intermittent, less predictable schedule.

Social and edible reinforcers. In an instructional program, any reinforcers introduced that are not usually available in the natural environment for completion of the response being taught must be replaced by naturally occurring consequences. Sometimes naturally occurring consequences do not have sufficient reinforcing value and will not initially maintain or increase a response being taught in a program. In this case, *contrived* reinforcers not usually available for the response must be temporarily employed during instruction to help establish the response and to increase the value of the natural consequence. The reinforcing value of the natural consequence is increased by being repeatedly associated with established reinforcers. Over time, the established reinforcer is faded from use and the behavior is maintained by the naturally occurring consequences.

For example, social reinforcers such as a nod of approval, a smile, a handshake, a wink, verbal praise, or a hand on the shoulder may be naturally occurring consequences that maintain a variety of behaviors in the natural environment. However, for some individuals, these social consequences may not have sufficient reinforcing value, and during instruction a contrived reinforcer such as food may be introduced. During training, each time the response is rewarded with food, a social consequence is also dispensed. In this manner, the social consequence gains reinforcing value by repeated association with the food. As the response is established, the food reinforcer is faded from use as the social reinforcer begins to maintain the response.

Because food is not a naturally occurring reinforcer for the majority of behaviors performed in the natural environment, it is infrequently used during instruction and is usually employed only when other consequences do not have sufficient reinforcing value.

Whenever possible during instruction, it is desirable to use reinforcers that are the same as, or very similar to, those that maintain the response in the natural environment. Contrived reinforcement systems such as tokens should be employed only when more naturally occurring consequences are not sufficiently reinforcing.

Descriptive praise. Social praise in the form of general, positive comments about a person is a relatively common form of reinforcement. Descriptive verbal praise involves a positive comment plus a concise and explicit description about the specific aspects of the performer's response that are being reinforced. Consider, for example, a child who is learning to copy words from the chalkboard. After several attempts, his still chaotic product may elicit a general social praise comment, such as "Good boy, that looks better." A comment of this nature may increase the learner's general level of motivation to perform the task, however, s/he is not told which aspect of his/her performance is "better." As a result, s/he may make an invalid assumption and work to improve some irrelevant or trivial aspect of the task. In addition, a general comment such as, "You're really pretty smart," may be at odds with the child's self-concept. This discrepancy may have an adverse effect, especially if the learner feels that s/he is being manipulated.

A suitable descriptive praise comment in the printing exercise may be in the form, "That's better, you've got eight letters on the line," or "Great job, you've closed all of your a's and o's." Descriptive praise does not evaluate the learner, but explicitly identifies positive aspects of his/her performance. Thus, the praise is not discrepant with the learner's self-concept, but provides him/her with objective evidence to construct a positive self-image. In addition, the learner is taught to identify and evaluate important characteristics of his/her performance. This information is the basis of self-control: self-evaluation, recording, and reinforcement. These skills increase the likelihood that the response will be generalized and maintained. Descriptive praise may be awarded for: (a) paying attention, "Excellent, you're looking right at the book"; "Janet knows where to look, she's watching my hand"; and (b) hard work, "I'm very pleased, you've been working for ten minutes"; "Wow, look at Louise, she's finished three problems." Descriptive praise can and should be used with most types of reinforcement.

Descriptive praise and rules. Descriptive praise may be used in conjunction with a set of positively stated rules describing the minimum essential behaviors prerequisite to a particular instructional situation. Approximately five rules should be developed to briefly describe what the learner *should do* rather than what s/he *should not* do. For example, the rules might state: "Sit to learn," "Look at the book," and "Hands to yourself." Students are rewarded for reciting the rules before the lesson begins. This exercise prompts appropriate behavior before instruction starts. When appropriate behavior does occur, it is rewarded with descriptive praise in which the rule is restated, "John knows how to look at the book." Descriptive praise is occasionally used in conjunction with stronger reinforcers. In this manner, descriptive praise that repeatedly restates a rule and that is associated with strong reinforcers strengthens the rule and may lead to its internalization by the learner. This technique is used in television advertising, where brief phrases such as "Things go better with . . ." are repeatedly stated in a positive context. The evidence seems to indicate that advertising strongly influences consumer behavior.

Specify, praise, and ignore. The combined use of rules and reinforcement is part of a powerful technique that Becker, Engelmann, and Thomas (1975a) refer to as the "specify, praise, and ignore" strategy. By specifying a rule, a teacher prompts appropriate behavior; by reinforcing occurrence of the behavior, the teacher increases the likelihood that it will recur. Ignoring, not reinforcing, inappropriate behavior decreases the probability that it will recur. Removal of a previously available reinforcer such as teacher attention is called *extinction* and is used as a means of weakening undesirable behaviors. The method is very effective, if the teacher's attention to the inappropriate behavior is its major or only source of reinforcement. When an inappropriate behavior occurs, the teacher can attend to it and, for example, tell the child not to get out of his/her seat, or the teacher can attempt to put the behavior on extinction by ignoring it and praising children who are in their seats.

Ironically, telling a child to sit down—focusing on inappropriate behavior—may increase the frequency of out-of-seat behavior. Madsen, Becker, Thomas, Koser, and Plager (1968) conducted a study in a first-grade classroom in which the children were out of their seats on the average of three times in a ten-second interval. When the teacher increased the frequency of telling the children to sit down, out-of-seat behavior *increased* to an average of 4.5 times per ten-second interval. This phenomenon is called the *criticism trap*. Because the children actually sit down after the teacher speaks to them, the teacher is misled to believe that his/her disapproval of inappropriate behavior effectively reduces the behavior. However, because the children find teacher attention reinforcing, they are likely to stand up more often to gain more teacher attention. The "specify, praise, and ignore" procedure is designed to avoid the criticism trap, focus on positive behavior, and build a positive relationship between the teacher, the learner, and instruction.

Extinction. Ignoring inappropriate behavior (a form of extinction) is generally effective when used in conjunction with the specification and reinforcement of appropriate behavior. However, extinction procedures are sufficiently complex to warrant separate discussion. Putting a behavior on extinction—withholding reinforcers previously available for its performance—is usually a slow process. Often there is difficulty identifying and gaining control over the reinforcers that maintain the behavior. Characteristically, when the reinforcers are initially withdrawn, the frequency, duration, and/or intensity of the behavior may temporarily increase. Sometimes the increase may be intolerable, leading to a breakdown in the program. Eventually, without reinforcement, the behavior will decrease, but there may be periods of *spontaneous recovery* during which there is a sudden, temporary increase in the behavior. If reinforcement is inadvertently reintroduced during the extinction process, the intermittent reinforcement will strengthen the behavior and counter the attempts to weaken it. Extinction procedures are generally less problematic when used in conjunction with "specify, praise, and ignore"; nevertheless, one should be aware of, and attempt to cope with, the difficulties that may occur.

Activity and tangible reinforcement. When verbal praise and feedback about results are not sufficiently reinforcing consequences, other types of reinforcement, such as activity or tangible reinforcers, may be used as the basic reinforcers. These reinforcers are used in conjunction with descriptive praise and social reinforcement to increase the reinforcement value of the social and verbal methods and to derive the benefits associated with them. Also, even when verbal praise and feedback are effective reinforcers, occasionally it may be desirable to alternate various reinforcers to avoid *satiation.* Satiation describes the loss in reinforcement value of a consequence when it is available too frequently and/or too abundantly. To avoid satiation and to maximize reinforcement, a variety of reinforcers is used. There are many types of activity reinforcers. Children who perform well may be given a pass to use the pencil sharpener whenever they wish; they may be awarded a period of time set on a timer to work on hobbies or crafts in an activity center. High performers may be given a headset to listen to popular radio or TV programs. Other rewards may include using a typewriter, eating lunch with the teacher, a two-minute break to talk to a classmate, or the opportunity to operate the film projector, hand out materials, or be first in line. Tangible reinforcers also come in various forms, such as hobby crafts, recreation and school materials, trinkets, toys, or performance certificates. "Hard workers" may be allowed to sit at a special desk with a cushion and carpet, or work in a private study booth. Students showing improvement may be given colored paper to write on, or novel pens, pencils, and erasers. Sulzer-Azaroff and Mayer (1977) provide a very comprehensive list of edible, tangible, and activity reinforcers for children and youth.

Token reinforcement. Unfortunately, several problems arise when activity and tangible reinforcers are used. First, it is impossible for a teacher to carry around the variety of tangible reinforcers that might be appealing to different learners involved in various tasks. In addition, if tangible or activity reinforcers were dispensed during a task, they would disrupt instruction. These difficulties may be overcome with the use of a token reinforcement system. In a token economy, tokens together with descriptive praise are used to reinforce desired behaviors. The tokens (poker chips, checkmarks, etc.) are accumulated by the learner to be *cashed-in* at a designated time for a variety of *back-up* reinforcers. These back-up reinforcers (activity, tangible, or edible reinforcers) are selected so that for all students in a group, at all times, there will be at least one reinforcer that will be attractive to each learner. Tokens may be cashed-in at a token store; they can be used to bid on reinforcers at periodic auctions, or they can be used to purchase lottery tickets for weekly draws of reinforcers.

How to use reinforcers.

1. Reinforcers should be awarded as soon as possible following the emission of a response. The closer in time that a reinforcer is to the response, the easier the performer will learn the relationship between his/her behavior and its consequences. If a period of time passes between a response and the reinforcer, an intervening behavior may be inadvertently reinforced.

2. During initial teaching trials, whenever possible, reinforcement should be dispensed on a continuous schedule where each response is reinforced. Initially, with handicapped individuals, reinforcement should be dispensed for at least 80 percent of the responses. With continuous reinforcement, the relationship between a response and its consequences is readily apparent and acquisition of a new response is relatively rapid. If it is not always possible to dispense continuous reinforcement immediately following each response, descriptive praise may be used in conjunction with other types of reinforcers to make the learner aware of the relationship between his/her behavior and the reinforcer.

3. A continuous schedule of reinforcement leads to rapid acquisition of a response, but may also lead to satiation. The consequence may lose its reinforcing value, if it is made available frequently or in large supply. Also, continuous reinforcement characteristically does not lead to a very high or durable rate of

response, and it is not very resistant to extinction. If reinforcement is withdrawn, the rate of response returns relatively rapidly to its pretraining level. To overcome these difficulties, after the response has been established with the aid of continuous reinforcement, an intermittent schedule of reinforcement is gradually introduced. With a variable ratio schedule, reinforcers are awarded after varying numbers of appropriate responses. Most reinforcers in the natural environment are awarded on a variable ratio schedule in which many responses are performed between each reinforcer. A variable ratio schedule of reinforcement characteristically leads to a high and stable rate of performance that is most resistant to extinction.

4. The shift from a continuous to an intermittent schedule of reinforcement and the shift to less frequent and more unpredictable reinforcement should be done carefully to insure that the qualitative aspects of the behavior are maintained as the frequency, intensity, and/or duration of the response are increased.

5. Whenever possible, when a new response is being taught, the same reinforcers should be used that typically will maintain the response in the natural environment. Reinforcement within a training program should be based upon an analysis of: (a) the various types of reinforcers available in the natural environment, (b) the frequency with which the reinforcers are dispensed, (c) the amount of reinforcer dispensed, and (d) the exact nature of the response that is reinforced. Although a variety of reinforcers and schedules may initally be used to teach a response, and generalize and maintain the response, reinforcement within the training environment should be made congruent with that available within the natural environments.

6. Before beginning instruction: (a) to avoid satiation, a hierarchy of preferred rewards should be established, and (b) to provide a proportionate distribution of reinforcers, a decision should be made as to the amount and type of reinforcer to use for varying levels of task difficulty. Increasing reinforcement *after* a difficulty has been encountered should be avoided. This procedure may inadvertently teach the learner to have difficulty so as to obtain an increase in reinforcement.

7. Reinforcement should be made contingent (available *only*) upon the occurrence of a desired behavior. If a consequence, to be made available for the occurrence of a difficult behavior, is readily available for a variety of responses, the learner will not be motivated to perform the difficult behavior to obtain the reinforcer. However, if the consequence is available only after the difficult behavior is performed, and if the consequence is reinforcing to the learner, s/he will be more inclined to perform the difficult behavior to obtain the reinforcer.

8. During instruction, reinforcement should be dispensed: for perseverance in the face of difficulty, for the amount or duration of effort expended, for successive improvements in performance, for obtaining the correct answer, and for the absence of inappropriate (off-task or disruptive) behavior. Before beginning a task, rather than telling learners what not to do, they should be reinforced and thereby reminded of past successes, as a prompt for future performance. Also, rather than attending to children who have performed inappropriately, children who have performed adequately should be reinforced and used as models for the other children.

9. Instructional activities should be sequenced so that desirable tasks follow (reinforce) the completion of less desirable tasks. This procedure is called the Premack Principle (Premack, 1959).

10. Descriptive praise should be used in conjunction with all types of reinforcers during the acquisition stage of instruction.

11. As a new response is being established, a shift should be made from: (a) extrinsic to intrinsic reinforcement, and (b) external to self-evaluation and reinforcement.

12. Typically, no reinforcement is presented during pre- or post-tests and probes made during instruction. The object of these tests is to evaluate the learner's ability to perform without assistance. Note, however, that if a newly acquired response has been operating on a continuous schedule of reinforcement, the response may be extinguished during testing trials in which no reinforcement is available. This difficulty may be avoided by introducing an intermittent schedule of reinforcement before conducting tests.

Introducing variety into instruction. The selection and variation of suitable program materials and formats can increase and maintain interest, attention, and motivation. In Chapter Three, the benefits derived from alternating different types of tasks, e.g., verbal and manual, during a single lesson were discussed. Alternating dissimilar tasks permits: (a) recovery of the psychological and/or physiological requirements of one skill while the other skill is being exercised, and (b) distributed practice of each skill, and increased maintenance of performance over time. Also, the variation of stimulation decreases boredom and fatigue, and heightens and maintains motivation.

Becker, Engelmann, and Thomas (1971) have described a number of methods for increasing motivation. They suggest that selecting or creating material with unusual, dramatic, surprising, or even silly content is a big step towards motivating learners. The authors describe the following story used to teach addition facts.

> This is a story about Bob.
> Bob started out with four teeth.
> He went to sleep and when he woke up,
> What do you think happened?
> He had grown five more teeth.
> Wow! How many teeth did he end up with? (p. 120)

Summary:
> He started with four teeth.
> He grew five more.
> How many did he end up with?

Presenting a *challenge* can increase enthusiasm for instruction. The teacher challenges the students when s/he says, "'This is a tough one, I don't think you will be able to do it . . .' After the children get it right, the teacher acts surprised, 'I didn't think you could do that. You guys really are smart today'" (p. 123). "Well, I'll bet you can't get this one." "When teaching rules, use of the rules is demonstrated with a few examples, then the students are challenged to find examples where the rule is not true" (p. 125).

Motivation may also be increased through the use of *competition*. Tasks that require considerable practice and repetition may be converted into "competitions" between the students and the teacher. Becker *et al.* (1971) suggested that the teacher draw a score box on the chalkboard. "Every time I win, I'll put a mark up here. Every time you win, I'll put a mark down here . . . . What's one plus two? Three. I win. I'll bet I can get more points than you." The teacher gets ahead in the early part of the competition but lets the children win more and more as the race proceeds. The teacher should act as if winning were really important. "You were just lucky on that one, I'm still going to beat you" (p. 124).

To maintain interest and focus attention during review and drill of *established* skills, the teacher may purposefully embed errors in the presentation. *Catch me, if you can.* For example, "the teacher might misread a word or an arithmetic problem" (p. 125). The teacher earns points if his/her errors are not discovered, and the students win points for "catching the mistakes."

Learners may compete with themselves. Timers may be used in a race to *beat-the-clock* by maintaining or increasing accuracy of a task while decreasing the time required to complete it. Records may be maintained so that students may also compete with their earlier performances by trying to increase the number or difficulty level of tasks completed within a fixed time interval. Usually, competition between students should be avoided unless students with equal abilities are being matched. A competition of this type should give the participants equal opportunity to win. If each participant wins occasionally, his/her perseverance, interest, and effort will be intermittently rewarded and strengthened.

Suspense and *anticipation* may also heighten interest. Becker *et al.* suggest that the teacher should hint that something special is coming, but not reveal what it is. Picture materials for a lesson should be kept out of sight until it is time to use them. "Let the children know that you have something for them to see, but don't show them what it is" (p. 124).

Teacher style is an important influence in maintaining interest and enthusiasm. The completion of one task or set of materials and the introduction of the next may be an uneventful occurrence, may be anxiety producing, or the event may provide the opportunity for excitement and adventure. The manner in which the teacher presents the materials will determine the expectations (self-fulfilling prophecies) and efforts expended by the students. Similarly, because of the manner in which Detroit presents their new cars each year, adults are willing to work thousands of hours to purchase one of the cars.

The "sales promotion" of new instructional materials in the classroom might begin with an enthusiastic review of the major skills learned in the previous materials. The students are told how proud the teacher is of their accomplishments. They are reminded how hard the material first looked and how smart they were to have learned it. Individual learners and their accomplishments are reviewed. And then, as a reward, the students are told that they will be allowed to work with the new material. Some of the interesting features are previewed. Some of the skills to be learned and their benefits are described.

Becker, Engelmann, and Thomas (1971) claim that variations in pacing, rhythm, loudness, and pauses are essential elements in attention-holding presentations. Pacing and its effects were discussed in Chapter Three. Rhythmic variations provide variety while consistent use of rhythm can increase retention. Rhythm is used as a mnemonic device in, "Thirty days hath September, April, June, and November . . . ." Bereiter and Engelmann (1966) suggested that instructional statements and rules be presented with a consistent rhythm. Rhythm assists the learner to recall the statement. Also, when rhythm is used in a group choral response, a break in the rhythm will identify individual students in need of assistance. Variations in loudness may be used to avoid a monotonous oral delivery and to prompt attention to important parts of the message. For example, in DISTAR Arithmetic (Engelmann and Carnine, 1975), the equality rule is emphasized in the following manner, "You MUST end up with the same number on this side aaannnd on the other side" (p. 17).

Pauses are used to focus attention and give the learner time to prepare his/her response. One place where a pause is used is between a signal like, "Everyone listen" (pause), and the presentation of a task, "We are going to count to four." By varying the length of the pause, enduring attention to the task is strengthened (Becker, Engelmann, and Thomas, 1971). A second point where pausing is used is between the time that the teacher presents a task command, "We are going to count to four" (pause), and the signal to respond, "Count to four" (p. 123). The children see the teacher as playing a game in which s/he is trying to catch them not attending. If some children respond at the wrong time, the teacher can act as if s/he tricked them, "I caught you that time" (p. 125).

Variation may also be provided by alternating between group and individual responses. The students are likely to be attentive when they are uncertain when they will be asked to respond. Attention may also be maintained through the use of *embedded messages*. The teacher quietly inserts a verbal message into his/her dialogue, "Everyone shut your eyes," everyone with their eyes shut is then reinforced for listening carefully, "You may go to recess early."

Simulation provides variation and a practical experience with life-like events. Rather than abstract discussion or the use of pictures, actual social (role playing) or physical events or materials can be presented. Active involvement with these experiences may increase interest and enhance generalization and maintenance. These benefits may also be obtained by providing practice in a variety of settings.

Instructional *games* enhance interest and motivation. Games may involve one or more students and the teacher, individually or in teams. Dull or repetitive practice or drill exercises may be enlivened when presented in a game format. To be successful, games should not simply be an entertaining activity only vaguely related to skill acquisition, generalization, and maintenance. A game should require attention as well as application and practice of skills and knowledge in the same manner and sequence required to achieve the goal under natural environmental conditions. Also, the game should offer the participants intermittent reinforcement for the successful steps taken to achieve the goals of the game. This reinforcement will maintain interest and reward persistence. Williams and York (1978) suggest that games allow practice to become "fun activities." Rather than have severely handicapped children repeatedly practice buttoning a jacket, the authors suggest that the learners play dress-up games. The game not only increases the fun of learning, but also provides the learner with the normal variations in the task that s/he will find in the natural environment. When games are used to provide variety and assist the achievement of instructional goals, care should be taken to maximize performance of essential skills and minimize nontask related activities.

Williams and York (1978) recommend that instructional toys, games, music, and songs be selected on the following bases. The tasks should be novel or offer results that are not always predictable. Tasks should be matched to the functional level of the learner. The tasks should involve active participation and manifest cause-and-effect relationships. The skills and knowledge employed should be of functional value to the learner.

Caution must be taken to insure that the variety of stimulation introduced to increase learner motivation does not produce confusion through inconsistency. If changes are made to the essential features of a task, the task changes and the learner must modify his/her performance accordingly. Thus, the learner may not be receiving practice of the responses initially taught. If changes are made to non-essential characteristics of the task, the learner's attention may be distracted and s/he may focus attention on irrelevant features. This problem is of particular importance to handicapped learners who may have difficulty attending to relevant variables.

When introducing variety, one must insure that continuity of essential details is maintained from trial to trial. If required, prompt the learner to attend to the discriminative features of the task before beginning instruction. Bereiter and Engelmann (1966) advise that the sentence structure and word choice used in instruction be held constant. Uniformity of instruction is extremely important, the authors suggest, because children backwards in language tend to concentrate on the key words in a sentence—usually the nouns. Initially, introduce variation into instruction slowly and in small amounts only after a newly acquired response has become relatively well established.

In summary, interest, attention, and motivation may be increased and maintained by: (a) requiring active participation rather than passive observation, (b) continuing a high rate of overt learner response permitting frequent practice and reinforcement, (c) alternating individual and group responses, (d) building suspense and attention by randomizing who will be asked to respond next, (e) alternating easy with difficult tasks, (f) alternating topographically different tasks, (g) alternating old and new materials and a rapid and slow pace, as well as (h) using games, simulation, challenges, competitions, "catch me, if you can," "beat-the-clock," suspense, embedded messages, and variation in teacher style.

Chapter 5

Instructional Methods: Two

Contents

A Generic Model of Instruction

To assist mnemonics, the model described below is referred to as the OIRRC model of instruction. The letters represent the five steps of instruction: *o*rient, *i*nstruct, *r*espond, *r*epeat, and *c*onsequate. Each of these *steps* is used in a slightly modified form during three *stages* of instruction. The stages are: (a) task introduction, (b) assisted practice, and (c) unassisted practice or testing. The model is a derivation and modification of instructional methods described by Becker, Engelmann, and Thomas (1971), Hofmeister and Gallery (1977), McCormack *et al.,* (1976), Tawney and Hipsher (1972), Williams, Coyne, DeSpain, Johnson, Scheverman, Stengert, Swetlik, and York (1978), and Williams and York (1978).

Table 5.1 shows the five steps of the generic instruction model in the three stages of instruction. Each asterisk indicates that a change in the step has been made from the preceding stage. In stages A and B, the orient and instruct steps are identical. During the respond step in stage A, the response is modeled; in stage B, the response is performed by the learner with assistance, in stage C, the assistance is withdrawn.

In the following paragraphs, the general characteristics of the model are discussed and the use of the model is illustrated in the teaching of a verbal and a motor chain. A *readiness signal* indicates who is to orient (an individual child or the group) to a stimulus; for example: "Everyone"; "John"; "Ready." The *stimulus material* is the apparatus, if any, that is used during the ensuing instruction and may include: lesson presentation books, objects, pictures, or a chalkboard. The *focusing prompt: 1* is optional. This prompt is designed to focus auditory and/or visual attention on particular aspects of the stimulus material. There are two types of focusing prompts. The first type, stimulus modification, involves *highlighting* or temporarily increasing the saliency of discriminative features. Alternatively, the saliency of nondiscriminative features may be decreased. Artificial prompts such as arrows may be used to point out discriminative features. The second type of prompting involves *changes* in teacher behavior. The teacher may provide verbal prompts to indicate to the learner where and how to attend, for example, "Look at the dot." Using gestural prompts, a teacher may point to or trace one or more discriminative features of a stimulus. The teacher may also use a physical prompt to help the learner point and thereby attend to important parts of the stimulus. The use of both types of focusing prompts are more fully discussed in the upcoming chapter on concept instruction.

Table 5.1

Steps	A Task introduction	B Assisted practice	C Unassisted practice or testing
1. Orient	Readiness signal Stimulus material Focusing prompt: 1 (optional)	Readiness signal Stimulus material Focusing prompt: 1 (optional)	Readiness signal Stimulus material *No focusing prompt
2. Instruct	Task command Task confirmation: 1 Consequate	Task command Task confirmation Consequate	Task command *No task confirmation *No consequate

3. Respond	Model
	
	Focusing prompt: 2
	(optional)
		*Response signal
		
		*Prompt–verbal or lead
		  –gestural
		  –physical
			Response signal
			
			*No prompt

4. Repeat	Instruct and respond
	steps
		Instruct and respond
		steps
		
		Fade prompts–focusing
		  prompts
		  –task con-
		  firmation
		  –response
		  prompts
			Instruct and respond steps
			
			*No prompts

5. Consequate	task confirmation: 2	Task confirmation: 2 *Reinforce *Correct	*If practice: reinforce or correct If test: no reinforcement or correction

Table 5.1.   Shows five steps of generic instructional model in three stages of instruction.

The *task command* indicates *who* is to respond, for example, when the teacher is going to model a response, the initial part of the task command is, "My turn." When an individual is to respond, the task command becomes, "Your turn," or "John's turn." "Your turn" is also used during group instruction when the entire group is to respond. The second part of the task command indicates what response is to be made, for instance, "Count and end up with *12*," or "Put the block *on* the box."

A *task confirmation* is obtained wherever possible and involves gaining a verbal confirmation of the task command from the learner. The confirmation insures that the learner knows what response is expected. Thus, the task command is linked to, and becomes a discriminative stimulus for, the response. To *consequate* a response, one must either reinforce or correct the response, as appropriate. *Modeling* involves the demonstration of an act by a teacher, trainer, peer (pupil or trainee), or shill (confederate of the teacher). Modeling is reviewed in Chapter Four.

The *focusing prompt: 2* is optional. This prompt is built into the teacher's demonstration and is designed to focus attention on critical features of the model. A verbal prompt may be involved, such as "Watch my hand," or particular emphasis may be placed on an important word such as the last number in a series, for example: one, two, three, FOUR. A gestural prompt may be used, such as pointing to an important characteristic of a demonstration. A physical prompt of pointing the learner's finger may be employed to focus attention. Artificial prompts may also be used; for example, clapping one's hand between each word in a verbal chain.

Task confirmation: 2 is designed to strengthen the relationship between the task command and the response by restating the task command following the response. For example, after the teacher models a counting response, s/he would say, "I counted to NINE." After the learner has performed a response, the teacher joins a task confirmation together with verbal praise to provide descriptive praise, "Good! You counted to NINE!"

The *response signal* is made by the teacher to indicate *when* the task is to be performed. A response signal may be verbal and/or manual. The teacher may say, "Now," or "Your turn," and point to a learner, or the teacher may snap his/her finger or clap hands to signal when to respond. The response signal comes after the "ready" signal in the following manner: "Ready" (pause) response signal. The pause is designed to give the learner time to formulate his/her answer and to avoid impulsive or guessing responses. In group instruction, a sufficient pause is allowed to let the slowest person in the group prepare his/her answer. The group is then able to respond in unison following the response signal. A unison response is imperative in group instruction to insure that one learner is not merely imitating another rather than preparing his/her own response. A failure to respond in unison may indicate the need to test the skills of learners who responded too slowly.

Prompting, fading, and *reinforcement* are discussed in Chapter Four. Note that, initially, reinforcement *directly* follows each and every response both in the respond and the repeat steps. Later, reinforcement becomes more intermittent but is still presented directly following each response for which it is dispensed.

Application of the model in teaching a motor chain is described below. The model is designed for low functioning individuals, but it can be modified for more experienced learners. Steps that may be eliminated for advanced students are indicated by an asterisk. Some or all of these steps may be eliminated during some or all of the instruction. Congruent with an errorless approach, all of the steps should be included in the initial stages. As instruction proceeds, each of the indicated steps may be faded from use.

Where required, the first step of task introduction may involve review or precorrection of previously taught skills, rules, or information. The purpose of these procedures, as fully described elsewhere in this text, is to focus attention on critical features of the task and/or to return prerequisite skills or knowledge to competency level.

For example, when teaching a learner to make the first loop in tying shoe laces, it may be desirable to review the prerequisite skills of: (a) pinching a lace with the thumb and forefinger using either the left or right hand, and (b) pinching a lace either in the middle or at the end. Initially, these skills would be reviewed using the "unassisted practice format" in stage C of the generic teaching model. If the skills were performed at competency level, instruction of the new skills would proceed. If the skills were not performed at competency level, an "assisted practice format" (stage B) would be employed. Examples of these formats are described below where the learner is being taught to make the first loop in tying shoe laces.

Stage A: Task introduction
Step 1: Orient   (a) Readiness signal: "READY."[1]
                    (b) Stimulus material: (present shoe)[2]
                    (c) *Focusing prompt: 1, "LOOK AT THE LACES."
Step 2: Instruct (a) Task command: "MY TURN, I'M GOING TO MAKE A LOOP."
                    (b) *Task confirmation: "WHAT AM I GOING TO MAKE?" [a loop][3]
                    (c) *Consequate: "RIGHT, I'M GOING TO MAKE A LOOP."
Step 3: Respond (a) Model: I.   (*grip* left lace in fist),
                                 II.   (*pull* left lace up *until straight*),
                                III.   (*pinch end* of right lace between thumb and forefinger of right hand),
                                 IV.   (*pull* right lace up *until straight*),
                                 V.   (*pinch middle* of right lace with thumb and forefinger of left hand), and
                                 VI.   (with right hand, *bring end* of right lace *to bottom* of right lace)..
                    (b) Focusing prompt: 2 (The model may be accompanied by a very brief verbal prompt to focus on the action involved in each step. The verbal prompts are italicized in the modeling step.)
Step 4: Repeat (The instruct and respond steps are repeated as many times as are required.)
                    (a) Instruct: "AGAIN; MY TURN; I'M GOING TO MAKE A LOOP."

---

1. The teacher's verbal responses are printed in capital letters within quotation marks.
2. Directions to the teacher are shown within parentheses (. . .).
3. Learner verbal responses are shown within brackets [. . .].

(b) Task confirmation: "WHAT AM I GOING TO MAKE?"
[a loop]
(c) Consequate: "RIGHT, I'M GOING TO MAKE A LOOP."
(d) Respond: (Model I-VI, as above)
(e) (Repeat instruct and respond steps as many times as are required for the learner to benefit from the model.)
Step 5: Consequate—Task confirmation: 2: "I MADE A LOOP IN THE LACE." (Trace left forefinger around loop.)

Stage B: Assisted practice
Step 1: Orient (a) Readiness signal: "READY"
(b) Stimulus material: (present shoe)
(c) *Focusing prompt: 1, "LOOK AT THE LACES."
Step 2: Instruct (a) Task command: "*YOUR TURN,* YOU ARE GOING TO MAKE A LOOP."
(b) *Task confirmation: "WHAT ARE YOU GOING TO MAKE?" [a loop]
(c) *Consequate: "RIGHT, *YOU* ARE GOING TO MAKE A LOOP."
Step 3: Respond (a) Response signal: "O.K., MAKE A LOOP." (The learner is assisted, as required, to complete modeled steps I-VI.)
(b) *Prompt: (If required, the verbal prompts used during the model are repeated at each step of the model I-VI.) (If required, a gestural prompt is used in conjunction with the verbal prompt, e.g., point to the middle or end of the laces.) (If required, a physical prompt may be used in conjunction with the verbal prompt, e.g., the learner's hand may be moved to facilitate pinching in the right location.)
Step 4: Repeat (a) (The instruct and respond steps are repeated.)
(b) fade prompts—focusing prompts
—task confirmation
—response prompts
(Fade the prompts in the manner described in Chapter Four.)
Step 5: Consequate: Task confirmation and reinforcement (after each correct response, reinforce with descriptive praise). "GOOD, YOU MADE A LOOP." (Other types of reinforcers: food, tokens, etc., may be used in conjunction with descriptive praise.) Correction: (After each incorrect response, use one of the correction procedures described later in this chapter.)

Stage C: Unassisted practice or testing
Step 1: Orient   (a) Readiness signal: "READY"
                   (b) Stimulus material: (present shoe)
Step 2: Instruct (a) Task command: "YOUR TURN, YOU ARE GOING TO
                       MAKE A LOOP."
Step 3: Response signal: "O.K., MAKE A LOOP." (The task command *and*
                       the response signal may be abbreviated to: "O.K.,
                       make a loop.")
Step 4: Consequate: "GOOD JOB, YOU MADE A LOOP."

Application of the model to teach a verbal chain is demonstrated below. In the example, a learner is taught to ask for a
particular person at a telephone number that s/he has reached.
Only stage B, assisted practice, is described.

Stage B: Assisted practice
Step 1: Orient   (a) Readiness signal: "LET'S BEGIN."
                   (b) Stimulus material: (touch the telephone)
                   (c) Focusing prompt: 1 (not required)
Step 2: Instruct (a) Task command: "YOUR TURN, WHEN *THEY* SAY
                       'HELLO,' *YOU* SAY, 'MAY I SPEAK WITH JOAN,
                       PLEASE'."
                   (b) Task confirmation: "WHEN *THEY* SAY HELLO, YOU
                       SAY?" [may I speak with Joan, please]
                   (c) Consequate: "GOOD, WHEN THEY SAY 'HELLO,'
                       YOU SAY, 'MAY I SPEAK WITH JOAN, PLEASE'."
Step 3: Response signal: "I'LL DIAL, YOU LISTEN." (they answer)
                       "HELLO." [may I speak with Joan, please]
         Prompt: (If the response is incomplete, or inaccurate, or if the words
                       are out of order, use leading and reply in unison
                       with the learner, "MAY I SPEAK WITH JOAN,
                       PLEASE." Leading may also be used to assist the
                       learner initially to make the task confirmation.)
Step 4: Repeat   (Repeat instruct and respond steps.)
                   —fade prompts: fade prompt if used at task confirmation.
                   —fade response prompt.
Step 5: Consequate: "WELL DONE, WHEN *THEY* SAID HELLO, YOU
                       SAID, MAY I SPEAK WITH JOAN, PLEASE."
                       (Reinforce after each correct response.)

Small-Group Instruction

In some respects, group instruction offers several advantages over individual instruction requiring one teacher for each learner. Group instruction may be employed if each of the following conditions is met. It must be possible:

(a) to deliver instruction within a relatively small area within which the response of all learners can be continuously monitored;

(b) to provide appropriate assessment, feedback, reinforcement, assistance, and correction, quickly and effectively to facilitate individual development without retarding group progress. Bereiter and Engelmann (1966) recommended that teachers not work with an individual child in a group for more than 30 seconds. The authors also suggested that, if it is desirable for each individual learner to have the opportunity to respond separately, tasks should be structured so that each task requires five seconds or less for its completion.

It must also be possible:

(c) for all individuals within the group to perform in unison so that learners unable to respond independently in the correct manner, do not simply imitate the responses of other learners.

Group instruction is particularly suitable where learner responses are verbal. Situations requiring a motor response, however, can sometimes be structured to accommodate group instruction. The size of the group is contingent upon the ability of both teachers and learners to comply with the conditions described above. In some cases, group instruction with handicapped learners may involve two or three learners. With other tasks and/or learners, it may be possible to accommodate ten to 12 learners within a single group.

Some of the advantages of group instruction are listed below.

1. Several studies have shown that overt, verbal responses (choral responses) improve performance when compared to non-vocalized responding (Abramson and Kagan, 1975; Durling and Schick, 1976; Frase and Schwartz, 1975).

2. Choral responding permits rapid identification of individual difficulties: failure to respond or incorrect responding. Thus, problems may be rapidly corrected so that learners

do not receive extended practice performing incorrect responses.

3. Because all individuals within a group receive practice each time a choral response is performed, more individual responses are made per unit of time than would be possible if the teacher had to teach each individual separately. Also, because incorrect responses are promptly corrected, correct responses are practiced at a higher rate than would otherwise be possible.

4. Obviously, if a single teacher can deliver instruction simultaneously to a group of learners, and if these individuals are able to progress at the same, or at a more rapid pace, group instruction is more economical than individual instruction.

5. In a group situation, learners who perform competently may be used as models for individuals requiring assistance. Thus, the model is given the opportunity to practice a newly acquired response; s/he is rewarded by being asked to model the response, and assistance is provided to a learner experiencing difficulty. An additional advantage of being able to use learners as models occurs in the area of behavior management. When a learner performs in a manner counter to instruction, the teacher may directly correct the individual's behavior. However, focusing on inappropriate behavior may lead to the "criticism trap" in which an inappropriate behavior, when repeatedly corrected, increases in frequency because of the attention it receives. In addition, if attention is drawn to inappropriate behavior, other children may begin to imitate the behavior. An alternative method of coping with inappropriate behavior in a group situation is to ignore the inappropriate behavior and reinforce a learner who is responding appropriately. With this technique, appropriate behavior is modeled, a positive atmosphere is maintained, and a child whose appropriate behavior might have been taken for granted (put on extinction) is reinforced.

Engelmann and Osborne (1976) have made several suggestions

to improve group instruction. They recommend that the ratio of group to individual responses be, respectively, 85:15 percent. The authors also suggest that when learners are seated in a semi-circle around a teacher, the best performers should be seated in the periphery with low performers seated directly in front of the teacher. When teacher attention is focused on low performers, s/he will be able to assess when to: (a) prompt, (b) use correction procedures, (c) proceed to individual evaluation (after the group response is firmly established), and (d) move to the next task. Engelmann and Osborne also suggest that when a child makes an error on an individual response, the correction should be made by the entire group. When one child makes a particular mistake, it is likely that the other children could also make the same mistake, especially since the error has just been modeled. Thus, the most efficient way to correct the error is to correct the entire group. Even if other children are able to perform the response, they may benefit from the additional practice. After group correction, the child who initially made the error is retested.

Testing Procedures

In an effective instructional program, testing and teaching are continuous and complementary activities. Testing begins with a *pre-test* of the learner's ability to perform to the standards and under the conditions described in the terminal behavioral objective. If the learner's performance is satisfactory, another instructional program and terminal behavioral objective are selected. If the student fails to perform the objective adequately, an *entry level test* is administered to determine if the learner possesses the skills required to begin the instructional program. If the entry level test is passed, a *placement test* is administered to assess which, if any, of the skills taught in the program are already in the learner's repertoire. This information is used to avoid teaching the learner what s/he already knows. For example, if a student can already adequately perform the first three enabling skills in a strand, instruction will begin at the fourth enabling skill. Also, if a student can perform the seventh enabling skill in the strand, this skill may be *skipped* from instruction. A placement test involves two phases of testing. In the first phase, the learner's ability to perform each *subskill* is assessed. Second, if a learner is unable to perform a particular subskill adequately, his/her ability to perform each of the *enabling skills* leading to the subskill is evaluated. A *post-test* is administered following completion of an instructional program. The post-test is parallel to the pre-test. A post-test may assess performance under various conditions and may, in effect, be a test of *generalization.* In addition, a post-test may be administered on several occasions following completion of instruction and will function, thereby, as a *maintenance* test.

Each of these tests involves an evaluation of the learner's ability to perform in the manner described in a behavioral objective. All instructional assistance and reinforcement are withdrawn. The conditions described in the objective are presented, and the learner is required to perform in the specified manner to the prescribed standards or criteria. This type of testing is referred to as criterion-referenced testing, where the behavioral objective represents a criterion that the learner must achieve.

If each behavioral objective is only tested once, the results of the test may reflect chance variations in performance rather than the learner's actual ability to perform the objective. For example, a learner who might otherwise have passed a test may fail because of random error in his/her performance. Alternatively, s/he may have correctly performed the test by chance. Therefore, to obtain a reliable measure of a learner's performance, two or more parallel test items should be developed for each objective. With multiple-choice test items, where the likelihood is high that a learner could perform correctly by guessing, a sufficient number of parallel test items must be developed to insure that the performance exhibited exceeds what would have been expected by chance alone. Also, because of the variability of performance exhibited by some handicapped children, the test items may be administered on several occasions.

Some behavioral objectives describe various conditions under which the learner is to perform. In this case, two or more test items should be developed to assess performance under each condition. Where a number of test items are employed, some behavioral objectives specify the number, percentage, or number of consecutive items that must be correctly performed. In any case, whenever a number of test items are used, a *cut-off point* must be established beyond which performance may be assumed to exceed chance expectation and reflect actual achievement of the objective.

Tests may also be *embedded* within the instructional program. *Progress* tests are constructed in the same manner as those described above and assess achievement of enabling objectives and subskills. *Probes* may be used to assess generalization of a newly learned skill or acquisition of an untaught skill through incidental learning. Skills acquired through incidental learning may be omitted from further instruction. Perhaps the most important tests are the *diagnostic tests* embedded within each lesson. Ideally, diagnostic tests alternate with, and evaluate, each step of instruction. The purpose of the test is to assess: (a) if a particular skill or piece of knowledge has been acquired, (b) if the information or skill learned can be repeatedly, rapidly, and accurately expressed, and (c) if errors are made, what type, and which correction procedure is required.

Errors and Correction Procedures

Frequent assessment of learner progress within each lesson permits repeated reinforcement and strengthening of newly acquired responses. Frequent assessment also permits early identification and correction of errors. If errors are not quickly corrected, learners experiencing difficulties may repeatedly practice an incorrect response. Once an error occurs, the probability increases that the error will recur, particularly if the correct response is unknown. Research indicates that correction of errors rather than simply ignoring them leads to more effective instruction. Carnine (1975c) reported that during arithmetic instruction, correcting errors in contrast to ignoring them, was associated with 55 percent greater accuracy during training and 48 percent higher accuracy on the post-test.

In the following discussion, a review is made of a number of errors that commonly occur during instruction and the corresponding correction procedures for each type of error. Some of the ideas described have been adapted from Engelmann and Osborne (1976), Tawney and Hipsher (1972), and Williams and York (1978).

Orienting errors occur after a readiness signal, such as "Look at me" or "Look at this," if the learner either fails to orient or attends to the wrong stimulus. If the student has previously demonstrated the ability to respond appropriately to a readiness signal, the signal currently being used may be inadequate. In this case, the orienting error may be corrected by increasing the intensity of the readiness signal and/or by introducing a prompt such as pointing to discriminative features of the stimuli. Alternatively, in group instruction, if a learner fails to attend because s/he was involved in a distracting activity, reinforce an individual who did attend appropriately; then reintroduce the readiness signal and reevaluate the learner's orienting response. In individual instruction where a learner resists orienting to the task, *time-out* procedures may be employed. Rather than reinforcing the learner's resistance by focusing on it, the teacher may, temporarily, withdraw all reinforcement for a brief period of time before repeating the readiness signal. The success of this approach is contingent upon the teacher's attention and the instructional process being more reinforcing to the learner than being ignored by the teacher and having instruction terminate. An alternative procedure involves the use of a physical prompt where the learner's head is physically turned by the teacher to focus on the stimulus. This technique may also be useful when a learner's attention is lost or s/he fails to track the teacher's demonstration. Physical prompting is also employed with learners who are being taught for the first time how to attend to, and track, a demonstration.

If a student responds, says "yes," without examining the stimuli, a series of trials may be presented on which the "yes" response is consistently incorrect. Care must be taken not to alternate the presentation so that the inappropriate strategy of saying "yes" without attending is strengthened by intermittent reinforcement.

A *latency* of response error occurs when an individual in group instruction, who is expected to respond on signal with the group, responds too early or late. Where the response is too early, the learner is asked to "wait for the signal," and the task is repeated. If the learner persists in responding too early, two alternative correction procedures may be used. Another performer in the group may be chosen to act as a model who waits for the signal before responding. Descriptive praise such as, "Good waiting for the signal," may be used to reinforce the model. Several trials involving one or more performers may be employed. Alternatively, *overcorrection* procedures may be used. The learner who responded too early may be prompted to respond on signal; after the response has been learned, s/he may be required to practice the response repeatedly.

When a response is made too slowly, several considerations may be made. First, it must be established whether or not the student has had sufficient time to formulate a correct response. This hypothesis may be rejected, if a greater time allotment does not produce an improvement in behavior. Second, it may be determined that the learner begins to respond on signal, but that his/her response *rate* is too slow. In this case, feedback is provided, "Too slow," and additional trials are presented. If the rate of response does not increase, *shaping* procedures may be employed. This technique is discussed more fully later in this chapter. During shaping, the rate of response is increased over several stages. First, the learner is reinforced several times for performing at his/her current average rate, then only responses that occur at a slightly more rapid rate are reinforced. The criterion for reinforcement is successively shifted until a suitable response rate is achieved.

Occasionally, a performer may make the right *type* of response, but the wrong response of that type. For example, s/he may make a touching response as requested, but touch the wrong object. Where this type of error occurs, the teacher says, "No! (pause) *this* is *x*" (touch the correct object); the position of x is randomized and the learner is again directed to "Touch *x*." The exclamation, "No!" should be emphatic but nonaversive. The purpose of the feedback is to let the learner know that the response was inappropriate and to avoid inadvertent reinforcement of the response. The "pause" acts as a period of nonreinforcement and increases the significance of the word "No!" Bereiter and Engelmann (1966) suggest that a teacher should be completely unambiguous in letting the child know when his/her response is correct or incorrect. Subtle feedback may not be understood.

After the learner has been given a second opportunity to "Touch *x*," if s/he still fails to respond appropriately, the failure may result from an inability to discriminate *x* from *y*. In this case, the discriminative features of *x* may be increased and the correct response *modeled*. Another learner or the teacher may be used as a model of the correct response. If the teacher models the correct response, s/he says, "My turn; Touch *x*," and then models the correct response. If the learner responds during the teacher's model in reply to the task command, "Touch *x*," the trial is begun again and greater emphasis is put on "My turn." In addition, if required, the learner may be given a physical prompt to prevent him/her from responding at the wrong time.

If the failure to respond appropriately continues, as a result of a discrimination problem, further modifications may have to be made to the stimuli. Perhaps stimulus *y* should be modified or replaced to ease the discrimination. If the failure continues for other reasons, a physical prompt may be employed in which the learner is physically "put through" the correct response.

Where the learner makes the right *type* of *verbal* response, for example, labeling, but provides the wrong label, different correction procedures are required than would be used with incorrect *motor* responses. When a performer incorrectly replies, "yellow," to the question "What color is this?" the correct response may be modeled. The teacher would say, "My turn; What color is this? *Red.*" The learner is then given the opportunity to imitate the model in response to the question, "What color is this?" *Leading* may be used instead of or following the model. To lead a response, the teacher makes the response in unison with that made by the learner(s). For example, if the learner has had difficulty responding with the word "elephant," the teacher might simultaneously lead and shape the response by "stretching" the word, e.g., "ehhlehhffaant." As the learner and teacher repeatedly sound the word in unison, it is slowly returned to its proper pronunciation. When children are learning to make multi-word responses, leading by chaining and stressing key words is probably more effective than simply modeling the response (Carnine, 1977; Risley and Reynolds, 1970; Twardosz and Baer, 1973).

Where a learner makes the wrong type of response, for example, touches rather than picks up an object, the response may be modeled or physically prompted as illustrated earlier. Where the name of the object is given, rather than its color, the response may be corrected by modeling or leading.

Response bias errors occur when a student repeatedly exhibits a preference to choose stimuli incorrectly on the basis of some irrelevant characteristic, such as position, color, or size of the object. This type of error may be corrected by establishing a situation in which another position or color is consistently the correct choice. The student is then taught, through modeling or physical assistance, to make the correct choice. The problem with a response bias is that the learner's error response, if not corrected, is being maintained on an intermittent schedule of reinforcement.

Interception is a method of coping with various types of errors. Incorrect responses are anticipated and prevented from occurring; the response is corrected, perhaps with the aid of prompts, and the correct response is reinforced. With this approach, the learner does not receive practice making an error response, and the correct response is strengthened. Bereiter and Engelmann (1966) describe several examples of interception. If a task requires a learner to make a visual discrimination and the learner has not inspected the material, the teacher can assume that a guessing response is about to be made. The guessing response can be intercepted by the directive, "Look *carefully* at *both* of them." If the task requires several steps in reasoning and the learner begins to respond immediately, it is likely that the reasoning process has been short-circuited. The response may be intercepted by the directive, "Think of each step first." Carnine (1977) suggests that when children follow several steps to determine an answer, corrections in which the teacher asks questions about the steps tend to be more effective than merely modeling the correct response (Siegel, 1976; Siegler and Liebert, 1973). Cuvo, Leaf, and Borakove (1978) used a nonspecific prompt, such as "What's next?," to promote consideration of each step in a janitorial program designed for the mentally retarded.

In a task where errors are anticipated, *precorrection* or pretraining may reduce the occurrence of errors. Fink (1976) used precorrection. First-grade students who made frequent decoding errors were asked to identify the vowel sound before they read a word. The percent of words accurately read averaged 15 percent without precorrection and 55 percent with precorrection. Precorrection may involve modeling or the review and rehearsal of prerequisite skills or strategies.

When an error is corrected and the new response is practiced only once, the error and the correct response may have an equal probability of recurring. *Overcorrection* procedures may have to be used to increase the probability that the correct response will recur. In overcorrection, the learner continues to practice a response repeatedly following his/her initial demonstration of competence in performing the response.

During *initial* learning, a correction should not be punitive, nor an occasion for shame or coaxing such as "Come on Harold, think." If a learner performs incorrectly, s/he should be given brief, explicit, and emotionally neutral feedback. A punitive correction *may* be used when a learner repeatedly makes errors on a task that s/he has previously mastered; punitive corrections should be used sparingly (Carnine, 1977). Haring (1977-1978) describes a corrective procedure called the *mandate*. This technique is used only when the teacher is *certain* that the learner is able to perform a behavior and is deliberately not doing so, and when a positive consequence will not control the behavior. In the mandate, physical guidance is used as an aversive consequence for an error or a lack of response. The mandate is done rapidly and forcefully and is designed to be aversive. Haring also describes *error drill* as an aversive correction procedure. Error drill involves the repeated correction of previously made errors.

Williams and York (1978) suggest that although errorless

learning is advantageous during initial instruction, errors should be allowed to occur during later phases of a program. The authors recommend that students be permitted to make errors and learn how to respond to them after they have been made. Students should be taught strategies for detecting and correcting errors without the need for teacher intervention. These experiences will increase the ability of a learner to cope with conditions found in the natural environment.

For each instructional program and group of students, a cut-off point should be predetermined; if the number of errors equals or exceeds this limit, instruction should be temporarily withdrawn while the program is reviewed. The program should be evaluated to determine: (a) if all prerequisite skills have been taught, (b) if the prerequisite skills currently can be performed competently, (c) the suitability of the instructions and prompts, and (d) the appropriateness of the step size. In some cases, a single step in a program may have to be analyzed into a number of smaller steps. Perhaps, too, a modified method of performing the task may have to be adopted.

Forward and Reverse Chaining

In Chapter Three, the joining together of S-R links into a chain was discussed in relation to the topic of instructional sequencing. Four different types of instructional sequencing were identified: (a) forward and (b) reverse (c) cumulative sequencing, as well as forward and reverse (d) successive sequencing. In the following paragraphs, methods are discussed for employing prompting and reinforcement procedures to join S-R links into a chain regardless of the instructional sequence used. Table 5.2 displays the forward and reverse, cumulative and successive chains involved in teaching a learner to print the word "Mary." Note that at each step of the reverse cumulative chain sequence, the learner is only required to perform the final link to complete the entire task. That is, in the first step, s/he is given "Mar-" and is required only to provide the "-y." Note also that in the first four lessons of the reverse successive chain, the S-R links may be taught in any order. In fact, it may be advantageous to teach easier S-R links first and leave more difficult links to be taught later.

Table 5.2

Activity	1	2	3	4	5	6	7	8	9
					Step				
A. Forward Cumulative Chain									
Teach	M	a		r		y			
Chain			Ma		Mar		Mary		
Practice				Ma		Mar		Mary	
B. Reverse Cumulative Chain									
Given	Mar	Ma	Ma	M	M				
Teach	y	r		a		M			
Chain			ry		ary		Mary		
Practice		y		ry		ary		Mary	
C. Forward Successive Chain									
Teach	M	a	r	y					
Chain					Ma	Mar	Mary		
Practice								Mary	
D. Reverse Successive Chain									
Given					Mar	Ma	M		
Teach	M	a	r	y					
Chain						ry	ary	Mary	
Practice					y	ry	ary	Mary	

Table 5.2. Teaching "Mary"; four types of chaining sequences.

In the following discussion, a forward cumulative sequence is used to demonstrate the manner in which prompting and reinforcement are used to join the S-R links: M, a, r, and y into a chain. The method illustrated is equally applicable to all chaining sequences. Assume throughout the discussion that the generic teaching model employing readiness signals and task commands, etc., is used to teach each of the individual letters.

Step 1:   Teaching "M."

$$S_{TC}^{D} - \begin{bmatrix} S^P \\ R_M \end{bmatrix} - S^+$$

The discriminative stimulus (S^D) in this situation is the task command (S_{TC}^{D}), "PRINT MARY." Verbal, gestural, and/or physical prompting stimuli (S^P) are used, as required, to assist the response (R) of printing the letter "M" (R_M). The reinforcement (S^+) is dispensed on a continuous schedule. The step is repeated until "M" reaches criterion. The prompts are then faded from use, and reinforcement is shifted to an intermittent schedule.

Step 2:   Teaching "a."

$$S_{TC}^{D} - \begin{bmatrix} S^P \\ R_a \end{bmatrix} - S^+$$

The task command, "PRINT 'a,'" is provided and prompts are employed, as required. Reinforcement is initially dispensed on a continuous schedule. The step is repeated until "a" reaches criterion. The prompts are faded from use, and reinforcement is shifted to an intermittent schedule.

Step 3:   Linking "M" and "a."

$$S_{TC}^{D} - R_M - S^P - R_a - S^+$$

The task command, "PRINT MARY," is provided as are prompts, when required. No reinforcement is provided after "M." Initially, continuous reinforcement is dispensed after "a," and then a shift is made to an intermittent schedule as "Ma" approaches criterion. This is the basic step in chaining. Because the letter "M" has been previously associated with reinforcement, and because of the temporal relationship of "M" to reinforcement at the end of the chain, the letter "M" acquires a reinforcing function. That is, completion of the letter "M" reinforces the printing response. Also, because the letter "M" has been repeatedly followed by the letter "a," that is, followed by reinforcement, "M" begins to act as a discriminative stimulus indicating that if "a" follows "M," reinforcement will be received.

When teaching a learner to print the word "Mary," prompts and reinforcers initially used to teach each letter are faded from use as the individual responses are linked together. In its final form, the chain begins with the task command, is followed by each of the S-R links in order, and finishes with a reinforcer.

$$S^D_{TC} - R_M - R_a - R_r - R_y - S^+$$

As is characteristic of all chains, each S-R link begins to act as a reinforcer for the immediately preceding step and as a discriminative stimulus for the next step in the chain.

Shaping

Whereas chaining involves the joining together of a number of S-R links into a chain, shaping involves the modification of a single behavior. There are two types of shaping: (a) where the frequency and/or duration of a behavior is progressively increased or decreased through a series of steps, or (b) where the topography of a behavior is modified through a series of steps from one form to another.

Shaping is used: (a) when a desired behavior is not in an individual's repertoire, and/or (b) when a desired change in behavior is very large, *and* when in (a) and (b) the change cannot be directly instructed or prompted, *or* in (b) where, if the change were demanded, a negative behavioral response would be occasioned. In these circumstances, shaping is a very effective procedure. However, shaping is a slow and labor-intensive process that should be employed only when other techniques, such as prompting and instruction, are not effective.

Shaping may be employed to: (a) increase the *duration* of a behavior, such as the learner's attention span, and (b) increase the *rate* of behavior, for example, the number of arithmetic problems correctly calculated per unit of time. Alternatively, shaping may be used to *decrease* the rate or duration of a behavior, for example, decrease the time taken to assemble radio components in a sheltered workshop. Shaping is also used to change the *topography* of a behavior. For example, in speech therapy the word "water" might be shaped from its initial form "wa-wa" to "watah" and finally to "water" (Martin and Pear, 1978).

In each of these examples, the existing form of a behavior is initially reinforced, then the criterion for reinforcement is shifted, and a slightly modified form of the behavior is required to obtain reinforcement. The behavior is slowly modified from its initial form through a series of successive approximations to its final form. Modification of the behavior is achieved through the use of prompting, shifting criterion, and differential reinforcement techniques. The steps involved in shaping are described below.

1. *Establish a terminal behavioral objective.* The terminal behavioral objective describes the final form of the observable, measurable behavior that the shaping program is designed to develop, the *conditions* under which the behavior is to be performed, and the *standards* that are to be achieved. A well defined behavioral objective helps to insure that each of the enabling steps in the program is a *successive approximation* of the objective. For example, if the goal was to increase the number of addition problems calculated in a fixed interval of time, several considerations would have to be made to establish a suitable behavioral objective. First, there is a great variety of different types of addition problems, such as sentence or pictorial problems, those involving concrete objects, or numerical problems with two or more addends in a vertical or horizontal format. Addends may have single or multiple digit(s), and the operation may or may not involve regrouping. Also, there may be several response variations. The value of one or more of the addends may have to

be calculated in problems in which the sum is already provided; answers may have to be selected from a multiple-choice format, verbalized, or written by hand. A behavioral objective for a shaping program to increase the rate of calculating addition problems may be written as follows.

> Given 30 addition problems, each with two single-digit addends in a vertical format, with a sum less than or equal to 18, the learner will write the correct sum of at least 20 of the problems in an eight-minute interval on five consecutive trials.

2. *Identify entry level behaviors.* Entry level behaviors are those behaviors already in the learner's repertoire that are currently the closest approximation of the terminal behavioral objectives. These are the behaviors that are shaped through successive approximations to the terminal behavioral objective. Alternatively, if the goal of the shaping program is to increase the frequency or duration of a response, the entry level or starting point of the program is the average frequency or duration (as appropriate) of occurrence of the response before shaping begins. For example, in the shaping program described above, to increase the number of addition problems calculated, the learner on five pretraining trials may correctly calculate six, eight, seven, six, and eight addition problems. The average number of correctly calculated problems is seven. Therefore, seven is the entry level behavior at which the program is begun. Initially, the learner will be reinforced for correctly calculating at least seven addition problems.

3. *Determine the successive approximations.* Before beginning a shaping program, it is desirable to describe the successive approximations or enabling steps the learner will be required to make in progressing from his/her entry level to the terminal behavioral objective. The process of describing the successive approximations is one of plotting the learner's development from his/her entry to the terminal levels and establishing the *step size* of each successive approximation. Step size refers to the amount of shift in criterion from one approximation to the next. The step size should be as large as possible, but as small as necessary. That is, the step should be large enough to permit rapid development from one step to the next, while avoiding the tedium of making

small steps when larger steps are possible. Each step must also be small enough for the learner to adapt to the shift in criterion, with or without prompting, in a relatively short period of time. If the step is too large, the learner may experience a relatively long period during which s/he receives little reinforcement. This situation may cause extinction of earlier approximations of the terminal behavior. For example, where the object is to increase the learner's rate of calculation of the sum of addition problems from an average of eight to a minimum of 20 per eight-minute interval, the successive approximations selected may be: 8, 9, 11, 13, 16, 18, 19, and 20. The shift in criterion is relatively small in the beginning. The initial goal is to make demands upon the learner that are readily within his/her reach; also, the goal is to reward the learner highly for exerting more effort in the desired direction. Later, as the program becomes established and the learner has been repeatedly reinforced for improving, larger shifts in criterion may be made. However, towards the end of the shaping program, where improvements in performance may be more difficult to make, relatively small shifts in the criterion are made.

4. *Select appropriate prompts.* Verbal, gestural, modeling, physical, and/or artificial prompts may be selected in most situations. Several guidelines for selecting prompts should be followed. Prompts should be employed only when the desired response cannot be performed without assistance, and the least amount of prompting should be used to occasion the response. Prompts should be selected that most effectively occasion the desired response; effective prompts require the least amount of time and effort and are readily faded from use. In the example previously discussed, to increase the rate of calculating addition problems, a teacher may use verbal prompts in the form of pretask instructions along with a timer on the learner's desk set to ring in eight minutes.

5. *Accelerate the entry level behavior.* When a shaping program is designed to modify the *form* of a behavior, the first step involves increasing the rate of performance of the entry behavior. If required, prompts may be used to occasion the behavior. Initially, a continuous schedule of reinforcement is used. Later, to

further increase the rate of performance, an intermittent schedule may be employed.

6. *Use differential reinforcement.* Differential reinforcement is used to increase the frequency of occurrence of a form of the entry level behavior that best approximates the terminal behavior. However, if a closer approximation of the terminal behavior occurs spontaneously, "bonus" reinforcement is dispensed to strengthen the behavior. Differential reinforcement is difficult to use when a learner is responding at a high rate. Nevertheless, to be effectively employed, reinforcement must be dispensed immediately following a desired response. Otherwise, the learner may be inadvertently reinforced for the wrong behavior, and successive approximations of the desired behavior may not be achieved.

7. *Fade the use of prompts.* As the rate of the entry level behavior is brought to a satisfactory level, any prompts employed to occasion the behavior are progressively faded from use.

8. *Shift the criterion for reinforcement.* As a rule of thumb, move to the next step in the program when the learner performs the current step correctly 6/10 trials (Martin and Pear, 1978). For example, if the learner on 6/10 trials achieves criterion by correctly calculating the answers to eight addition problems and exceeds or fails to reach criterion on the remaining four trials, shift the criterion for reinforcement. The learner would then be required to correctly calculate ten addition problems within an eight-minute interval on 6/10 trials. Prompts and differential reinforcement are used to shape the remaining steps in the program.

9. *Move to environmental reinforcers and contingencies.* When the behavior has been modified to comply with the terminal behavioral objective, all prompts are removed and the type and schedule of reinforcer are modified to correspond with naturally occurring contingencies.

10. *Diagnose problems.* (a) If the response rate, accuracy of performance, or attention to task decrease, the task may be too easy or difficult for the learner. If the task is too easy, steps in the program may be combined to accelerate the response rate. If the task is too difficult, steps in the program may be analyzed into

smaller steps. (b) If a previous approximation to the terminal behavior is extinguished and a new behavior is not emitted, the shift in criterion to a new approximation may have been made too early. It may be necessary to return to an earlier approximation and restore previous learning. The adequacy of the prompts and reinforcers used should also be examined. (c) If, after the criterion has been shifted, the learner persists in performing the previously learned response, rather than shifting to the next approximation, training may have continued too long at the earlier level. Alternatively, the prompts used to occasion the next approximation may not be adequate.

Skinner and Krakower (1968) developed a series of writing workbooks based on shaping. In the *Write and See* series, the learner begins by tracing letters. Gradually, portions of the letters are faded out and the learner is required to fill in increasingly more of each letter. A special pen is used, and the paper has been chemically treated. As a result, the performer receives immediate feedback and reinforcement for his/her response. A black mark is made when the letter is correctly formed, and an orange line is drawn when an error occurs.

Lovaas, Koegel, Simmons, and Long (1973) reported on an extensive and successful shaping program to teach speech and conversational skills to autistic children. Allyon (1963) conducted one of the classic shaping programs. He worked with an institutionalized psychotic woman who, on the average, wore 25 pounds of extra clothing. Previous attempts to get her to remove her clothing had been unsuccessful; removal was not readily prompted and other techniques might have occasioned a negative behavioral response. Therefore, shaping techniques were employed. Over an 11-week period, the amount of clothing worn was reduced by successive approximations to three pounds. On the first step of the program, the woman was weighed before she was allowed into the institutional dining room. If her weight was 23 pounds more than her body weight, she was reinforced by being permitted to enter. If she was overweight, she was not granted entry—an example of differential reinforcement. Over time, the woman was required to wear successively less clothing to enter the dining room.

Stimulus Generalization

Stimulus generalization or transfer of a response refers to performance of the response under conditions that are different from those in which the response was initially acquired. Conditions in the two environments may vary in terms of: (a) the materials used; (b) the people present (peers, parents, teachers, employers, and/or strangers); (c) discriminative cues (social, physical, or language); (d) extraneous stimuli; and (e) reinforcement or feedback. These differences in conditions are likely to impede generalization. One of the major goals of training is to have a response taught in the presence of one set of stimuli (the training environment) performed in the presence of another set of stimuli (usually the natural environment) that has similar or identical discriminative stimuli.

The process of generalization is separate from, but related to, the process of maintenance. Generalization may occur concurrent with, or subsequent to, initial training. Maintenance of a newly acquired response, if it occurs, takes place following the termination of training and refers to the continued performance of a response in the training situation and/or in the other environments to which it had originally generalized. Many of the procedures used to promote generalization also enhance maintenance.

Numerous researchers and research reviewers have concluded that generalization and maintenance over persons and across settings do not occur automatically with the acquisition of a new response (Cooke, Cooke, and Apolloni, 1976; Kazdin, 1975; Stokes and Baer, 1977; Walker and Buckley, 1972). It has become axiomatic that behavior change in children is reversible and situation-specific (Conway and Bucher, 1974). There is a need to systematically program generalization and maintenance, rather than passively expect them to be an outcome of training (Stokes and Baer, 1977; Walker and Buckley, 1972; Warren, 1977).

A traditional learning deficiency of the mentally retarded has been the inability to use previously learned experiences in new or unique situations (Denny, 1964; Schworm and Abelseth, 1978; Wehman, 1976). The problem is particularly pronounced with individuals classified as trainable, mentally retarded or lower

(Murdock, Garcia, and Hardman, 1977). Unfortunately, even demonstrably effective techniques for producing generalized language changes among normal populations are not always useful when applied to the mentally retarded (Cooke, Cooke, and Apolloni, 1976).

Cooke, Cooke, and Apolloni (1976) suggested that the ability to express language in a natural setting be adopted as a primary criterion for evaluating language intervention approaches with the mentally retarded. Williams, Brown, and Certo (1975) recommended that if the success of a program is to be evaluated in terms of a student's performance across different environmental configurations, then the objective for each major skill taught in a program should stipulate how and where the skills should be performed. For example, when one-to-one correspondence skills are being taught to severely handicapped individuals, the objective might specify: "'Give one . . . to each . . .,' or 'Give every . . . a . . .,' or 'Put a . . . in each . . .'." These task commands would be presented by at least three different control figures (e.g., teacher, parents, and peers) across at least three settings (e.g., classroom, playground, and home) and across at least three functional tasks (e.g., setting the table, passing out cookies, and dealing cards).

One approach to achieving generalization, *sequential modification,* has been described by Stokes and Baer (1977). In this approach, when a new behavior has been taught to criterion, generalization is assessed. If generalization is absent or deficient, the new behavior is systematically and sequentially taught in each of the environments in which generalization is desired. Obviously, this approach is time-consuming and costly. Furthermore, research evidence is available indicating that such extensive training is not required to achieve generalization. Frequently, it is necessary to train a learner in only two or three situations to produce generalization of a response to additional surroundings. For example, when Griffiths and Craighead (1972) provided articulation training to a 30-year-old retarded woman, generalization to a residential setting did not occur until training procedures were instituted at the cottage. However, following training at the cottage, the behaviors automatically generalized to a classroom.

When Murdock, Garcia, and Hardman (1977) provided articulation training to trainable, mentally retarded children, generalization of the responses to additional environments did not occur until training was provided in at least one additional setting. Some subjects were trained in two or three settings. All subjects performed the newly acquired responses in five settings. Unfortunately, because different trainers were involved in each context, one cannot be certain which variable produced the generalization: the different training settings, the different trainers, or the combination of different settings and trainers. Handleman (1979) described a study in which autistic children were taught to make verbal replies to common questions. When training took place on a one-to-one basis in a cubicle, no generalization was observed. When the training took place as the trainer and each child moved through six locations in the school, generalization was observed in six locations in each child's home. There was no apparent relationship between the number of trials to criterion and the various training settings. Stokes and Baer (1977) concluded from their review of the literature that although little research has been reported, "consistent optimism should follow examination of the studies showing generalization after training in only a few settings" (p. 356).

Unfortunately, the highly structured training environment that is most conducive to initial acquisition of a response may be least conducive to generalization of the response. In the training environment, the removal of distracting stimuli and the consistent use of instructional procedures: discriminative stimuli (cues or instructions), reinforcement, and feedback, provide a contrived simplicity and continuity of stimulation that are not found in the natural environment. According to the notion of a stimulus generalization gradient, well established in the literature, as the training environment becomes increasingly different from the natural environment (special education), generalization is less likely to occur.

To overcome the difficulties of generalizing from a training milieu to the natural environment, as learning progresses, the training environment may be systematically transformed to approximate the characteristics of the natural environment. This process is preceded by a thorough study of the natural environment to determine the *variety* of ways that the responses to be trained are prompted, performed, and reinforced in various contexts and circumstances. Note should be made also of the number and type of irrelevant stimuli that may distract from, or be confused with, discriminative stimuli.

The training situation should provide the learner experience with the range of stimulus variations found in the natural environment. Thus, as training proceeds, more people, non-essential stimuli, interruptions, variations in materials, sequence changes, different types and schedules of reinforcement, and a variety of instructions or other cues may be progressively introduced as the training environment approximates the variation and complexity of the natural environment.

A relatively simple, but effective, study by Clark, Boyd, and Macrae (1975) demonstrated the procedure of providing experiential variation. In their study, six mildly retarded individuals were trained to complete job application forms. During each training session, students were taught one item of biographical information, such as name or address. They then practiced on at least four different forms. As a post-test measure of generalization, the students were given an unfamiliar job application form on which they correctly completed an average of 70 percent more items than they had on the pre-test.

Langone and Westling (1979) suggested that vocational training programs for the moderately and severely retarded should regularly substitute equivalent functional materials. They cite an example of a janitorial program in which liquid cleaners occasionally would be substituted for powder cleaners.

Williams, Brown, and Certo (1975) recommended that changes in programs for the moderately and severely handicapped be made gradually as large changes either fail to elicit the desired behavior or may change the nature of the response. Progressive and systematic change of the environment should be made while maintaining the topography of the behavior under different environmental conditions. Wehman, Abramson, and Norman

(1977) recommended that teachers provide adequate transition time when introducing changes, as there are likely to be some initial increases in inappropriate behavior, or decreases in appropriate behavior. If these changes in behavior are anticipated, suitable management and instructional changes may be made to minimize any possible disruptive effect as the behavior is brought under the control of the new stimuli.

Conway and Bucher (1974) point out that a frequently encountered difficulty in a treatment program is that children appear to make inadequate use of discriminative cues that exist in the environment. This difficulty may arise in the initial training situation, in the modified training situation, and/or in the natural environment. The problem may be corrected by highlighting or increasing the saliency of the discriminative features common to each environment. These features may be emphasized by directly embellishing the stimuli or through the introduction of artificial prompts that draw attention to the discriminative features. Of course, these prompts must be faded from use as the learner is taught to respond in the presence of naturally occurring stimuli. Also, when there is a similarity between stimuli that signal when a response is appropriate and stimuli that should not signal the occasion to perform, the learner should be taught to discriminate these stimuli. If the learner is unable to discriminate these features, s/he may inadvertently be put on extinction, or perhaps be punished for performing the newly acquired response not yet firmly established in his/her repertoire.

One method of modifying the training milieu to approximate the natural environment is to vary the reinforcement contingencies. Continuous or frequent and prompt reinforcement facilitates rapid acquisition of a new response; however, the natural environment is usually characterized by infrequent and delayed reinforcement. Usually, too, different types of reinforcers are used during training than are found in the natural environment. Ferster (1972) suggests that generalization of a treatment program is doomed unless there is a viable plan for natural reinforcers to take on and maintain a new response. Conway and Bucher (1974) suggest that, in general, we are relatively ignorant about the typical contingency relations operating in the natural environment. Even under the best circumstances, there are likely to be major differences between contingencies in treatment settings and those in the natural environment.

To approximate the reinforcing conditions in the natural surroundings, during training it is usually necessary to vary the frequency, delay, amount, and type of reinforcers used. Artificial reinforcers such as food, tokens, and verbal praise are systematically decreased while naturally occurring reinforcers such as head nods, smiles, and visual attention are introduced. At the same time, continuous and rapid reinforcement is shifted to an intermittent and delayed schedule. Also, through pairing of artificial and natural reinforcers and through direct instruction, the learner is taught to identify the naturally occurring reinforcers and their contingency relationship.

Generalization is facilitated when the learner is taught a functional skill that is instrumental in producing reinforcing consequences for the individual and/or the people around him/her. A skill of this nature is likely to be occasioned, reinforced, and maintained in various contexts. Some behaviors taught to the handicapped may be functional and permit task completion, however, they also may be sufficiently deviant in nature to elicit a negative response from other people in the environment. Baer and Wolf (1970) describe the process of *trapping*, whereby the behavior taught to an individual is sufficiently reinforcing to the people around him/her that they automatically and naturally reinforce the behavior and assist its generalization and maintenance. The authors described an example of trapping in which social interaction skills were taught to a preschool child. Initially, the other children at the preschool were taught to interact with the child and reinforce his/her appropriate responses. With time, the natural consequences of interaction took control of the child's behavior.

Seymour and Stokes (1976) taught institutionalized girls to solicit reinforcement for acceptable behavior. When their work was objectively good and when a staff person was nearby, the girls were taught to call the adult's attention to their good work.

Self-evaluation, performance recording, and reinforcement may assist the generalization and maintenance of behaviors. Johnson (1970) and Johnson and Martin (1973) have shown that children's behavior is more resistant to extinction through self-regulation procedures than it is through external regulation. Although maintenance of behavior change has been demonstrated within the same setting by use of self-control procedures, no evidence is yet available demonstrating generalization to new settings. This topic deserves further study.

As was mentioned earlier, the use of more than one trainer may enhance generalization. Stokes, Baer, and Jackson (1974) established a greeting response in four retarded children. When the response was established by one trainer, generalization did not usually occur. When a second trainer worked in conjunction with the first, the greeting response generalized to 20 members of the institutional staff who had not been involved in the training. Similar results were observed by Garcia (1974) when a conversational speech form was taught to two retarded children. The responses did not generalize until they were taught by two trainers. Langone and Westling (1979) suggested that to foster generalization of the prevocational and vocational skills of mentally retarded students, it may be desirable to make temporary shifts in teaching assignments. Different teachers would supervise the skills being learned by various groups of students.

Different teachers and people in the general environment may use a variety of language, social cues, and reinforcement procedures that may confuse a student trained by one teacher (Schworm and Abelseth, 1978; Wehman, Abramson, and Norman, 1977). McCormick and Elder (1978) examined the consistency of adult speech directed towards young children. They found that a mother and father referred to a Mickey Mouse watch as: Mickey Mouse, tic toc, watch, clock, and Mickey. A small child's shirt was called a sweater, shirt, toy, clothes, and a horseshoe, referring to the design on the front of the sweater. Greer, Anderson, and Davis (1976) found that institutional staff were inconsistent in the manner in which they labeled common objects. In one situation, the authors observed that pants were referred to as trousers, jeans, slacks, and overalls.

In some cases, the use of more than one teacher may incidentally teach the learner to respond under the variety of conditions that may occur later in the general environment. In other cases, it may be necessary to program the learner to respond to specific variations in conditions. Williams, Brown, and Certo (1975) described systematic changes that should be made to verbal instructions while training severely handicapped individuals. The authors suggested that learners should be taught that some modifications to a verbal instruction should all occasion the same response: "Pick up . . . (many, several, a lot, or a bunch)," other changes should occasion different responses, ". . . (Touch, Give me, Point to, or Take) the ball." The learner must be taught to discriminate the different types of changes that are most likely to occur in the general environment.

In some situations, it may be possible and desirable to modify the environment into which the newly trained behavior is to be generalized. Where little reinforcement for behavior is available, prompting and reinforcing newly acquired responses may be increased, while punishment, or reinforcement for a failure to perform adequately is removed. Initially, maximum opportunity should be provided to respond and be reinforced. With handicapped children, whose gains may be small and infrequent, new behavioral acquisitions may go unnoticed and adults may continue to respond towards the children in habitually unreinforcing ways. As a result, the new behaviors may inadvertently be put on extinction. Alternatively, over-protective parents may prevent a retarded individual from expressing his/her new capabilities. These difficulties may be overcome by teaching parents, teachers, and peers to encourage expression of new skills and to notice and reinforce spontaneous emission of the responses.

Summary. There is considerable evidence to demonstrate that generalization does not occur automatically with the acquisition of a new response and that it must be systematically programmed. Traditionally, the mentally retarded have experienced difficulty generalizing newly acquired responses from the training milieu to the natural environment. Various methods of facilitating generalization have been reviewed: (a) sequential modification: if generalization does not occur, provide training in each generalization environment; (b) using more than one initial training situation; (c) modifying the training environment to approximate the nature of the natural environment: (I) varying the materials used, (II) varying the amount, type, frequency, and delay of reinforcement, and (III) teaching the learner to respond to variations in language cues; (d) prompting discriminative stimuli in the training and natural environments; (e) differentiating discriminative from similar, nondiscriminative stimuli; (f) teaching functional skills that are mutually reinforcing to the performer and the people around him/her; (g) teaching the performer to solicit reinforcement; (h) teaching self-evaluation, recording, and reinforcement; (i) using more than one trainer; and (j) modifying the environment into which the newly learned behavior is to be generalized.

Review of Concepts and Procedures
Covered in Chapters Four and Five

Before proceeding into new material, review the following concepts and procedures discussed in Chapters Four and Five. Use a paper and pencil as applicable: (1) define or explain; (2) provide a novel example; (3) describe where, when, and how to apply or evaluate; and (4) discuss advantages and disadvantages of each term. As a term is being reviewed, cover all of the other terms to avoid giving yourself clues. If you are unable to recall the information *rapidly* and *accurately*, refer to the listed page number(s) and review the material; page numbers with major references have been underlined. Note troublesome terms and put them into a maintenance schedule for repeated review after successively longer periods of time.

Subject   Page No.

Spontaneous recovery, 104
Errorless learning, 88, <u>89</u>, 98, 119, 132-133
Imitative prompts, 89
Extra-stimulus prompting, 94-96, 98

Placement test, 125-126
Topography of a behavior, 136, 137, 145
Generalization test, 126
Task confirmation, 117-118, 120-122
Advantages of group instruction, 123-125
Post-test, 126, 145
Shaping, 129-131, 136-141
Successive approximations, 137-139, 141
Forward chaining, 133-136
Orienting errors, 128
Reverse cumulative chaining, 133-136
Stimulus generalization, 142-150
Latency of response error, 129

Chapter 6

Development of an Instructional Program:
An Example

Contents
1. Developing an instructional program to teach students to ride a public bus.

   Step a.   Learner evaluation.

          b.   Selecting and ordering goals.

          c.   Literature review.

          d.   (I) Conditions analysis.

               (II) A prosthetic adaptation.

          e.   Performance analysis.

          f.   Writing the terminal behavioral objective.

          g.   Constructing a flowchart.

          h.   Constructing a lattice ridgeline.

          i.   Performing a hierarchic learning analysis.

2. A program prospectus: Public bus transportation training program: 1.
3. Sample lessons.

Developing an Instructional Program
to Teach Students to Ride a Public Bus

This chapter applies the instructional techniques described in the preceding chapters to develop a program to teach handicapped students the skills required to ride a public bus. Figure 1.2 and the checklist at the end of Chapter One provide a summary of the preliminary stages of instructional design and the development and evaluation of a terminal behavioral objective. Figure 2.9 and the checklist at the end of Chapter Two describe the steps involved in performing a task analysis. Chapter Three discusses various methods of instructional sequencing. Chapters Four and Five illustrate a variety of instructional methods used to teach, generalize, and maintain skills. The application of each of these procedures is illustrated in the development of the following instructional program designed to teach the skills required to ride a public bus.

Steps 1 and 2: Learner evaluation; selecting and ordering goals. The bus riding program that follows has been developed for a hypothetical group of handicapped students. Usually the preliminary steps leading to program development involve an evaluation of learner skills in many different areas of performance. The purpose of the evaluation is to identify: (a) performance areas of relatively high or low achievement; (b) specific prerequisite skills that have been mastered; (c) successive steps or skills on the ladder of development for which the learner has achieved the prerequisites; and (d) the general importance, functional value, and developmental priority of specific skills. Assume for sake of discussion that in the present circumstance an evaluation of this nature has been completed and that the following instructional goal, one of many, has been selected for the particular group of students that had been evaluated.

Instructional goal: To teach the learner to travel independently on a public bus between home, school, or workshop and return.

Step 3: Literature review. The following references provide an example of the types of instructional programs and research articles that one might review in preparation for the development of an instructional program to teach the skills required to ride a public bus. A review of this nature provides information about (a) the behavioral objectives developed in other programs, (b) the number, type, and sequence of skills taught, (c) the various instructional methods employed, and (d) the efficacy of these methods with particular types of handicapped learners.

Certo, N., Schwartz, R., and Brown, L. Community transportation: Teaching severely handicapped students to ride a public bus system. In N.G. Haring and L.J. Brown (Eds.), *Teaching the severely handicapped.* New York: Grune and Stratton, 1977.

Hughson, E.A., and Brown, R.I. III—A bus training program for mentally retarded adults. *British Journal of Mental Subnormality,* 1975, *21,* 79-83.

Lupei, J.D. Riding a public bus. In D.R. Anderson, G.D. Hodson, and W.G. Jones (Eds.), *Instructional programming for the handicapped student.* Springfield, Illinois: Charles C. Thomas Publisher, 1975.

Neef, N.A., Iwata, B.A., and Page, T.J. Public transportation training: In vivo versus classroom instruction. *Journal of Applied Behavior Analysis,* 1978, *11,* 331-344.

Step 4 (a): Conditions analysis. The conditions analysis is conducted in conjunction with a performance analysis. A conditions analysis is designed to determine the number, type, and variation of conditions that occur and that may influence performance of a task. The results of a conditions analysis of riding a public bus follow.

Conditions analysis	Common variation of conditions
1. Bus stop:	
a. sign	—discriminative features: color, design, and location. —similarity with other signs. —nearness to curb.
b. location	—distance from home, school, or workshop. —at side of road or within a terminal area.
c. waiting area	—open; —fenced queuing maze; —enclosure: waiting hut, —benches.
d. people	—none, few, or many, —from the general population, peers, or acquaintances of the learner. —queued or randomly dispersed. —waiting for the same or different buses.
2. Bus:	
a. discriminative features	—color, surface design, size, shape, name of bus line, destination label, number and location of destination labels and route numbers (front, side, or rear of bus).

          —similarity among different types of buses.

b. doors
—front and/or rear entry or exit;
—automatic opening, treadle operated, or push response type.

c. fare
—exact change required;
—if exact change required, amount, number, and type of coins;
—change provided;
—tokens or bus passes accepted;
—meter box, change tray, conductor;
—transfer.

d. seats
—available or not available, upon entry or while traveling;
—location of seats: window, aisle, or along the side, at the front and/or rear of the bus.

e. people
—sitting on window or aisle seats;
—standing at the front or rear of the bus;
—exiting at the same or different stops;
—from the general population, peers, or acquaintances of the learner.

f. stanchions
—horizontal (across ceiling) or vertical (floor to ceiling);
—hanging hand-grips,
—within reach;
—grip-loops on the back of seats.

g. exit alarm
—buzzer or bell;
—cord or button operated;
—at each seat and at doors.

3. Destination cue
—may be on curbside or roadside of bus;
—building: McDonald's restaurant, gas station, or school;
—street names or numbers;
—salience of discriminative features;
—number, amount, and types of advance warnings.

Step 4(b): A prosthetic adaptation. A prosthetic analysis, part of the conditions analysis, is designed to identify methods for temporarily substituting or improving a missing or dysfunctional part or process to make possible or improve an individual's level or type of functioning. The following prosthetic adaptation, a "travel guide" (Figure 6.1), eliminates the need for the learner to:

(a) count coins, if exact fare is required,

(b) recall and read the destination name and/or number of the bus,

(c) recall the color and surface design of the bus or bus stop sign,

(d) recall the destination cues.

The travel guide offers several advantages:

(a) individuals of relatively low levels of functioning can participate in the instructional program,

(b) the time taken to complete the program is shorter than if the recall and fare counting skills had to be taught,

(c) any combination of silver coins can be used to make up the exact fare,

(d) the three parts of the prompt fold into a single width to readily fit within a pocket or purse.

The travel guide is comprised of a coin counter, a bus selection prompt, and a destination cue. Each of these devices is described below. The *coin counter* permits the learner to use any combination of silver coins to make up the fare. In the example shown in Figure 6.1, two coin configurations are displayed, A and B: more configurations could be added or a single configuration could be used repeatedly to help the learner count the exact fare.

The configuration is used in the following manner. The shape of each coin has been impressed into a piece of solid plastic so that nickles, dimes, and quarters can be inserted level with the surface of the configuration. The impression of the dimes has been colored to prompt discrimination of that shape. Each configuration permits the learner to count any combination of nickles, dimes, and quarters up to a total of 25 cents. The following combinations of coins will fit into each configuration: five nickles *or* one nickle and two dimes, *or* one dime and three nickles, *or* a

Figure 6.1

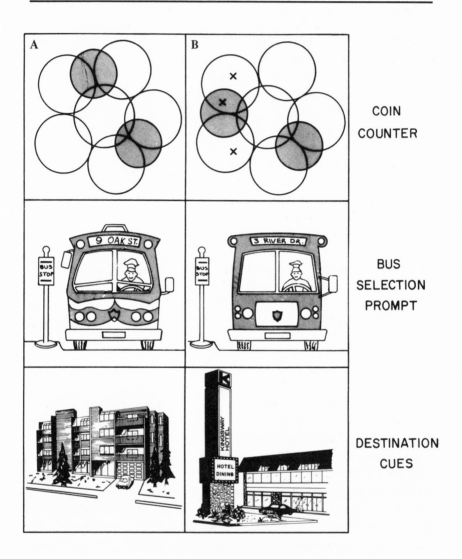

Figure 6.1. Travel guide.

25 cent coin. When a combination of coins totaling 25 cents has been inserted into the configuration, no additional coins can be inserted. Also, no coins will "fit" firmly into the wrong impression. If a bus fare requires a combination of coins of less than 25 cents or between 25 and 50 cents, one or more of the impressions in the configuration can be filled-in with a plug so that only coins of the desired denomination will fit into the configuration. For example, if the fare is 40 cents, configuration A is left open, while the three impressions indicated by "X's" in configuration B are filled-in. When coins are inserted in the remaining impressions, the only combinations possible are: three nickles, *or* one nickle and one dime. Thus, the total of the two configurations is 40 cents.

The *bus selection prompt* is a color photograph of the front of the bus that the learner is required to take and includes a picture of the bus stop sign. The photograph is inserted into a protective plastic pocket. This prompt is useful when there are two or more buses and/or signs to be discriminated. The picture shows the color, number, and destination label of the buses going to, and returning from home, school, or workshop.

The *destination cue* is a color photograph of the geographic location where the learner should pull the cord to indicate his/her wish to alight from the bus.

Steps 5 and 6: Performance analysis; writing the terminal behavioral objective. The results of the performance analysis are summarized in the flowcharts that follow (see Figures 6.2 to 6.8). A terminal behavioral objective describes the observable, measurable behaviors that a learner should be able to perform at the end of an instructional program. The objective also describes the conditions ("the givens") under which the learner must perform, and the standards of performance that s/he must achieve. The objective that follows describes the terminal behavioral objective for the public bus riding program.

Given: 1. A valid public transportation bus pass and/or coins of various denominations with a total less than, equal to, or exceeding that required for bus fare, and

2. A public bus stop sign within 250 meters from home, school, and/or workshop.

    (a) the sign is located 50-150 cm from the curb;
    (b) people may or may not be waiting at the bus stop;
    (c) if people are waiting at the bus stop, they may be queued or randomly located at the bus stop;
    (d) the return trip to and from home, school, or workshop does not require a transfer.

3. A number of public transportation buses stop at the bus stop at various intervals.
    (a) the buses are of similar color, size, and model; entry is permitted only through the front door.
    (b) the destination of each bus is displayed by name and/or number on the front of each bus.

4. When the appropriate bus comes to the bus stop:
    (a) people may or may not exit before entry is possible;
    (b) people at the bus stop may be waiting for various buses and none, some, or all of the people may enter any of the buses;
    (c) if there are people at the bus stop and/or on the bus, they will be comprised of people from the general community rather than the learner's classmates, or fellow trainees.

5. On the bus:
    (a) there may or may not be people standing;
    (b) all seats may be filled, or window and/or aisle seats may be available at the front and/or rear of the bus;
    (c) after a period of time, seats may become available near the front and/or rear of the bus; other people may be closer to the seats than the trainee is; also, there may be insufficient time to sit before the destination is reached;
    (d) exit is permitted from the rear door only;
    (e) the doors may open automatically, or they may be operated by a foot treadle or push bar;
    (f) passengers may exit at various destinations requiring the learner to adjust his/her position in a seat or on the aisle;
    (g) exit alarm buzzers or bells are accessible to each seat and door and are operated by a pull cord or a push button;
    (h) a travel guide with a coin counter, bus selection prompt, and destination cue is provided.

The learner, alone, without assistance, companionship, or obtrusive supervision will:
    (1) obtain and prepare the fare, exact change, if required;
    (2) go to, and wait at, a bus stop;
    (3) board the appropriate bus;
    (4) pay the fare;
    (5) sit in a seat or stand in the aisle as is appropriate;

(6) look for the destination cue;

(7) when the cue is sighted, ring the alarm; and

(8) exit at the destination.

The task of traveling from an origin to a destination and return will be performed on six consecutive occasions randomly distributed over a one-month period; performance must comply with the following standards.

1. When waiting, boarding, seating, or exiting, the learner will give each person ahead of him/her in the line-up the opportunity to respond first before proceeding to perform each step of the task.

2. Where it is necessary for the learner to move past people who block the passage, the performer will excuse himself/herself and allow at least three seconds for the person to respond appropriately before moving past.

3. Where other people excuse themselves to gain passage, the learner will temporarily move aside to permit passage.

4. The learner will not exhibit deviant behavior such as hand flapping, rocking, talking or singing to one's self, nose picking, smoking, genital stimulation, eating, violent behavior, or similar non-normative behaviors that would attract attention or alienate other passengers.*

5. When seated, the learner will occupy only the amount of space assigned to one person.

6. When standing, the learner will hold on firmly with *both* hands, and will not lean or fall against other people.

7. When moving down the aisle, while the bus is in motion, the learner will hold onto the stanchion, the back of seats, and/or the overhead bar or grip.

8. The learner will not put his/her hands upon other passengers.

9. The learner will activate the exit alarm in response to the correct geographical destination cue: McDonald's restaurant, street sign, gas station, etc., rather than respond to the incidental or customary exit of another person.

10. After activating the exit alarm, the learner must be ready to exit when the bus stops, be at the appropriate door (if rear exit only), or in the line-up to exit from the door.

---

*In accord with the principles of normalization, when the passengers on the bus are comprised of people from the general community, the behaviors referred to above may be normatively and circumstantially defined in accord with the manner in which the average person on the bus performs under various conditions. Different communities or sets of circumstances may establish normative standards of behavior dependent upon cultural and socio-economic influences.

11.   Barring any unusual event, the learner will not seek assistance or confirmation from fellow passengers or the bus driver.
12.   When paying the fare, the learner will use the coin box, change tray, or bus pass as required, and will give the driver time to make change or return the bus pass before proceeding.

Step 7: Constructing a flowchart. A flowchart summarizes the results of the conditions and performance analyses. The flowchart provides a graphic representation of the sequence of subtasks required to complete the task described in a terminal behavioral objective. The flowcharts that follow, Figures 6.2-6.8, display the numbers, types, and sequences of subtasks involved in the various conditions associated with riding a public bus. The flowchart is the product of the instructional designer's efforts to:

(a) think-through and actually perform the task,
(b) analyze the task being performed by novice and accomplished performers under various conditions, and
(c) review the conditions and skills described in the literature.

Step 8: Constructing a lattice ridgeline. The subtasks in a flowchart are collapsed onto the ridgeline of a lattice. Later, a hierarchic learning analysis is performed on these subtasks to determine what enabling skills are required to perform each subtask. The bus riding program is comprised of seven instructional modules:

(a) getting the fare ready;
(b) arriving at the bus stop;
(c) boarding the bus;
(d) paying the fare;
(e) looking for a seat;
(f) waiting for the destination; and
(g) exiting from the bus.

Figure 6.9 illustrates the manner in which the subtasks in module 2, "arriving at the bus stop," are numbered and alphabetized in preparation to collapse the flowchart onto a lattice ridgeline. The ridgeline formed of the subtasks in module 2 is displayed in Figure 6.10.

Step 9: Performing a hierarchic learning analysis. In a hierarchic learning analysis, a subskill is analyzed into the enabling skills: S-R

Figure 6.2

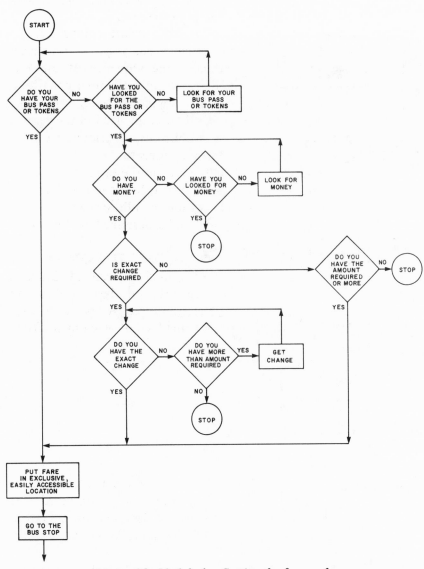

Figure 6.2. Module 1: Getting the fare ready.

Figure 6.3

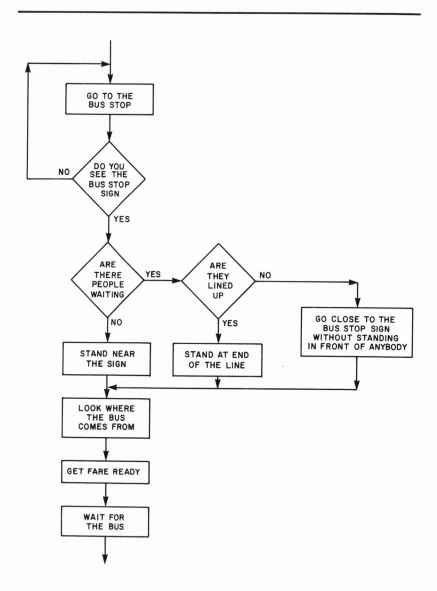

Figure 6.3. Module 2: Arriving at the bus stop.

Figure 6.4

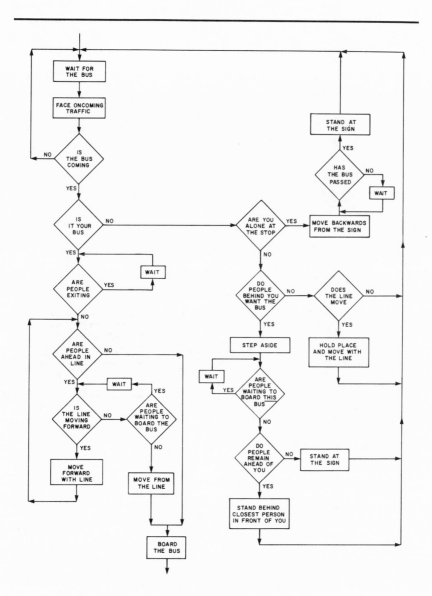

Figure 6.4. Module 3: Boarding the bus.

Figure 6.5

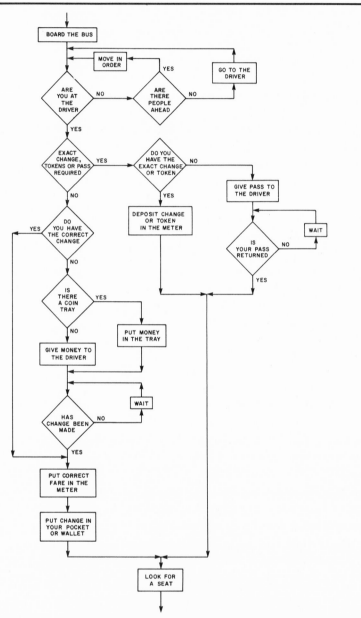

Figure 6.5. Module 4: Paying the fare.

Figure 6.6

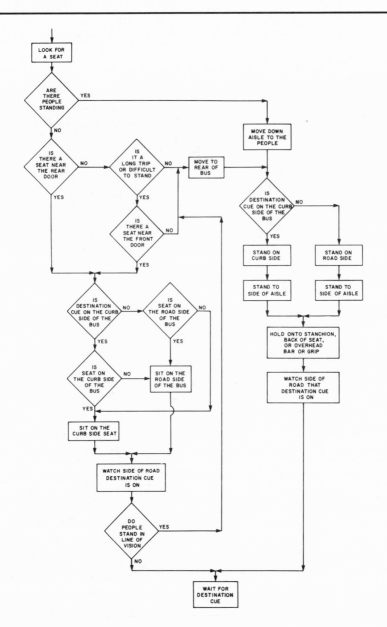

Figure 6.6. Module 5: Looking for a seat.

Figure 6. 7

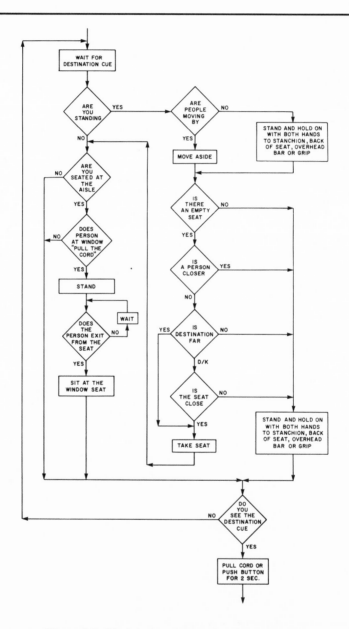

Figure 6.7. Module 6: Waiting for the destination.

Figure 6.8

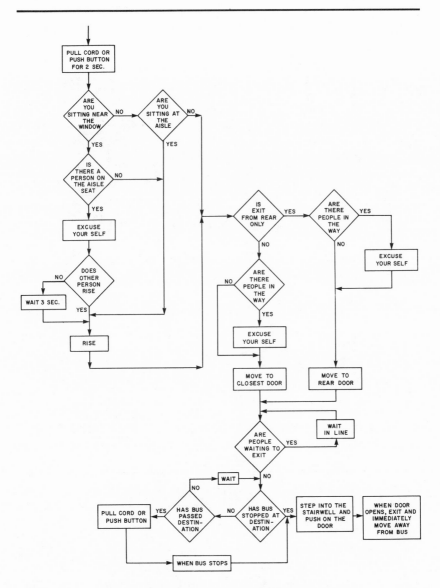

Figure 6.8. Module 7: Exiting from the bus.

Figure 6.9

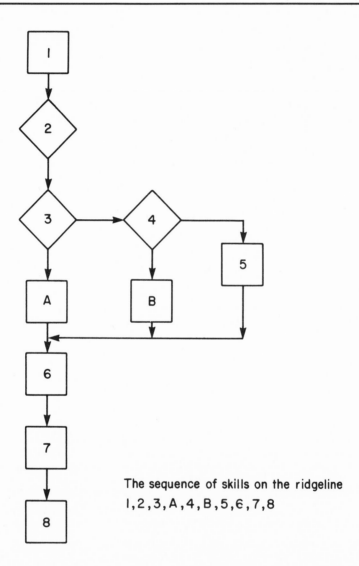

The sequence of skills on the ridgeline
1,2,3,A,4,B,5,6,7,8

Figure 6.9. Preparing to collapse the subskills in module 2 onto a ridgeline.

Figure 6.10

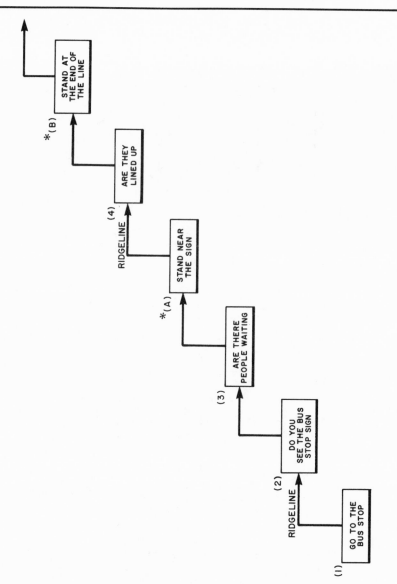

Figure 6.10. Lower part of ridgeline for module 2: Arriving at the bus stop.

Figure 6.11

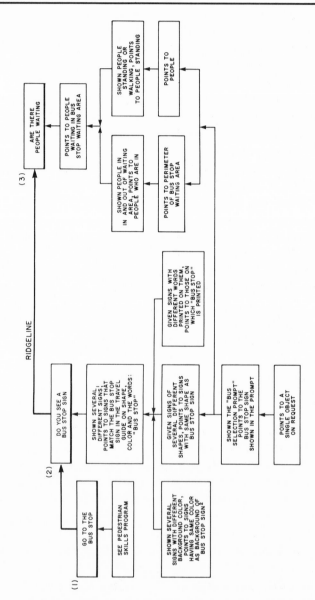

Figure 6.11. Hierarchic learning analysis of lower part of module 2: arriving at the bus stop.

links, chains, discriminations, concepts, rules, and problem solving strategies that an individual must learn to move from his/her entry skill level to acquire each subskill. Since the present program was developed for a hypothetical group of learners, no entry level skills have been established. Figure 6.11 displays the results of a hierarchic learning analysis of the lower part of module 2: "arriving at the bus stop."

A program prospectus forms the preface of an instructional program. The prospectus provides sufficient factual, empirical, and evaluative information about the program to permit a teacher to determine: (a) precisely what skills are taught, (b) what methods of instruction are employed, (c) what skills are required to administer the program, (d) what group of students the program was designed for, (e) what student entry level skills are required, (f) how successful the program has been in teaching specific groups of students, (g) how the success rate compares with that of other programs that teach the same skills, and (h) the time and material costs that are involved. The program prospectus that follows describes the Public Bus Transportation Training Program: 1.

Program Prospectus

1. *Program title.* PUBLIC BUS TRANSPORTATION TRAINING PROGRAM: 1.

2. Instructional goal: To teach the learner to travel independently on a public bus between home, school, or workshop and return.

3. *Terminal behavioral objective.* Ordinarily, the terminal behavioral objective for public bus transportation, described earlier in this chapter, would be restated at this point in its entirety. However, for sake of brevity the objective is omitted.

4. *Learner population.* This program is designed for "low functioning" handicapped learners, for example, the trainable, mentally retarded, who possess the requisite entry level skills and for whom learning to ride a public bus independently is an instructional priority in view of their level of development in all major areas of performance.

5. *Learner entry level skills.* These skills should be defined in

the form of behavioral objectives that describe the social, psychological, academic, sensory, physical, communication, and vocational skills that are prerequisite to entry into the program. The learner must be able to reach criterion on the following behavioral objective describing pedestrian skills.

Crossing the street. Given: (a) the intersection of a four-lane, through street (with approximately x-vehicles per minute) and a secondary street (with approximately y-vehicles per minute), (b) stop signs on the secondary street, (c) no stop sign or light on the through street, (d) no crosswalks on either street, (e) situations with and without pedestrians, and (f) a speed limit of 60 km/h or less, the learner will walk across the through street to the nearest opposite corner. The learner will: (a) take one step from the curb when there is no moving traffic within M-meters in the first, left lane and cross the first lane and each successive lane when there is no moving traffic within M-meters in the lane to be crossed. Where there is a moving vehicle within M-meters in the lane to be crossed, the learner will either wait on the curb, stand at the curb, or wait just behind the dividing line of the lane to be crossed. Running or changing direction of travel is not permitted. The learner will demonstrate the behavior without assistance and in the presence or absence of other pedestrians who may or may not conform to the same procedures. The behavior must be exhibited and unobtrusively evaluated at four different street corners on six consecutive occasions randomly distributed over a three-week period.

Behavioral objectives should also be listed that describe the learner's ability to (a) cross intersections that are controlled by traffic and/or pedestrian traffic lights, and (b) walk several blocks along a route from home, school, or workshop to a bus stop and return. If a learner can perform these behavioral objectives, s/he has adequate general academic, intellectual, sensory, and psychological skills to benefit from the bus riding program. More specific skills that are required are: (a) sufficient motor skills to board a public bus without assistance and to support one's self while standing in the aisle and holding on with both hands throughout the duration of a ride of k-kilometers; (b) freedom from uncontrolled seizures; (c) freedom from deviant behavior such as hand flapping, rocking, talking or singing to one's self, nose picking, genital stimulation, touching people, and violent behavior; and (d) sufficient visual and intellectual skills to learn how to discriminate sameness between two samples of either colors, shapes, or letters, and to match geographic and structural landmarks observed from the bus with a picture of the same location.

6. *Teacher qualifications.* This program may be administered by teachers, paraprofessionals, or parents who have previously successfully taught other skills to several members of the population of learners and who have completed the following steps.

Before administering this program, (a) complete the sample lesson described in the section on "general instructional procedures," (b) preread the entire program, and (c) practice the instruction, feedback, correction, and reinforcement procedures for each lesson. Delivery of appropriate instruction, feedback, reinforcement, and correction procedures should be rapid and accurate before the program is implemented with members of the target population.

7. *Program rationale.* The skills of riding a public bus to and from school, home, recreation center, and/or workshop are part of the normalization process. The individual who learns these skills: (a) increases his/her ability to function independently, (b) extends the limits of his/her environment, and (c) increases the amount and type of stimulation and the frequency with which s/he will observe the modeling of various types of normative behaviors. The learning of bus riding skills reduces the responsibility of parents, guardians, and teachers and increases the possibility of the learner participating in independent living, recreation, and employment.

8. *Instructional model.* This program employs a direct instructional approach. Instruction is preanalyzed and sequenced into graduated steps. Teacher interactions are prescribed. Each step of instruction integrates techniques of behavioral and instructional management: reinforcement, feedback, and correction procedures. Behavioral techniques such as shaping, chaining, prompting, and fading are also employed. Behavioral objectives describe the goals of instruction. The instructional sequence has been developed through the process of task analysis, and experimental procedures have been employed to validate the sequence. Criterion-referenced tests evaluate performance at each level of instruction.

9. *Instructional administration.* Instruction is conducted on a one-to-one basis of one teacher to each student. Most of the

instruction takes place in a classroom using simulated materials and conditions; the final steps of instruction are administered in the natural environment. The program follows a linear sequence where all students follow the same steps of instruction. However, individualization is possible. Beginning students who have already acquired some of the skills taught in the program may begin instruction at skill levels commensurate with their entry level skills. Students may progress at an individually suitable rate. Correction procedures are shaped to individual needs. Students receive as much practice as they require at each step of instruction.

10. *Program modules.* The program is comprised of the following instructional modules:

(a) getting the fare ready;
(b) arriving at the bus stop;
(c) boarding the bus;
(d) paying the fare;
(e) looking for a seat;
(f) waiting for the destination; and
(g) exiting from the bus.

11. *Program limitations.* The program does not train the learner to:

(a) travel with peers,
(b) transfer from one bus to another,
(c) cope with unusual circumstances such as rerouting of the bus, or removal of the destination cue,
(d) cope with being lost,
(e) interact verbally with fellow passengers (except to excuse one's self when seeking passage), and
(f) get from home, school, or workshop to the bus stop.

12. *Instructional materials.* The following materials are required for administration of the program:

(a)   a life-size, simulated model of the floor plan of a public bus,
(b)   exterior walls of the bus constructed from cardboard,
(c)   windows are cut into the walls,
(d)   simulated and functional front and back doors,

- (e) chairs or benches to represent typical seating,
- (f) a life-size coin meter—appropriately situated,
- (g) a life-size coin tray—appropriately situated,
- (h) a "bus driver,"
- (i) a buzzer or bell cord or button fixed to the wall above each seat and within reach,
- (j) a 12v. D.C. buzzer or bell and battery,
- (k) a slide projector and a series of slides projected adjacent to either the curb or roadside of the bus, as appropriate, showing a sequence of locations along the route,
- (l) a standard bus stop sign,
- (m) a simulated bus stop waiting area,
- (n) a group of individuals to wait at the bus stop and/or ride the bus,
- (o) a 7cm x 7cm picture of the public bus that travels from the origin to the destination bus stops and pictures of the return buses. Both pictures show the front of the bus, its number and destination label, and a picture of the bus stop signs,
- (p) a picture of the destination point at which the exit buzzer or bell should be activated, and
- (q) a plastic coin counter (as previously described).

13. *Formative and summative evaluation.* This program has been successfully employed by teachers, teachers aides, and workshop personnel with the following individuals.

- (a) Workshop personnel implemented the program with 25 adult, trainable, mentally retarded persons: CA: 18-36 yrs.; IQ: 37-49. The program was administered individually for 20 minutes daily. Results: the program took from 12-32 hours to complete; the average time for completion was 17 hours. Eighteen of the students met all of the standards described in the criteria. Three students were transferred from the workshop and failed to complete training. Two students failed to complete the program during the allotted time; 80 percent of the modules they attempted were completed successfully. The two remaining students met all standards in the terminal objective except that of exiting from the bus at the right spot. These students failed to pay sufficient attention to the destination cue and on 30 percent of the trials traveled beyond their destination.

The results of summative evaluations in which the program is compared with the results obtained by other programs should also be reported in the program prospectus.

14. *Instructional costs.* The following costs have been estimated from the results of the studies reported above.

program manual	$ 45.00
materials (equipment)	17.00
labor (construction) $5/hr. for four hours	20.00
operating costs	
training staff $6/hr. for 15 hours	90.00
bus fare @ 50 cents/trip for ten trips	5.00
total cost to train first student	177.00
total cost per student thereafter	$ 95.00

15. *Assessment procedure.* The following tests are included in the program package.

(a) A *pre-test* of the ability to perform the terminal behavioral objective for the program.

(b) An *entry level skills test* provides an assessment of the presence of the skills required to begin the program.

(c) The *placement tests* indicate where to begin instruction in the program and facilitate homogeneous grouping of students.

(d) The *diagnostic tests,* embedded in each lesson, reveal particular learner problems and corrective procedures.

(e) *Probes* are interspersed throughout instruction and evaluate the learner's incidental acquisition and generalization of skills; this information permits some students to "skip" selected steps in the program.

(f) *Post-tests* (mastery tests) assess achievement of the terminal behavioral objective.

(g) The purpose of the *generalization* and *maintenance* tests is obvious.

16. *General instructional procedures.* This section of the prospectus serves three purposes. The first purpose is to provide the reader with a *brief* explanation of the major instructional techniques incorporated into the program. For example, three short, explanatory paragraphs may be written to describe prompting, fading, and chaining procedures. The second purpose of this section is to remind the reader that the program has been established by means of a thorough study by experts of both the subject matter and the learner population. The reader is also reminded that the methods have been carefully and repeatedly validated during field testing with teachers, aides, parents, workshop personnel, and a variety of students. As a result, the product is considered to provide the optimum method for teaching skills included in the program to the learner population for whom the program was designed. In conclusion, the reader is admonished to follow carefully, without modification, each of the prescripted procedures and sequences exactly as they are written in the Teacher's Manual. It is explained that because of the complexity of the program, the ultimate significance of a single element in the program may not be readily apparent. Thus, a minor modification early in the program may have major consequences during advanced instruction.

The third and most important purpose of this section is to explain to the prospective teacher how to employ those parts of the program over which s/he may exercise administrative control. Although many aspects of the program are not subject to modification, the teacher does have discretionary control over when and how to use other instructional and behavioral management techniques such as pacing, reinforcement, correction procedures, etc. This section, therefore, is designed to explain clearly and concisely how and when to employ each of these techniques. Examples and sample exercises are provided. The sample exercises are designed to be practiced by the teacher with the assistance of a colleague whose participation has been prescripted into the exercise so that a variety of typical correct and incorrect responses will be exhibited. Additional references that the teacher may consult are also listed.

A Sample Lesson

A hierarchic learning analysis of the use of the "coin counter" employed in module 2 of the bus riding program reveals the chain of behaviors displayed in Figure 6.12.

Part A of Lesson 16 in the Teacher's Manual for the bus riding program, shown below, illustrates the manner in which some of the skills in the "coin counter" chain are taught. The lesson illustrates the "assisted practice stage" of the generic teaching model described in Chapter Five. In the lesson, teacher responses are printed in capital letters within quotation marks, for example, "READY"; directions to the teacher are printed in lower case letters within parentheses, for example, (touch the coin), and learner responses are printed in lower case letters between brackets, for example, [yes]. Note, that the "task confirmation and consequation" steps that would usually follow step (d) have been faded from use during earlier lessons.

Lesson 16

Part A: USING THE COIN COUNTER

   subtasks: 2, 4, and 5, "Does it (the coin) fit?"

1. *ARRANGEMENT*
   (a) Place the coin counter on the table in front of the learner.
   (b) Put a nickle, dime, and quarter in a random array in front of the learner.
2. *PROCEDURE*
   (a) O.K., LET'S USE THE COUNTER.
   (b) (put a dime into the quarter hole)
   (c) LOOK AT THIS COIN (point to the dime)
   (d) YOUR TURN: DOES IT FIT?
   (e) (Put forefinger of learner's dominant hand on top of the coin and attempt to move the coin back and forth in the hole.)
   (f) DOES IT FIT? (point to learner)
3. *CORRECT RESPONSE*
   [no] – YOU'RE RIGHT, IT DOESN'T FIT.
4. *ERROR RESPONSE*
   [yes] – NO! (Pause) IT DOESN'T FIT.
   CORRECTION
   (a) *MY TURN*, DOES IT FIT?
   (b) (Put forefinger on top of coin; move the coin back and forth in the slot.)
   (c) (pause) NO! IT DOESN'T FIT.

Figure 6.12

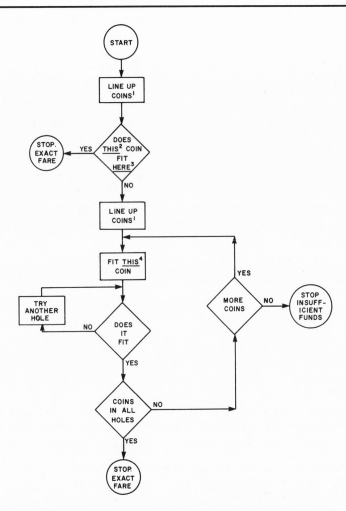

Figure 6.12. Flowchart of subskills involved in using a coin counter.

Note: 1. *Coins are lined-up from right to left, from large to small.*

Note: 2. *The largest coin.*

Note: 3. *The quarter hole.*

Note: 4. *The smallest coin.*

In successive parts of Lesson 16, the following tasks are presented to teach the learner to discriminate if a coin "fits" into a coin impression. Each task is taught in the same manner as described above.

a. The dime is put in the quarter slot.
b. The dime is put in the dime slot.
c. The nickle is put in the nickle slot.
d. The dime is put in the nickle slot.
e. The nickle is put in the quarter slot.
f. The quarter is put in the quarter slot.
g. The quarter is put in the nickle slot.

As was mentioned in Chapter Three, various phases of instruction of a variety of skills from different parts of a lattice may be included within a single lesson. For example, different parts of Lesson 16 may involve: (a) acquisition of the ability to discriminate if a coin "fits" in a coin hole, (b) review of newly acquired skills related to seat selection, and (c) maintenance trials of the visual discrimination of 35mm slides showing examples and nonexamples of destination cues. Inclusion of this variety of skills within a single lesson provides variation in the pace of instruction, the type of response required, the stimulus materials used, and the difficulty of the task. This variety of stimulation increases interest and motivation, as well as maintenance of learning; recovery time is also provided for skills that when practiced lead to boredom and fatigue.

A page from the instructor's manual of Hofmeister and Gallery's (1977) program for teaching shoelace tying is shown in Figure 6.13. The program employs the use of illustrations showing the instructor how to use physical prompts. In Engelmann and Osborne's (1976) program DISTAR, each page of the instructor's manual is comprised of the teacher's script, instructions to the teacher, and illustrations used by the student; some pages also describe one or more correction procedures.

Figure 6.13

I: Perfect! You made a loop! Now pick up the right lace with this hand and put it around the loop.
(Help the learner put the right lace around the loop.)

L: (Wraps the right lace around the loop with the instructor's help.)

L: (Pushes the lace through with the instructor's help.)

I: That's the way to wrap! Now push the lace through with this finger.
(Help the learner push the lace through with his index finger.)

L: (Pulls both loops.)

I: You did a good job pushing! Now hold this loop with this hand . . .
(Help the learner hold the left loop with his left hand.)

. . . and this loop with this hand . . .
(Help the learner grasp the right loop with his right hand.)

. . . and pull!
(Help the learner pull.)

I: You did it. You tied your shoe!

> **REDUCING HELP:** Repeat Step B, reducing the amount of help, using the *Tell-Help, Tell-Touch, Tell-Point, Tell* method in Lesson 1. When the learner responds correctly to *Tell*, proceed to Step C.

> **NOTE:** If the learner is having difficulty with the laces, use *long, stiff* laces, for example, made of rawhide.

Figure 6.13. Part of a teacher's manual for teaching shoelace tying.

Chapter 7

Concrete Concepts:
Analyzing, Sequencing, Teaching, and Testing

Contents
1. An introduction to concepts.
2. Examples and nonexamples.
3. Discriminative and nondiscriminative characteristics.
4. A summary and explanatory review of guidelines for teaching concepts.
5. Using pictures to teach concepts.
6. Prompting and pretraining.

An Introduction to Concepts

A concept is comprised of a set of objects, events, or symbols, or their characteristics or relationships that have been classified in a single category on the basis of common features. Members of the class are referred to by a particular name or symbol. Some examples of various types of concepts are listed below.

1. Objects: apples, cars, elephants, hammers, theaters, vehicles, and mammals.
2. Symbols: numbers, musical notes, and words.
3. Events: melting, kneeling, and hibernating.
4. Object or event characteristics: shiny, round, hot, smooth, sour, happy, quickly, large, complex, and nervous.
5. Object or event relationships: close, in, under, previous, third, early, and more.

An individual has been taught a *concrete* concept when s/he learns to *classify* (make one consistent response such as point to or label) all examples of the concept presented during instruction and any examples of the concept not presented during initial instruction.

Classification of examples of a concept involves two processes: (a) *generalization*, where a student learns to make the same response (e.g., pointing) to examples that were or were not present during instruction; and (b) *discrimination*, where the learner makes one consistent response to all examples of a concept, and makes other responses to all nonclass members including those not displayed during instruction. For example, an individual may demonstrate his/her ability to discriminate examples of fox terriers, chihuahuas, and wolfhounds from domestic cats, pigs, and leopards by pointing only to members of the concept class "dog." However, the individual has not demonstrated acquisition of the concept of "dog" until s/he generalizes initial learning by pointing to members of the class "dog," such as whippets, German shepherds, and pekingese, not included in initial instruction, while discriminating (not pointing to) tigers, lions, and racoons.

Concepts are defined by the *discriminative* characteristics possessed by all members of the class. Discriminative characteristics are also called relevant, defining, critical or criterial features, attributes, or traits. The discriminative features of a drinking cup are listed below:

(1) an object occupying a 63-800 cm^3 space,
(2) enclosed on the side and bottom with a solid or semi-solid,
(3) nonpermeable wall,
(4) 2mm-1cm thick,
(5) free standing on a
(6) flat base,
(7) having an opening of 16-100 cm,
(8) on the upper side, and
(9) capable of holding a liquid volume of 63 milliliters to eight deciliters.

Members of a concept may also possess *nondiscriminative* features. The nondiscriminative properties of a concept may be referred to as irrelevant, variable, or noncriterial or noncritical variables or characteristics. The nondiscriminative features may or may not be possessed by a particular example of a concept and where they do exist, they may be changed without affecting the classification of the example. Some of the nondiscriminative features of cups are listed below:

(1) color,
(2) surface design: flower pattern, plain, or geometric,
(3) material: plastic, metal, or glass,
(4) handles,
(5) shape: cylindrical, square, or irregular,
(6) size (within the range specified), and
(7) surface qualities: opaque, clear, or solid.

When *deductive* methods are used to teach concepts, a learner is presented with a definition that describes the discriminative features of a concept. The learner applies the definition to discriminate *examples* from *nonexamples* of the concept. A cup is a relatively common concept and most children learn to identify a broad variety of examples of cups at an early age. Few children, however, would be able to use a definition to identify an example of a cup. The definition of a cup contains a number of concepts that are frequently unfamiliar to children who, otherwise, are able to discriminate cups from noncups. Similarly, adults can readily classify examples of a large number of concepts; however, they would likely have difficulty providing a definition for any one concept that would include all examples and exclude all nonexamples of the concept. Anderson and Faust (1974) suggest that it is difficult to define the discriminative features of a concept as simple and as common as that of a ball; both a marble and a shot-put possess the two critical features listed by *Webster's Third New International Dictionary* (1964) and yet neither is characteristically called a ball.

Concrete or tangible *concepts* are taught by presenting a learner with examples. Usually, a range of examples is provided. For instance, to teach the concept "car," a learner may be presented with three types of cars: (a) *large* luxury cars: Cadillacs and Lincolns, (b) *medium*-sized cars: Chevrolets, Plymouths, and Mercurys, and (c) *small* cars: Volkswagens, Hondas, and Datsuns. Given this range of examples, the student learns to *generalize* and identify as cars untaught examples, such as Chryslers and Dodges. These cars may have different nondiscriminative features (colors, ages, styles, and conditions) than the examples of cars presented during instruction; however, all of the cars will possess the same discriminative features. The learner must also learn to discriminate cars from noncars, such as buses, trucks, golf-carts, and motorcycles. The discrimination of cars from noncars, or *examples* from *nonexamples,* is usually taught by presenting examples and nonexamples to a learner either *simultaneously* (two or more at a time) or *successively* (one following the removal of the other). The learner is taught to respond in *one consistent manner* to examples (pointing, sorting, or labeling) and to respond in different ways to nonexamples. Thus, when the concept "cup" is being taught, examples of various types of cups and nonexamples such as glasses, vases, and cans would be presented. Each example of "cup" would possess all of the discriminative features described in the definition. The nonexamples of "cup" may possess none or some but not all of the discriminative features. The nondiscriminative features of size, color, material, and design may be possessed by either examples or nonexamples.

Some concepts are difficult, if not impossible, to learn without the use of a definition. These concepts are referred to as *defined* or *abstract* concepts. Defined concepts do not have concrete examples that can be recognized by their appearance. Some examples of defined concepts are: democracy, truth, city, and family. For instance, one cannot simply look at a group of people and validly identify them as a family without comparing the biological, social, and/or legal characteristics of the group to the characteristics specified in the definition of a family.

This textbook focuses exclusively on the teaching of *concrete concepts* and the use of *inductive* and *receptive* methods of instruction. In the *inductive* approach, the learner is given a number of examples and nonexamples of a concept. S/he is not told which characteristics are discriminative or how these characteristics are combined (combinatorial rule). To acquire a concept, the student must: (a) learn to distinguish discriminative from nondiscriminative characteristics, and (b) determine the relationship among the discriminative features. This approach, involving *complete learning* of attributes *and* combinatorial rules, is used with instructionally naive learners with poor language skills and/or a generally low level of intellectual functioning. The learner is taught to identify one discriminative feature at a time. Learners at higher levels of functioning may be told which attributes are discriminative; they must then learn the combinatorial rule (*principle learning*). Alternatively, they may be told which combinatorial rule is involved; in which case, they are required to learn which discriminative features are combined in the described manner (*attribute learning*). Or, the learner may be given a definition in which both the rules and their combinatorial relationship are described (deductive learning).

In the *receptive paradigm,* the learner is presented with a preselected number, type, and sequence of examples and/or nonexamples. With this approach, the learner's attention, discrimination, and generalization can be systematically controlled and progressively shaped. By contrast, in the *selective paradigm,* the learner is presented with several examples and nonexamples from which s/he may freely choose.

This textbook describes a behavioral model of instruction for teaching concepts. In the behavioral model, concept teaching involves two phases of instruction. The first phase is concerned with *discrimination learning* and the establishing of *stimulus control. Feedback* and *reinforcement* are used to *condition* a *response* (e.g., pointing, naming, or sorting) to occur in the presence of a *stimulus* object, event, or symbol (an example) possessing one or more *discriminative stimuli,* and to *extinguish* the response in the presence of stimuli (nonexamples) that do not possess all of the discriminative attributes. The second phase of instruction involves *generalization* training in which a learner is *reinforced* for responding in the same manner to stimuli (examples) not included in initial instruction that may have a variety of nondiscriminative attributes but possess all of the discriminative characteristics.

Types of concepts. There are various types of concepts defined in terms of: (a) the number of discriminative features (*unidimen-*

sional or *multidimensional* concepts), and (b) the *combinatorial* rules that describe the relationship among the discriminative features of multidimensional concepts. Bourne (1970) classified concepts into ten categories according to their combinatorial rules; a list of five of the most commonly occurring concepts follows.

1. Affirmative concepts: an example is defined by the presence of a single attribute, e.g., all red objects are examples. These concepts are *unidimensional*.
2. Conjunctive concepts: all red *and* square objects are examples. These concepts and those described below are *multidimensional* and have two or more discriminative features.
3. Inclusive disjunctive concepts: all objects that are red *and/or* square are examples.
4. Conditional concepts: *if* an object is red, *then* it must be square to be an example.
5. Biconditional concepts: red objects are examples, *if and only if* they are square.

Because concepts are defined in terms of both discriminative features and rules combining these features, there are three tasks involved in learning concepts. These tasks are:

1. Attribute identification: the combinatorial rule is given and the attributes involved must be discovered;
2. Rule learning: the attributes are known and the combinatorial rules must be discovered; and
3. Complete learning: both the attributes and the rules are unknown and must be discovered (Bourne and Dominowski, 1972).

Affirmative concepts with only one attribute are the easiest to learn. Bourne and O'Banion (1971) studied concept learning among children in grades 1, 3, 5, 7, 9, and college. The results of their study showed that for all grades the most difficult concepts to learn are biconditional, followed in order by conditional, disjunctive, and conjunctive. The majority of studies reported in the research literature has been concerned with conjunctive concepts; fewer studies have dealt with unidimensional concepts. At the elementary and secondary school levels of instruction, the preponderance of studies has been concerned with conjunctive and relational concepts (Clark, 1971). Conjunctive and disjunctive concepts are common to everyday experience (Bourne, Ekstrand, and Dominowski, 1971). The remainder of the chapter discusses *complete learning* of both the attributes and rules of affirmative, conjunctive, and disjunctive concepts.

Examples and Nonexamples

As was mentioned earlier, when concrete concepts are taught by the inductive, receptive approach, a variety of examples and nonexamples is presented to the learner so that s/he can learn to identify discriminative and nondiscriminative features. Discriminative features are common to all examples; nondiscriminative features may be possessed by both examples and nonexamples. There are a number of considerations to be made in the selection and presentation of suitable examples and nonexamples to optimize acquisition of a concept. Because the method used to present examples influences the nature of the examples selected, this topic will be discussed first.

Simultaneous and successive presentation. Examples and nonexamples of concepts may be presented successively (one after removal of the other) or simultaneously (two or more at a time). Students usually perform more successfully (reach criterion with fewer errors) when stimuli are presented in pairs rather than singly (Clark, 1971; Granzin and Carnine, 1977; Reese and Lipsitt, 1970). Clark (1971) suggested that there may be an advantage to presenting several examples at one time. For instance, when young children are being taught the concept of triangle, several triangles can be presented simultaneously so that the children can analyze the critical features of triangularity. Clark also suggested that four appears to be the optimum number of examples to be presented at one time.

Becker, Engelmann, and Thomas (1975b) recommended the presentation of several examples and nonexamples simultaneously (in pairs or in larger sets) so that there is an opportunity to examine their likenesses and differences. Hurley (1973, 1975) suggested that if several examples and nonexamples were to be shown on each trial, it would be better to present more examples than nonexamples. According to Westling and Koorland (1979), mentally retarded children learn discriminations more rapidly in a two-choice situation. The two-choice format, in an initial teaching situation, allows the learner to receive more reinforcement because of the higher probability of making a correct response. Mercer and Snell (1977) suggested that when examples and nonexamples are presented, they should be placed close together; increasing the distance between them (physically or temporally) decreases the discriminations made by mentally retarded children.

Presenting examples and nonexamples simultaneously and allowing them to remain in full view during the concept task increase the ease of concept acquisition more than that obtained by a successive withdrawal presentation (Bourne and Dominowski, 1972; Clark, 1971). In a simultaneous exposure, both examples and nonexamples are in view after the learner responds and receives feedback so that s/he can review the characteristics of the stimuli. This procedure puts less strain on the learner's memory, as s/he does not have to recall the nature of previously presented examples and nonexamples that would have been withdrawn if a successive approach had been employed. Bourne and Dominowski (1972) found that a mixed sequence of examples and nonexamples was consistently superior for teaching all types of combinatorial rules.

The approach to teaching concepts adopted in this text is to present examples and nonexamples simultaneously in pairs or in arrays of up to four examples and nonexamples. In the arrays, the number of examples presented is variable (unpredictable) and either equals or exceeds the number of nonexamples.

Using examples and nonexamples. Swanson (1972) presented examples and nonexamples of a concept to children in grade six. The presentation of both examples and nonexamples resulted in better recognition of new examples than occurred with the presentation of examples only. The errors that arose when nonexamples were removed from the presentation were errors of *overgeneralization* in which the children identified nonexamples as examples on a post-test.

When examples and nonexamples are presented on each trial, the examples show what characteristics define a concept; the nonexamples show what characteristics do not define a concept (Hurley, 1973, 1975). This situation occurs only when the nonexamples do not possess any of the discriminative qualities of the examples; this condition should prevail during the initial stages of concept instruction.

When examples alone are presented that possess both discriminative and nondiscriminative characteristics, a learner may have difficulty deciding which characteristics are discriminative. As additional examples are presented, in which the discriminative features remain constant while the nondiscriminative features vary, the discriminative features become more apparent because of their constancy. However, a disadvantage of the exclusive use of examples is that during successive presentations, the learner may have made several false assumptions about the number, type, and combination of features that were thought to have been discriminative. As these hypotheses must be successively formulated and tested, there is a heavy analytic and memory load upon the learner.

Alternatively, when pairs of examples and nonexamples are matched so that they are the same in all nondiscriminative respects and different in all discriminative characteristics, learner attention, from the beginning, is focused upon discriminative features. After the learner has identified the combination of discriminative features, variations in the value of these features may be introduced and nonexamples with some but not all of the discriminative features may be included. Klausmeier, Ghatala, and Frayer (1974) claimed that some studies have not shown significant benefits from the use of nonexamples simply because the nonexamples were not properly matched with examples.

When a learner is presented with examples that sample a range of values of a discriminative characteristic, s/he learns to generalize and identify as examples other objects having similar discriminative values to those presented. The boundaries of generalization are established when the learner is introduced to nonexamples that are selected from the ends of the range of discriminative values.

Thus, the student learns to discriminate examples from nonexamples.

When examples are selected to represent a range of discriminative values, they should be presented to the learner in a random order (Becker, Engelmann, and Thomas, 1975b). For instance, when the concept "car" is taught, if successively larger cars are presented, the learner may inadvertently be taught that "car" is something that is "larger" than the previously presented object. When examples and nonexamples are presented in a testing or teaching sequence, care must be taken to avoid any predictable relationship, such as progressively increasing or decreasing values, and alternating or repeating patterns or positions of the examples and nonexamples.

How many examples and nonexamples are required to teach a concept? Markle and Tiemann (1969) suggested that the minimum number of examples and nonexamples required to insure discrimination and generalization is a *rational set.* A rational set is comprised of sufficient examples to show variation in each nondiscriminative feature (generalization) and as many nonexamples as there are discriminative features (discrimination). Markle and Tiemann noted that the total number of examples and nonexamples required to bring a student to mastery was dependent upon several conditions.

One condition requiring further consideration is that one or more discriminative features may have a range of values where sufficient examples must be selected to represent the range, and where nonexamples must be chosen to define the ends of the range. Becker, Engelmann, and Thomas (1975b) have suggested that where a discriminative feature has a range of values: (a) examples should be selected from each end of the range, (b) nonexamples should be chosen that are adjacent to each end of the range, and (c) one or more examples should be selected from within the range.

Carnine (1975a) taught a group of preschoolers to identify three examples representing the ends and middle of a range of discriminative values. On a post-test, the children demonstrated that they had also learned to generalize or *interpolate* the concept by identifying as examples stimuli with discriminative values within the range of those initially taught. As well, the children had learned to discriminate or *extrapolate* and identify as nonexamples stimuli with values exceeding those of the nonexamples presented during training.

A study conducted by Tennyson and Rothen (1977) demonstrated that the number of examples and nonexamples required to teach a concept is not necessarily contingent upon the number of discriminative and nondiscriminative features, as suggested by Markle and Tiemann (1969). The results of the Tennyson and Rothen study demonstrated that the number of examples and nonexamples used in teaching should be based upon individual learner differences assessed in a pre-test of aptitude and attitude and an assessment of individual performance following the onset of instruction. In the study, students were given *fully adaptive* instruction based on pre-test and on-task measures, or *partially adaptive* instruction based only on on-task measures, or *nonadaptive* instruction. The nonadaptive instruction followed the guidelines recommended by Markle and Tiemann. In the nonadaptive approach, all students were given all items, whether they required them or not. The results of the study showed that the fully adaptive approach led to a more rapid achievement of criterion and higher scores on post-tests than either of the other two approaches. In the same manner, the partially adaptive instruction was superior to Markle and Tiemann's nonadaptive approach. When no attempt is made to adjust instruction, after initial learning has been achieved, students may lose interest in the task; the resulting deterioration in performance may reduce post-test scores. On-task measures for modifying instruction while maintaining a specific level of mastery can achieve significant gains in learning over those achieved by pre-test measures alone (Tennyson and Rothen, 1977).

The concept teaching technique described in the following chapter involves a modification of the Markle and Tiemann (1969) rational set procedure of selecting examples and nonexamples. The approach adopted also incorporates the recommendations made by Becker *et al.*, for representing a range of discriminative values and the Tennyson *et al.*, method of on-task adjustment of instruction. The method employed involves the selection of:

1. at least three examples to represent the range of values of each nondiscriminative feature, and

2. as many examples as there are discriminative features with fixed values.

3. Each example selected in 1 and 2 above is paired with a complementary nonexample.

    (a) When a nondiscriminative feature is being taught, both the example and the nonexample possess the same nondiscriminative features and some but not all of the discriminative features.

    (b) When a discriminative feature with a fixed value is being taught, the examples and nonexamples are identical except for the discriminative feature.

Pairing examples and nonexamples in this manner helps to focus the learner's attention on the significance of the particular discriminative and nondiscriminative features being taught.

4. When a discriminative feature with a range of values is being taught, at least three examples are selected to represent the range of values.

5. At least three nonexamples are matched with the examples selected in 4 above, to represent the ends of the range.

6. A sufficient number of sets of the pairs of examples and nonexamples described above are provided to give the learner enough practice to firmly establish the newly acquired discriminations and generalizations.

7. The incorporation of learning probes during instruction assesses incidental learning as well as generalization and maintenance and permits the learner to avoid unnecessary practice, to skip segments of instruction, and to otherwise accelerate his/her progress.

Discriminative and nondiscriminative characteristics. In concept learning when a learner is presented with a series of examples and nonexamples, s/he must learn to differentiate the discriminative and nondiscriminative features of the stimuli. Initially, the task is simplified by removing as many nondiscriminative features as possible from the stimuli (Bourne and Guy, 1968). This procedure reduces the number of characteristics that the learner is required to evaluate and increases the *salience* of the discriminative features. Later, as initial learning has been achieved, the nondiscriminative characteristics are reintroduced as the stimuli regain their natural qualities.

If examples and nonexamples differ on a number of discriminative features, children learn a discrimination rapidly. If, on the other hand, the stimuli differ on nondiscriminative features, learning is impeded. The interference of the nondiscriminative characteristics is especially marked with young children who are less able to disregard nondiscriminative information than are older children (Stevenson, 1972). Clark (1971) cited 40 studies in which it had been shown that as the number of nondiscriminative features increased, concept attainment decreased. Anderson and Faust (1974) suggested that to simplify the early stages of concept learning, nondiscriminative features should be temporarily eliminated; after criterion is reached with the "stripped-down materials," the discriminative features should be reintroduced. If the nondiscriminative features are not reintroduced, generalization of learning is greatly reduced (Modigliani, 1971). When nondiscriminative features are initially introduced, they should be displayed in both examples and nonexamples to demonstrate that the features are nondiscriminative. Brown *et al.,* (1973a) successfully used this procedure with severely handicapped children.

If the nondiscriminative features cannot be temporarily eliminated from the initial presentations, they should be held constant. That is, the learner should be presented with examples and nonexamples that possess the same nondiscriminative qualities. Clark (1971) suggested that if some nondiscriminative qualities are unavoidable, the stimuli should be modified so that: (a) nondiscriminative features are as different as possible from the discriminative features, (b) the nondiscriminative properties are made less obvious while the salience of the discriminative qualities is increased, and (c) the nondiscriminative features are made to show as much variation as possible from stimulus to stimulus, while the value of a discriminative property is held constant to show as little variation as possible.

Lubker (1969), in a study of concept learning among children, found that the presence of nondiscriminative features *within* a pair of examples and nonexamples impaired acquisition of a concept. Learning was relatively rapid when no nondiscriminative features were represented *between* or within pairs. The rate of learning was only slightly slower when there were *one or two between* pair nondiscriminative features and *no within* pair discriminative features. Learning was significantly slower when there were *one* or *two within* pair nondiscriminative features and *no between* pair nondiscriminative features.

Hillyard (1979) conducted a study of concept learning among preschool moderately and severely mentally retarded children. He found that holding the number of discriminative features constant while increasing the number of nondiscriminative characteristics resulted in increased generalization to novel examples not presented during original learning. Simply increasing the number of pairs of examples and nonexamples did not increase generalization.

The discriminative features of concepts may have fixed values or a range of values. The nondiscriminative features are always variable. A magnifying glass, for example, has the following discriminative features. At least one surface of the lens is convex (fixed); the amount of curvature is variable; the lens material is transparent (fixed); and the amount of magnification is variable. For both of the variable features, the range of variation is limited. The nondiscriminative features of a magnifying glass are the diameter of the lens and the type of mounting.

To teach a learner to identify a fixed discriminative characteristic, an instructional sequence must be designed to present a series of examples and nonexamples in which there are changes only in the fixed characteristic; although successive pairs of examples and nonexamples may have different nondiscriminative features, these features are held constant within each pair. To teach a range of values for a nondiscriminative feature, the instructional sequence must display a series of examples and nonexamples in which only the nondiscriminative feature changes while the discriminative characteristic remains constant. To teach a range of values for a discriminative feature, the instructional sequence must present a number of examples representing the ends and middle of the range of discriminative values being taught; also, it is necessary to present nonexamples to define the ends of the range of discriminative values (Becker, Engelmann, and Thomas, 1975b). When a range of values of discriminative or nondiscriminative features is being sampled, it is sufficient to sample selectively the boundaries and the middle of the range rather than attempt to exhaustively represent the range.

When teaching whether a particular characteristic is discriminative or nondiscriminative, the instructional sequence should display successive pairs of examples and nonexamples in which a single feature changes from one pair to the next. With this procedure, the learner can focus his/her attention on evaluating the significance of the change in the single feature (Bruner, Goodnow, and Austin, 1956). Granzin and Carnine (1977) studied concept learning of children in the second grade. The performance resulting from a sequence of examples in which only a single feature was varied from one example to the next was compared to the performance resulting from a sequence in which more than one feature was varied. The procedure employing a single feature change resulted in fewer trials to criterion and greater generalization to examples not presented during training.

The salience of the discriminative features of examples should be maintained or increased when a learner is being introduced to the nondiscriminative features of a concept. In this manner, the discriminative features remain the bases for identifying examples. Stevenson (1972) observed that the introduction of new, nondiscriminative features disrupted the performance of young children. The change in the stimulus resulted in a burst of activity, and the learner's attempt to select an example of a concept was made on the basis of the novel stimulation rather than on the presence of discriminative features (Bilsky and Heal, 1969; Turrisi and Shepp, 1969). New cues seem to distract and confuse the children, and their performance falters for a long period of time (Stevenson, 1972).

A Summary and Explanatory Review
of Guidelines for Teaching Concepts

1. Pairs of examples and nonexamples should be presented simultaneously to the learner. Advantages: fewer trials to criterion; better post-instruction generalization to new examples not presented during instruction; the examples indicate which characteristics define the concept; the nonexamples reveal which features are nondiscriminative.

2. Several examples and nonexamples may be presented at one time; more examples than nonexamples are preferred; the optimum number to present appears to be four. Advantage: the learner can observe which features vary among the stimuli (nondiscriminative) and which features remain constant (discriminative).

3. Examples and nonexamples should be presented close together in time and space. Advantages: facilitates comparison; reduces memory load.

4. Examples should be left in view long enough for the learner to analyze their features, respond, and evaluate the subsequent feedback. Advantages: maximizes the instructional value of the feedback; reduces memory load.

5. Ideally, in the initial stages of instruction, nonexamples should not possess any of the discriminative features. Nondiscriminative features that cannot be temporarily removed should be reduced in intensity and/or should be held constant in both examples and nonexamples. When nondiscriminative features cannot be eliminated, they should be made as different as possible from the discriminative features. The salience of the nondiscriminative features should be reduced, while that of the discriminative features should be increased. The nondiscriminative features should display wide variation in their values while the discriminative features are held constant. Advantages: increases the salience of the discriminative features; reduces the number of features the learner has to evaluate; accelerates the rate of acquisition of the concept; and reduces the possible interference caused by nondiscriminative stimuli.

6. After the combination of discriminative features has been

identified, nondiscriminative features may be introduced in both examples and nonexamples; also, discriminative features may be introduced in nonexamples. Advantages: the stimuli are more natural and represent the usual range of variations found in the general environment; also, this procedure increases generalization.

7. When nondiscriminative features are initially introduced, they should be displayed in both examples and nonexamples. Advantage: in the simplified conditions in which examples possess only discriminative features and nonexamples possess only nondiscriminative features, the introduction of any feature to both examples and nonexamples will rapidly lead to its recognition as a nondiscriminative feature.

8. To insure adequate generalization of a concept, an instructional sequence should present sufficient examples to sample the range of values of nondiscriminative and discriminative features; also, examples should be presented to represent the middle and ends of each range of values. To insure adequate discrimination of examples and nonexamples, the instructional presentation should include nonexamples selected from adjacent to the ends of the range of values of the discriminative features. Advantages: economy; a range of values can be taught with a select and representative sample of examples and nonexamples; an exhaustive sampling of values from throughout the range is not required.

9. Successive pairs of examples and nonexamples in a testing or teaching sequence should be presented in a randomized order. Any predictable relationship among the stimuli such as progressively increasing or decreasing values, and alternating or repeating patterns or positions should be avoided. Advantages: avoids teaching a misrule where the student inadvertently learns to discriminate examples from nonexamples on the basis of an insignificant but predictable change in value of a discriminative or nondiscriminative feature; reduces the chance factor of guessing the correct answer in testing.

10. During the initial stages of instruction, nondiscriminative features should be introduced *between successive* pairs of examples and nonexamples. Advantages: features introduced in this manner interfere less with the rate of acquisition of the concepts;

introduces and familiarizes the learner with changes in stimulus qualities before s/he has to be concerned with their significance.

11. To teach a fixed discriminative feature, the instructional sequence should present pairs of examples and nonexamples in which the only difference between the stimuli is the presence or absence of the fixed feature. Advantage: focuses attention on the discriminative feature and its fixed value in the example.

12. The range of values of a nondiscriminative feature may be taught through the presentation of a series of examples and nonexamples in which only the nondiscriminative feature changes while the discriminative features remain constant. Advantage: demonstrates that examples possessing all of the discriminative features are unchanged by variations in the value of nondiscriminative stimuli.

13. One feature at a time should be changed when successive pairs of examples and nonexamples are used to demonstrate that a particular feature is either discriminative or nondiscriminative. Advantages: the learner can focus attention on evaluating the significance of a single feature; fewer trials to criterion; and greater generalization to examples not presented during instruction.

Using Pictures to Teach Concepts

Pictures provide the principal means of representing and teaching concrete concepts. To teach the vast majority of concrete concepts, it is simply not practical to consider using the number and variety of real objects that would be required. Pictures provide a means of presenting a sequenced and controlled introduction of discriminative and nondiscriminative features. Very few studies have been reported on the effects of various types of pictures on the rate of concept acquisition, the number and type of errors committed, the extent of generalization, or the duration of maintenance. There is also little evidence in the literature describing the age level at which children typically acquire the ability to interpret various aspects of different types of pictures.

Some instructional programs use real objects before introducing pictorial representations of concepts. For example, in DISTAR Language 1 (Engelmann and Osborne, 1976), the concept "on" is first introduced when the teacher holds a pencil "on," "over," "next to," or "under" a table. Later, when both "on" and "over" are being taught, the children put their hands "on" or "over" their heads. Following this stage of instruction, "on" and "over" are pictorially represented by balloons and birds shown to be "on" or "over" a table or a girl. Presumably, the rationale for beginning instruction with real objects is to demonstrate that pictures represent real objects or actions.

Several difficulties may arise, however, with the use of real objects. When presented in a dynamic "social context," real objects possess many more irrelevant, uncontrolled, and potentially distracting features than would be found in a "simplified" picture from which nondiscriminative details have been removed and in which discriminative features have been highlighted. The reduction of irrelevant or potentially distracting sources of stimulation is particularly important among hyperactive, distractable, learning disabled children and among mentally retarded children who may have difficulty focusing on the discriminative aspects of a stimulus (Zeaman and House, 1963). Real situations may disrupt or inhibit awareness of the discriminative features of concepts (Marks and Raymond, 1951).

Can children recognize and interpret pictorial representations, or should they be introduced first to actual objects and events that are later pictorially represented? Gibson (1969) suggested that the differentiation of pictured objects is learned at the same time that the distinctive features of the real objects are learned. According to Gibson, features of an object will be recognized even by young children when they are presented in photographs or outline drawings. Kennedy (1974), after reviewing a number of studies of picture perception, concluded that neither advanced age, schooling, nor a specially high level of intelligence seems to be necessary for successful picture perception.

General comparisons of the results of instruction using either pictures or objects are difficult to make. Pictures may vary in several different ways, ranging from caricature or stylized depictions, simple line drawings with little, if any, internal detail, complex line drawings with considerable internal detail and shading, to black and white or color photographs. In addition, the pictures may represent static or dynamic events. Various types of pictorial representations may have a differential influence upon learners at various levels of development or intellectual functioning.

O'Connor and Hermelin (1961), in a study of picture perception, found that trainable, mentally retarded subjects were able to correctly identify outline figures. Hull, Barry, and Clark (1976) conducted a study of the learning of vocational concepts by adolescent learning disabled, educable mentally handicapped, and culturally deprived students. These researchers found no statistically significant difference in learning concepts with the use of line drawings, detailed drawings, photograms, photographs, 35mm color slides, or actual objects. However, they did find trends favoring line drawings and color slides as the most effective means of teaching concepts. In a second study, they found no significant difference in concept learning when line drawings or actual objects were used. Devore and Stern (1970) found that for boys there was no significant difference in gain scores which favored the use of concrete objects over pictures for teaching the names of common household articles. Direct experience with realistic material is usually not preferable to simplified pictorial representations in the form of line drawings or animated moving pictures that show only the important attributes of a concept (DeCecco, 1974; Travers, McCormick, Van Mondfrans, and Williams, 1964).

A study by French (1952) of the "picture preference" of 6-, 7-, and 11-year-old children found that the first-grade children consistently preferred relatively simple pictures while the older children preferred more complex pictures. Travers and Alvarado (1970) inferred that the picture preference exhibited by the young children in French's study was undoubtedly due partly to the inability of the children to structure more complex representations. Anderson and Faust (1974) suggested that although instruction should simulate reality as closely as possible, research shows that students learn more when instructional material is stripped of realistic but irrelevant detail. Travers and Alvarado (1970) concluded after a review of the literature that pictures in children's books designed for the lower grades should be realistic, yet simple, and of increasing complexity for higher grade levels.

Does the use of real objects and events lead to more rapid acquisition, generalization, and retention of concepts? Becker, Rosner, and Nelson (1979) studied the performance of preschool children randomly assigned to groups in which concepts were taught by pictures or objects. Neither the rate of acquisition nor the amount of retention was affected by the use of either pictures or objects. However, generalization of learning was influenced significantly. Generalization was assessed by having the children who had learned concepts through the use of objects identify new examples of the concepts (not presented during instruction) when the examples were displayed in either an object or a pictorial form. Similarly, children taught concepts through the use of pictures were asked to identify new examples of the concept presented in either object or picture form. Generalization in the object-object condition was lower than that in the picture-object or in the picture-picture condition. The items used to assess generalization ranged over four levels of elaboration. At level one, the objects used were white, two-dimensional forms depicting the basic outline; all extra features had been omitted. Objects at the fourth level of elaboration had as much detail as the training examples. The results of the study showed that generalization to items differing in level of elaboration from the training items was significantly better for children who had received concept instruction with pictures rather than with real objects. The authors hypothesized that picture training may have established a more abstract mental representation of the concepts that facilitated identification of unelaborated items. According to Becker *et al.,* object training may lead to greater reluctance to identify ambiguous items as concept examples.

Alternatively, there is considerable evidence to show that children with various types of learning problems, tested on short-term memory tasks, have better recall of three-dimensional stimuli than they have of two-dimensional representations (Iscoe and Semler, 1964; Kraynack and Raskin, 1971; Swanson, 1977; Swanson and Watson, 1976). In contrast, Brown and Scott (1971) concluded from their studies that recognition memory for pictures is extremely high even among preschoolers.

One possible difficulty with the use of pictures has been identified by Travers and Alvarado (1970), who claim that it is doubtful that children can recognize the *dynamic* aspects of pictures prior to the third grade. This problem is particularly important, as many pictures found in school textbooks are designed to depict movement or action. Movement is generally depicted in a static picture in several symbolic ways. A moving object may be represented as a blurred image; the rear contour of the object may be repeatedly traced along the path of movement to simulate successive impressions of the object, or a wake may be drawn that is similar to that shown behind a moving boat. Movement of an object may also be represented by depicting the object in a state of disequilibrium. To perceive movement in pictures, children must learn to interpret these conventions.

Several studies in which action concepts were taught to mentally handicapped children through the use of still pictures apparently have not resulted in the difficulties described by Travers and Alvarado. DeGraaf (1972) designed a successful program to teach action concepts to institutionalized, mentally retarded children ($\overline{X}$ IQ = 51, $\overline{X}$ M.A. = 7.5). He used 42 photographic slides with four line drawings on each. Stephens and Ludy (1975) compared the effectiveness of teaching 20 action concepts using photographic slides, motion pictures, and live demonstrations by teachers. The subjects in the study had an average IQ of 48 and an average M.A. of 4.7. The results of this study showed that the motion pictures produced greater gain scores than were achieved with the use of slides and live demonstrations. No significant difference in gain scores was found between the teaching of action concepts by line drawings or by live demonstrations. The authors found that the live demonstrations were less systematic and more complex than the slides and that the demonstrations were not as effective in holding the children's attention.

Perhaps the difference between the results of these studies and the observations made by Travers and Alvarado arises from small but significant differences in the type of still pictures or line drawings used. For example, Travers and Alvarado found that color enhanced the perception of dynamic features. Important differences may also have occurred in the manner in which the pictures were displayed. The topic is sufficiently important to warrant caution, further study, and more detailed description of the pictures and procedures used to teach concepts.

Some conclusions about the use of pictures to teach concepts. Although the research evidence concerning the use of pictures to teach concepts is far from definitive, several conclusions may be tentatively drawn.

1. A dynamic presentation of real objects may involve distracting movement in a complex social, physical environment in which it is difficult to systematically control variations in discriminative and nondiscriminative features of the concepts. During initial learning, particularly with children who are easily distracted, it is crucial to use simple stimuli in a nondistracting environment.

2. Young children prefer, can recognize, and can learn concepts from pictures and outline figures.

3. Care must be taken when representing dynamic events in still pictures. Some evidence indicates that the dynamic features of still pictures may not be recognized by children before they are in the third grade. Other studies have demonstrated the successful teaching of action concepts to young institutionalized mentally retarded children. Color appears to increase the perception of dynamic features. One study found no significant difference between the teaching of action concepts to mentally retarded children by live demonstrations or by static photographic slides.

4. For preschool children, there is no differential rate of acquisition or duration of retention of newly learned concepts when they are taught by use of objects or pictures. Generalization of newly acquired concepts is significantly improved with the use of pictures.

5. When pictures are used to teach concepts, an instructional sequence should initially display:

   (a) line drawings or outline figures, and
   (b) realistic rather than caricature or stylized representations.
   (c) Unessential shading and detail should be removed from the pictures.
   (d) Before depicting action in pictures, the instructional de-

signer should insure that the learner population can interpret the symbolic manner in which motion is represented.

(e) As learning progresses, the programmer should add successively more nondiscriminative detail to the picture to approximate a more life-like representation.

(f) Initially, when color is added to a picture as a nondiscriminative detail, an unsaturated hue may reduce distractability.

(g) In the final stages of instruction, the instructional program may employ photographs and real objects in which there is an uncontrolled variation in nondiscriminative features of the concepts.

Studies have shown that there is a marked tendency among children to fixate on a detail of a picture that is often of irrelevant significance (Travers and Alvarado, 1970). In a study by Alvarado, children were repeatedly, briefly presented with the same pictures. After each presentation, the children were asked what they had seen. There was a striking tendency for the young children to focus exclusively on one particular object in the picture and to fail to observe other items. On successive trials, the children repeatedly reported the same item.

Westling and Koorland (1979) described some of the problems associated with visual attention and discrimination among the mentally retarded. When learning attention and discrimination skills, mentally retarded individuals were not as competent as normal individuals of equivalent mental age. Mentally retarded individuals tended to focus on a limited number of stimulus characteristics. For example, they sometimes attended to the color of an object when it was more important to focus on its shape or configuration.

Many of the studies of picture perception have been conducted with children involved in spontaneous, unguided analysis of pictures. The evidence from these studies has shown that children frequently fail to notice critical features of pictures, focus on irrelevant details, dwell exclusively on one aspect of a picture, and have difficulty interpreting the depiction of motion. Picture perception may be enhanced through the use of various *prompting* devices that modify and guide the types of observations children make.

Prompting and Pretraining

Prompting. A minimum condition for receiving information from a picture is that the learner involved attend to it. Furthermore, the learner must be selective in what s/he attends to. Miller (1938) simply had a teacher point her finger at a picture to direct the attention of children in grade three to critical details. This simple technique significantly increased the observation of discriminative features made by the children. Zimmerman and Jaffe (1977) studied the teaching of several concepts to six- and eight-year-old children. During the demonstration, the teacher looked at each picture, pointed to the discriminative features, and then placed the picture in the proper group. For pictures of objects that rolled, the teacher made a circular gesture around the rolling surface. For pictures of pointed objects, the teacher traced her finger along the object to its point. For pictures of rectangular objects, the teacher traced one right-angle corner. These focusing procedures significantly improved the accuracy of sorting the pictures, and eliminated any initial performance differences between six- and eight-year-old children.

During lengthy instructional sequences, after visual attention has been repeatedly directed to critical features of a picture, the teacher's pointing response can be progressively *faded* from use as the learner is taught to continue to locate the discriminative features without assistance. Prompting may also take the form of stimulus *highlighting* where the salience of a discriminative feature may be temporarily increased to attract attention to it during initial teaching sequences.

Several researchers have also used a *fading-in* technique to increase the salience of critical features. In one study, an example of the concept "square" was presented as a bold outline figure while the nonexample of "square" was presented as a faded outline, thin line figure. Over successive presentations, the stimulus value of the nonexample was increased to that of the example (Cole, Dent, Eguchi, Fujii, and Johnson, 1964). Caron (1968) studied discriminations where children had to learn angularity and roundness to respond appropriately. During the early trials of instruction, outlines of the figures were barely perceptible. As the number of trials increased, the figures became more pronounced through a series of five steps. To emphasize discriminative features, a corner of each angular figure and its counterpart on the rounded figure were emphasized with black ink. In the early trials, only the critical features of the figures were readily discernible.

Magnifying the discriminative features of a stimulus while diminishing the value of nondiscriminative features is preferable to adding extra or artificial stimuli to focus on nondiscriminative features. An *artificial prompt,* such as color added to discriminative features, or the addition of a diacritical mark to a letter to indicate its phonetic value, may facilitate initial learning of a concept. As the use of the artificial prompt is faded, however, learning may deteriorate with the disappearance of the cue to which the response was attached. When artificial prompts are not used and the value of a discriminative feature is embellished, as the embellishment of the stimulus is faded, the response continues to be elicited by the remaining value of the stimulus.

Travers and Alvarado (1970) suggested another means of focusing attention on discriminative features and increasing a learner's recall of them. The authors recommended that the information presented in pictures be coded into words. According to these researchers, uncoded visual information does not retain very precise detail. A teacher, therefore, must focus learner attention on discriminative features of a picture and convert the crude visual information into a verbal form.

Pretraining. Pretraining can also be used to heighten a learner's awareness of discriminative stimuli. Clark (1971) reviewed a large number of studies in which it had been shown that a single exposure to verbal labels of discriminative features, prior to instruction, increased the ease of subsequent concept acquisition. Klausmeier, Ghatala, and Frayer (1974) suggested that giving the same name to a group of stimuli may induce subjects to look for common elements among them; the converse may also be true when different names are given to stimuli. Distinctive class labels reduce overgeneralization. When labels are familiar words, classification improves more than if labels are unfamiliar to the learner (Klausmeier *et al.,* 1974). Etaugh and Averill (1971) found that stimulus labels produced by students in a discrimination learning task did not have a superior effect on learning than labels produced by an experimenter, providing that the labels were meaningful to the students. There is considerable evidence to support the notion that concepts are better learned, recalled, and applied to new situations if the learner verbalizes to himself/herself the name of a discriminative feature (Clark, 1971).

Paivio (1971) concluded from a review of the literature that although labels can be helpful under certain circumstances, they do not consistently facilitate recognition of nonverbal stimuli. The emerging pattern, according to Paivio, is that verbal coding may be used effectively when learners find it difficult to store the nonverbal information in memory either because they have a poor verbal memory or because the stimulus is complex. However, verbal coding need not be used if the learner has a good memory, or if the stimuli are simple or familiar shapes or objects that can be stored as uncoded images, or if the verbal code is not readily available in the learner's response repertoire.

Clark (1971) found that preinstructional directions that focus student attention on the discriminative and nondiscriminative properties of stimuli increased the ease with which the concepts were learned. Discrimination learning can be greatly facilitated if a learner is told to "watch out for" variations in relevant dimensions of stimulation (Klausmeier, Ghatala, and Frayer, 1974). Frayer (1970) used questions to direct the attention of elementary school students to the discriminative features of geometric concepts. For example, for a quadrilateral, he asked, "Does this figure have four sides?" Questions of this type significantly improved performance over conditions where such questions were not used.

Mercer and Snell (1977) reported a study by Lobb in which the results of rewarded and non-rewarded pretraining were compared; the performance of the mentally retarded students studied improved when attention to a discriminative feature was rewarded. Preinstructional training to focus on discriminative characteristics of stimuli may be particularly important for mentally retarded students. Retarded children may have difficulty with simple concept learning tasks because of problems in learning to select and attend to specific stimulus dimensions (Zeaman and House, 1963).

Tighe and Tighe (1969) found that as the number of nondiscriminative characteristics increased in discrimination tasks, the mean number of trials to criterion increased markedly. However, children who were asked to make some same-different judgments prior to an experimental task learned a reversal shift with one and two nondiscriminative variables as easily as when there were no nondiscriminative variables present. Caron (1969) found that pre-instructional differentiation training with color and form significantly increased salience of these dimensions during training. Carnine and Silbert (1975) required beginning readers to practice sound-symbol correspondence of known difficulty prior to decoding words in which the relationship appeared. This procedure reduced the rate of errors made on subsequent trials. Fink (1976) studied first-grade children with IQ 68-72. He found that if the teacher pointed to previously misidentified graphemes representing vowel sounds in consonant-vowel-consonant (CVC) and CVCC words, and instructed children to say the sound immediately prior to sounding out the word, the number of words correctly read on the post-test was significantly increased.

Chapter 8

Developing Instructional Sequences
to Teach Concepts

Contents
1. Developing instructional sequences to teach concepts: affirmative (unidimensional) concepts; single, multidimensional concepts, and multiple, related noun concepts (cumulative instruction).
2. Generic methods for teaching and testing concepts.
3. Modifications for advanced learners.
4. Review of concepts and procedures covered in Chapters Six, Seven, and Eight.

On the following pages, methods are discussed for developing instructional programs to teach: (a) affirmative (unidimensional) concepts, and (b) conjunctive and disjunctive (multidimensional) concepts, and multiple, related noun concepts (cumulative instruction). The methods described are empirically derived; however, as Clark (1971) suggests, some caution should be exercised in applying the results of studies reported in the research literature. Some of the methods described in the literature have been tested in special, highly controlled, experimental situations with restricted samples of learners and limited numbers and types of concepts. The stimulus materials, and instructional procedures and sequences used in some studies have not been described in sufficient detail. As a result, the methods discussed on the following pages, although based on the best evidence available, offer a suggested starting point for designing instructional programs rather than a final solution for teaching concepts. These techniques have been employed to develop a number of concept teaching programs;

however, any application of these procedures must be validated and, if necessary, modified, to teach particular concepts to selected populations. Methods of formative and summative evaluation are described in Chapter Nine.

The techniques discussed in this chapter are designed for teaching concepts to instructionally naive learners who lack adequate language skills to benefit from a deductive approach to teaching concepts. An inductive, receptive approach to teaching concepts is described in which the learner is presented with a preselected number, type, and sequence of examples and nonexamples. A cumulative programming approach is employed where each discriminative and nondiscriminative feature is taught individually and sequentially. The instructional techniques of modeling, prompting, fading, feedback, reinforcement, and correction are used to teach the learner the discriminative features of concepts and their combinatorial rules.

The goal of this instruction is to assist the learner to achieve the *classification level* (Klausmeier, Ghatala, and Frayer, 1974) of concept acquisition. According to Klausmeier *et al.*, a learner at this level of achievement will respond in the same manner to two or more familiar and unfamiliar examples of a concept that may possess various nondiscriminative features. In addition, the learner will respond in a different manner to familiar and unfamiliar nonexamples than s/he did to examples of the concept. The learner will not necessarily be able to describe the basis of his/her discriminations and generalizations in terms of the presence of all discriminative features in the examples and the absence of one or more of these features in the nonexamples. At the end of the chapter, suggestions are made for adapting the instructional procedures to suit the needs of more advanced learners.

Affirmative (Unidimensional) Concepts

Affirmative concepts are those possessing a single discriminative feature. The presence of a particular discriminative feature affirms that an object is an example of a particular concept. Some examples of affirmative concepts are listed below; the list is not exhaustive.

1. Concepts of object relationships in space: refers to variables such as location, position, direction, or order of an object or objects. Some instances are: on, in, under, over, perpendicular, and near. Some, but not all, of these concepts have polar opposites, for instance: on-off and in-out.

2. Concepts of object properties: refers to the weight, size, state, shape, and surface properties of an object. Some instances are: long, wide, heavy, red, round, soft, curved, smooth, acute, and cold. Some, but not all, of these concepts have polar opposites, for instance: long-short and heavy-light. Many of the concepts can be stated in several forms: long-short; longer-shorter; and longest-shortest.

Some of the concepts listed in the above categories have poorly defined boundaries, and considerable subjectivity may be involved in determining whether or not an object possesses a particular discriminative quality. Examples of these concepts are: soft, smooth, long, and red. Other concepts have *well defined boundaries*, and little if any, subjectivity is involved in determining whether an object falls within the boundaries. For example, an object is either "on" or "off" a surface, or it is "*in*side" or "*out*side" the boundaries of a particular space; an angle is either greater or less than 90° and is, respectively, obtuse (and less than 180°) or acute. Affirmative concepts with *well defined boundaries* are taught in a different manner than concepts are that *do not* have *well defined boundaries.*

The following section describes the steps involved in developing an instructional sequence to teach affirmative concepts. During the discussion, an actual program is developed to teach the concept "long." This concept does not have "well defined boundaries." That is, an object is not "long" in any absolute sense. Whether or not an object is considered to be "long" depends upon the context within which it is viewed, and an object considered to be "long" in one context may not be judged as "long" in another context. The discussion also includes several brief points, indicated with an asterisk, that describe alternative steps for teaching concepts that do have well defined boundaries.

Step 1. Select stimuli to depict examples and nonexamples; use line drawings.

a. Select a set of stimuli in which the discriminative feature is salient and from which all nondiscriminative features have been eliminated or minimized. For instance, remove all color, shading, and unnecessary detail. Rectangles of the type shown in Figure 8.1 have been selected to depict "long." Note that the only difference between the two rectangles is in terms of the discriminative feature, length.

b. Define the range of values of the discriminative feature to be represented during instruction. For instance, the range of values selected to represent "long" and "not long" is displayed in Figure 8.2. The lengths A and E represent, respectively, the shortest and longest rectangles that will be compared. The most difficult discriminations the learner will be required to make are between adjacent lengths such as A and B, or D and E. The least difficult discriminations are between A and E, and A and D. In this set of rectangles, A will always be "not long," and E will always be "long." The remaining lengths will be judged as "long" or "not long," depending on which of the other lengths they are compared to. For instance, C is "long" when compared to A and B, but "not long," when compared to D and E.

c. Decide which nondiscriminative variables should be introduced during instruction and select three values to represent the range of each of the nondiscriminative features. The stimuli in Figure 8.3, for example, display three values of each of the nondiscriminative features of form and color. Note that all other nondiscriminative features such as shading and unnecessary detail have been removed from the stimuli in Figure 8.3. Note also that during instruction, the shoes, forks, and rectangles displayed in Figure 8.3 may assume any of the lengths shown in Figure 8.2.

Step 2. For concepts such as "long" that *do not* have *well defined boundaries*, begin pairing examples and nonexamples in the following manner. Initially, maximize the difference between examples and nonexamples on the discriminative feature to lessen the difficulty of the initial discriminations. Randomize the sequential *order* of the pairs of examples and nonexamples, and the spatial *position* of the examples and nonexamples in each pair. For instance, the following three pairs of examples and nonexamples have been selected from the range: A with D, E with B, and E with A. Each pair is comprised of members that are three or four lengths apart. The pairs represent the easiest possible discriminations.

Note that the sets of examples and nonexamples selected in steps 1 and 2 and each of the following steps are listed at the end of this section in an instructional sequence, designed to teach the concept "long." For example, the pairs of stimuli selected at step one: A-D, A-B, and E-A are shown as the first set of stimulus pairs in the sequence.

Figure 8.1

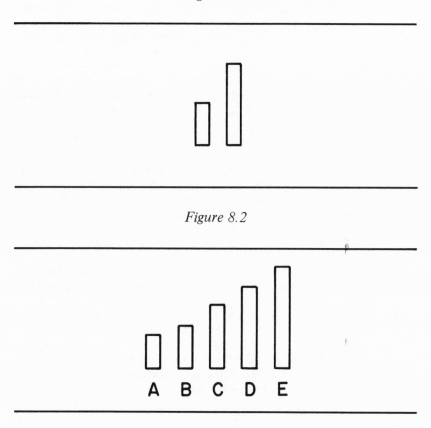

Figure 8.2

Figure 8.3

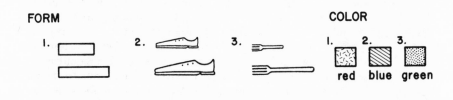

Step 3. Continue pairing examples (E) and nonexamples (NE); progressively lessen the difference between E^S and NE^S on the discriminative feature, and finally, teach the most difficult discriminations required. Randomize the order of the pairs and the position of E and NE in each pair. For this step, three pairs of E^S and NE^S have been selected to teach "long." The members of each pair are two lengths apart; three discriminations, a, b, and c, shown below, are of medium difficulty. Four pairs of E^S and NE^S were also selected whose members are one length apart; these pairs, d, e, f, and g, shown below, offer the most difficult discriminations.

Pairs of lengths   a. D-B   Discriminations of medium
                    b. C-E   difficulty
                    c. A-C

                    d. A-B   Discriminations of greatest
                    e. D-E   difficulty
                    f. D-C
                    g. C-B

Note that although the most difficult discriminations involved in this task are between adjacent lengths, in some tasks, the learner may not be required to make the most difficult discriminations possible. A learner should be taught to make the most difficult discriminations that are commonly found in his/her environment.

Step 2(a).* This step replaces step 2 for concepts that *have well defined boundaries.* Begin pairing E^S and NE^S; initially, *minimize* the difference between each E and NE on the discriminative feature to focus on the boundary discriminating E^S and NE^S. Randomize the order of the pairs of E^S and NE^S and the position of the E and NE in each pair. For instance, if the concept "in" was being taught, the three pairs of E^S and NE^S shown in Figure 8.4 could be used.

Step 3(a).* This step replaces step 3 for concepts that *have well defined boundaries.* Randomly select three or four E^S and NE^S that are various distances from the discriminative boundary. Randomize the order of the pairs and the position of the E and NE in each pair. For instance, to teach the concept "in," one might select the three pairs of E^S and NE^S illustrated in Figure 8.5.

Step 4. For steps 2 and 2(a), 3 and 3(a), develop a "sufficient" number of pairs of E^S and NE^S to teach and test the learner's discrimination. The "sufficient" number of pairs required will depend upon the nature of the learner and the amount of practice required to establish a newly acquired response. For the first trials, estimate the amount of practice required, and with increased experience with the learner population, add or subtract pairs of E^S and NE^S, as necessary. In any case, provide the learner with the most practice discriminating pairs of E^S and NE^S of medium and greatest difficulty.

Step 5. In steps 2 and 2(a), 3 and 3(a), if it was not possible to remove all

Figure 8.4

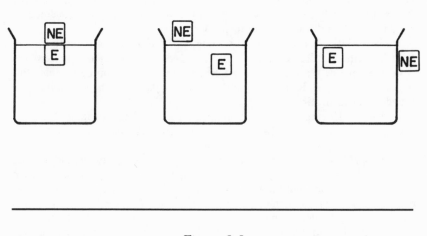

Figure 8.5

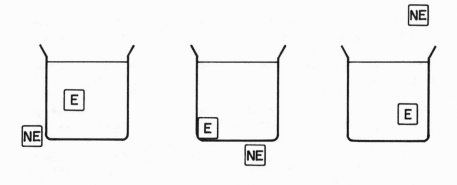

of the nondiscriminative (ND) features as recommended in step 1(a), hold any remaining ND features constant *within* and *between* all pairs of E^S and NE^S. In the present instance, for the E^S and NE^S selected to represent "long" and "in," all ND features have been removed.

Step 6. For concepts *without well defined boundaries*, select additional pairs of E^S and NE^S to introduce a ND feature such as color; select three values or forms of the ND feature to be introduced to represent the range of values. Figure 8.6 displays the three color values that have been selected to use during the teaching of the concept "long."

Initially, introduce one form or value of the ND feature to both E^S and NE^S; hold the feature constant *within* and *between* pairs. Then, present the nondiscriminative feature in pairs of E^S and NE^S of medium discriminability as defined in step 3. Randomize the order of the pairs and the position of the E and NE in each pair.

Pairs of lengths   a. C-E   both green (color is held constant
                    b. B-D   both green *within* and *between* pairs)
                    c. C-A   both green

*Step 6(a).** For concepts *with well defined boundaries,* introduce one form or value of the ND feature to both the E and NE in each pair; hold the ND feature constant within and between pairs. Randomize the order of the pairs of E^S and NE^S and the position of the E and NE in each pair. To teach "in," one might select stimulus pairs *similar* to those shown in Figures 8.4 and 8.5, the E^S and NE^S may be located in different positions. One color, for instance, green, would be introduced to all E^S and NE^S in all pairs.

Step 7. For steps 6 and 6(a), if there were ND features that were not removed from the E^S and NE^S during step 1(a), continue to hold these ND features constant *within* pairs; the ND features may be allowed to vary *between* pairs.

Step 8. If possible, and necessary to retain the salience of the discriminative feature, minimize the stimulus value of the ND feature being introduced. For instance, if the addition of the ND feature, color, could distract the learner and disrupt earlier learning, initially, introduce a muted shade of the color. Later, when it is predicted that the learner will have habituated to the addition of color, introduce saturated colors.

Step 9. If possible, and necessary for the reasons described in step 8, increase the stimulus value of the discriminative feature. For instance, to teach "long," one might prompt the difference in length in the manner depicted in Figure 8.7.

Note that an essential feature of the stimulus has been embellished, rather than adding an artificial prompt. This prompt can be progressively faded as stimulus control is transferred from the prompt to essential parts of the stimuli that remain after the prompt has been faded.

Step 10. In successive trials, let the previously introduced ND features that have been held constant in step 7, vary randomly *within* and *between* trials.

Figure 8.6

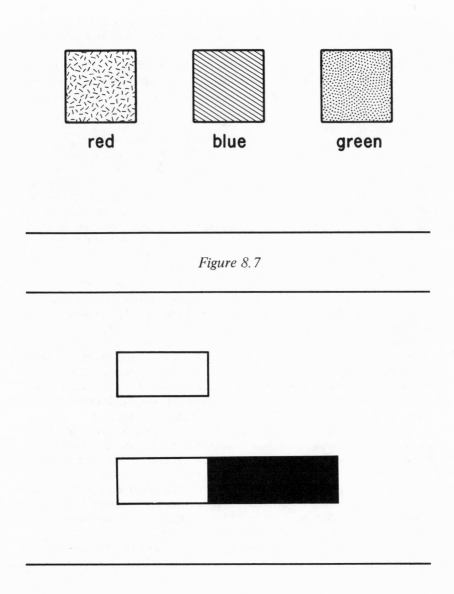

red   blue   green

Figure 8.7

Use discriminations of medium difficulty, as defined in step 3. Randomize the order of the pairs·of E^S and NE^S and the position of the E and NE in each pair. In the present program, no ND features were held constant at step 7.

Step 11. Sample the remaining two values of the ND feature introduced in step 6 or 6(a). Present all three values of the ND features first *between* and then *within* pairs. For ND features of concepts without well defined boundaries, use discriminations of medium difficulty as defined in step 3. Randomize the order of the pairs and the order of the E and NE in each pair. The pairs selected to teach "long" are:

Pairs of lengths   a. A-C   both blue   (three values of
                    b. E-C   both green color; color varies
                    c. D-B   both red   *between* pairs)

                    d. D-B   blue-red   (color varies
                    e. A-C   green-blue *within* pairs)
                    f. C-E   red-red*   *(unpredictable)

Step 12. Sample the range (three values) of the ND features introduced in step 6 or 6(a). Use all three values or forms of the ND features *within* pairs. For ND features of concepts without well defined boundaries, use discriminations of the greatest difficulty as defined in step 3. Randomize the order of the pairs and the position of the E^S and NE^S in each pair. The following pairs have been selected to teach "long."

Pairs of lengths   a. D-E   blue-green
                    b. B-C   red-green   (color varies
                    c. A-B   blue-blue* within trials)
                    d. D-C   green-blue *(unpredictable)

Step 13. Develop a "sufficient" number of pairs of E^S and NE^S to teach and test the learner's discrimination. Refer to step 4 for an explanation of a "sufficient" number of pairs.

Step 14. Repeat steps 6 or 6(a) to 13 while introducing variations in the ND features that were held constant in step 5. In the example of teaching "long," no ND features were held constant at step 5.

Step 15. Steps 16-22 retrace steps 6 or 6(a) to 13, while successive ND features such as shading, form, and internal detail are added one at a time.

Step 16/retrace 6 or 6(a). For concepts without well defined boundaries, introduce a ND feature, such as form; select three variations of the ND feature to be introduced to represent its range of values. Figure 8.8 indicates the three form variations that had been selected to represent the ND feature, form. Introduce one form or value of the ND feature to both E^S and NE^S; hold the feature constant *within* and *between* trials. Present the ND feature in pairs of E^S and NE^S of medium discriminability as defined in step 3. Randomize the order of the pairs and the position of the E and NE in each pair.

Figure 8.8

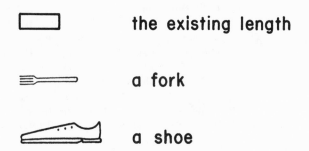

the existing length

a fork

a shoe

Pairs of lengths   a. A-C   shoe-shoe;   blue-blue.
                  b. C-E   shoe-shoe;   green-green.
                  c. D-B   shoe-shoe;   red-red.

Step 17/7. Hold previously introduced ND features (e.g., color) constant *within* trials. Color is held constant within trials as indicated above.

Step 18/8/9. Steps 8 and 9 refer to the procedures of minimizing the stimulus value of the ND feature while maximizing the stimulus value of the D feature. Review steps 8 and 9 for further details.

Step 19/10. In successive trials, let the previously introduced ND features that have been held constant in step 17/7 (e.g., color) vary randomly *within* and *between* trials. Also, introduce an additional form or value of the ND feature presented in step 16/6 or 16/6(a). Hold the newly introduced value or form of the ND feature constant *within* each pair. For ND features of concepts without well defined boundaries, use discriminations of medium difficulty as defined in step 3. Randomize the order of the pairs and the positions of the E and NE in each pair.

Pairs of lengths   a. B-D   fork-fork;   blue-green.
                  b. E-C   fork-fork;   red-blue.
                  c. C-A   fork-fork;   green-red.

Step 20/11. Sample the remaining range of values of the ND feature introduced in step 16/6 or 16/6(a). Use all three values or forms of the ND features first *between* then *within* pairs. For ND features of concepts without well defined boundaries, use discriminations of medium difficulty as defined in step 3. Randomize the order of the pairs and the order of the E and NE in each pair. The following pairs have been selected.

Pairs of lengths
a. E-C fork-fork; green-red. (form
b. D-B length-length; blue-green. varies
c. C-A shoe-shoe; red-red. *between* trials)

d. C-A fork-length; blue-blue. (form
e. E-C shoe-fork; red-green. varies
f. B-D length-shoe; blue-green. *within* trials)

Step 21/12. Sample the range of the ND features introduced in step 16/6 or 16/6(a). Use three values or forms of the ND features *within* pairs. For ND features of concepts without well defined boundaries, use discriminations of the greatest difficulty as defined in step 3. Randomize the order of the pairs and the position of the E^S and NE^S in each pair. The following pairs have been selected.

Pairs of lengths
a. C-B fork-shoe; blue-blue.
b. E-D length-fork; green-red.
c. A-B shoe-shoe; red-blue.
d. C-D length-shoe green-red.

Step 22/13. Develop a "sufficient" number of pairs of E^S and NE^S to teach and test the learner's discriminations. Repeat steps 6 or 6(a) to 13 until all nondiscriminative features have been introduced. For the concept "long," all of the ND features selected at step 1(c) have been presented.

Step 23. Change the format of the E^S and NE^S; do not present them side-by-side. Use discriminations of medium difficulty before those of greatest difficulty. In this instructional sequence, objects are introduced in a format similar to that in which objects may be found in the natural environment. See Figure 8.9.

Step 24. Introduce real objects and events in the natural environment. To demonstrate the practical utility of the concept "long," introduce the learner to a number of commonly occurring events in the natural environment in which there is some advantage to recognizing which object is "long."

Step 25. For students unable to learn without prompting, develop a parallel program incorporating prompting and fading, as required. A prompting and fading sequence may be introduced during all or part of the sequence. Introduce prompts only if the learner exhibits a "high" error rate.

Step 26. Develop a number of pairs of E^S and NE^S showing all variations in the discriminative and ND features to test maintenance of concept acquisition.

Figure 8.9

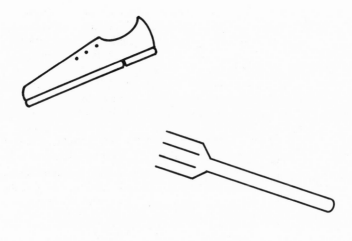

Step 27. List all of the pairs of E^S and NE^S developed in the preceding 26 steps into a "test-teach" sequence. See the following "test-teach" sequence designed to teach the concept "long."

Step 28. Validate use of the test-teach sequence with a sample of learners for whom the program was designed. Refer to Chapter Nine for a discussion of methods of program evaluation.

Multidimensional Concepts

Conjunctive concepts possess two or more discriminative features, all of which must be present for an object to be considered as an example of a particular concept. For instance, according to the American Association on Mental Deficiency, for an individual to be classified as mentally retarded, s/he must possess the following three discriminative features: (a) significantly subaverage intellectual functioning, *and* (b) significant deficits

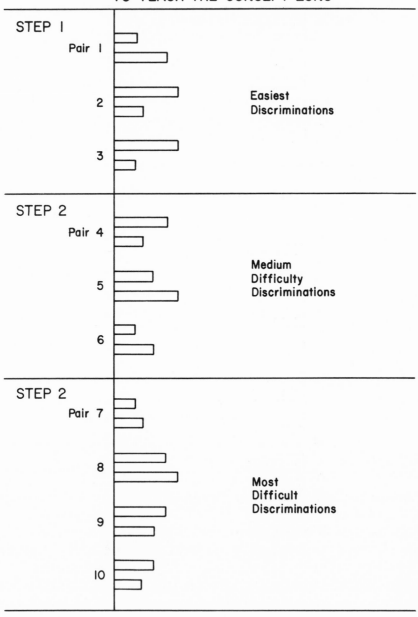

**TEST-TEACH SEQUENCE
TO TEACH THE CONCEPT LONG**

STEP 1

Pair 1

2

3

Easiest
Discriminations

STEP 2

Pair 4

5

6

Medium
Difficulty
Discriminations

STEP 2

Pair 7

8

9

10

Most
Difficult
Discriminations

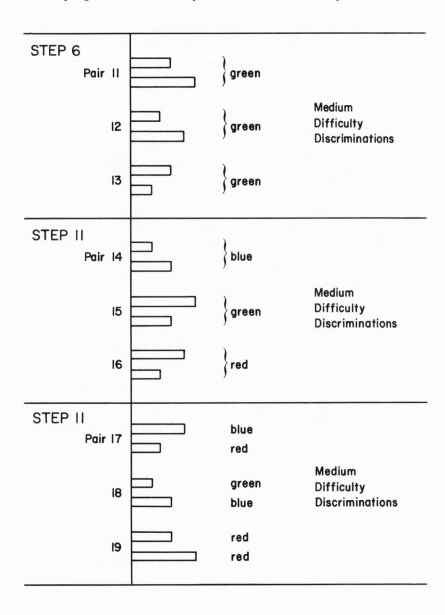

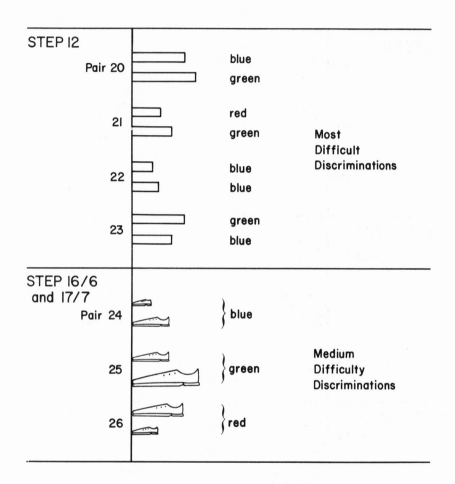

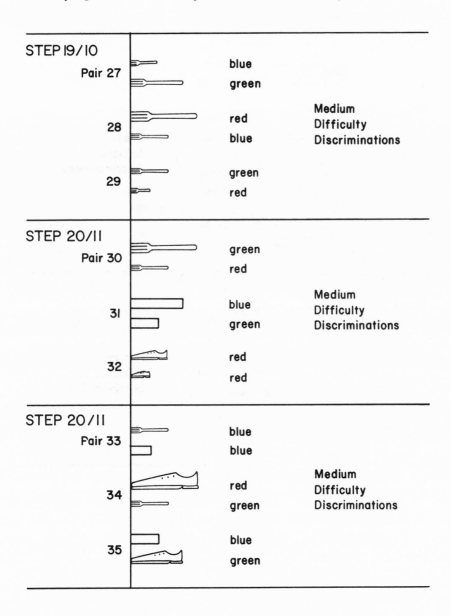

STEP 19/10		
Pair 27	blue	
	green	
28	red	Medium Difficulty Discriminations
	blue	
29	green	
	red	
STEP 20/11		
Pair 30	green	
	red	
31	blue	Medium Difficulty Discriminations
	green	
32	red	
	red	
STEP 20/11		
Pair 33	blue	
	blue	
34	red	Medium Difficulty Discriminations
	green	
35	blue	
	green	

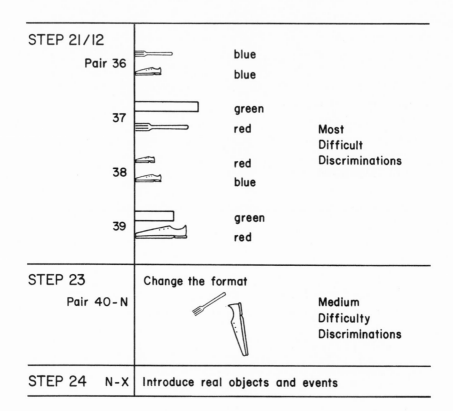

STEP 21/12

Pair 36   blue

               blue

37   green

               red   Most
                              Difficult
                              Discriminations

               red

38   blue

39   green

               red

STEP 23

Pair 40-N   Change the format

                              Medium
                              Difficulty
                              Discriminations

STEP 24   N-X   Introduce real objects and events

in adaptive behavior; in addition (c), these deficits must have been manifested during the developmental period. Thus, mental retardation is a conjunctive concept comprised of three discriminative features. An individual having only one or two of these features is not correctly classified as mentally retarded. Alternatively, disjunctive concepts are defined by two or more discriminative features either one, or both, of which must be present for an object to be classified as an example of a particular concept. Apples, for instance, possess some disjunctive features as they may be green *or* red or green *and* red.

The following discussion reviews methods for teaching: (a) single object (noun) concepts such as car, man, apple, dog, and tree; and (b) multiple, related (noun) concepts such as letters of the alphabet, geometric forms, groups of animals, and types of fruit. Single object (noun) concepts represent the general case for conjunctive concepts; each concept is taught independently and the acquisition of one concept does not usually affect the learning of other concepts, unless the concepts are hierarchically related. Multiple, related (noun) concepts are a special case of conjunctive concepts. Several of the concepts within a class of related concepts, such as geometric forms, possess a number of common or similar discriminative features. As a result, examples of various concepts within the class are likely to be confused with each other. For instance, parallelograms, rhombi, squares, and rectangles possess a number of common and similar features resulting in examples of one concept being confused with examples of each of the others. When a learner is being taught to identify one concept within a class of related concepts, s/he must also learn to discriminate examples of the concept from examples of each of the other concepts within the class. For instance, when a learner is being taught to identify examples of the concept "square," examples of circles, parallelograms, and rectangles are used as· nonexamples of the concept "square." The discussion that follows reviews methods of developing instructional sequences to teach single noun concepts and to teach multiple, related noun concepts.

Teaching single noun concepts. The following section describes the steps involved in developing an instructional sequence to teach single noun concepts. During the discussion, an actual program is developed to teach the concept "sector."

Step 1. Analyze the concept to be taught into discriminative (D) and nondiscriminative (ND) features. Determine if the D features have: (a) a fixed value or form, (b) a range of values or forms, or (c) two or more *alternative* values or forms (disjunctive case). For each D feature, describe the ND variations with which the D features are most likely to be confused. Figure 8.10 displays an example of the concept "sector."

The discriminative features of a sector, and the ND variations with which they are most likely to be confused are listed below, as are the ND features that are not confusing. Whether the D features are fixed or have a range of values is also indicated.

Discriminative features	*Confusing ND variations*
a. Circle–fixed.	Vertical or horizontal ellipse; square.
b. Sector is in quadrant one–range.	Sector is in quadrant two, three, or four.
c. Sector radiates from the center of the circle–fixed.	Sector radiates from above, below, in front of, or behind the center.
d. Central angle of the sector $\leq$ 90°–range.	Central angle $90° \geq 360°$.

Remaining ND features

a. Size of the circle: any size.
b. Color of the sector: any color.

Step 2. Remove all ND features from the stimuli, or select stimuli that have as few ND features as possible. Where ND features remain, hold them constant in both examples (E) and nonexamples (NE). In the case of the concept "sector," the ND features of size of the circle and color of the sector have been held constant in all introductory E[s] and NE[s].

Step 3. Select the most informative discriminative feature. The initial task for the learner is to differentiate D from ND features. Initially, there are many features that could be erroneously identified as D. By providing the learner with as much information as feasible, right at the beginning of instruction, it is possible to avoid having the learner formulate and later correct a number of invalid hypotheses about which features are D. In the example of "sector," if the learner is initially taught that "the sector is in quadrant one," s/he learns that: (a) the quadrant is a D feature, (b) in an E the sector is in quadrant one, and (c) the sector may be anywhere in quadrant one. Having all of this information, the learner is less apt to formulate invalid hypotheses about the D features of "sector."

Step 4. If the discriminative feature selected in step 3 has a range of values,

Figure 8.10

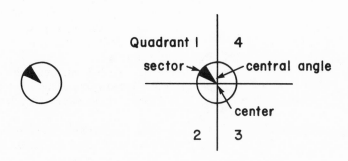

proceed as follows. If the D feature has a fixed value, advance to step 4(a). As indicated in step 1, the D feature, "the sector is in quadrant one" has a range of values, therefore, continue as follows. Introduce one D feature at a time. For each D feature with a range of values or forms, select at least four E[S] to sample the range of values: one E from each end of the range; one E near the middle of the range; and one E randomly located within the range. In steps 4 and 5 when introducing a D feature: (a) hold all untaught D features constant across successive pairs, (b) hold all previously taught D features constant within a pair, but (c) vary previously taught discriminative features from pair to pair. Four examples of "sector" are displayed in Figure 8.11; these E[S] show the range of positions of the sector in quadrant one.

Step 5. For each example selected in step 4, choose a corresponding NE: one NE adjacent to each end of the range; one NE near one end of the range; and one NE located randomly away from the ends of the range. Note that in Figures 8.11 and 8.12 the E "a" selected in step 4 is matched with the NE "a" selected in step 5. Also note that the pairs of E[S] and NE[S] selected in steps 4 and 5 comprise a *"set."*

Step 4(a). If the discriminative feature to be introduced has a fixed value rather than a range of values, proceed as follows. Introduce one fixed D feature at a time. For each fixed value or form of the D feature, select one E to match each of the respective, potentially confusing ND variations defined in step 1. In steps 4(a) and 5(a) when introducing one D feature: (a) hold all untaught D features constant across successive pairs, (b) hold all previously taught D features constant within each pair, and again (c) vary previously taught D features from pair to pair.

Figure 8.11

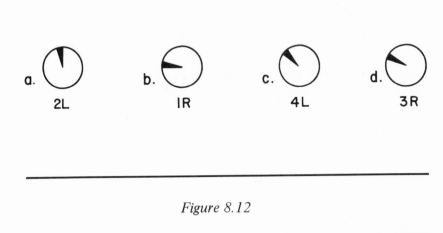

a. 2L   b. IR   c. 4L   d. 3R

Figure 8.12

Step 5(a). Match each E selected in step 4(a) with a NE chosen to represent one of each of the potentially confusing ND features described in step 1. Make each NE identical to the E except for the value or form of the confusing variation that is being introduced. Make the confusing value or form introduced in the NE similar to that of the D feature in the E to focus attention on the critical differences between D and ND features.

Step 6. If there are more discriminative features to be introduced that have a range of values or forms, select the next most informative D feature, such as "the central angle of the sector is less than or equal to 90°," and return to step 4, above. Figure 8.13 displays the four examples selected in step 4 above to illustrate that the central angle of a sector is ≤ 90°.

Step 7. To select NE^S to match the E^S chosen in step 6, follow the procedure described in step 5, above. The NE^S illustrated in Figure 8.14 have been selected according to the method described in step 5.

Step 8. If there are more D features to be introduced that have a range of values, repeat steps 4 and 5. If there are D features remaining that have a fixed value, follow the method described in steps 4(a) and 5(a). In step 1, the "circle" was described as a *fixed* D feature of a sector, therefore, return to step 4(a), above. In step 1, it indicated that the fixed, discriminative feature "circle," has three nondiscriminative, potentially confusing variations: a vertical or horizontal ellipse and a square. Therefore, according to the procedure described in step 4(a), one example has been selected to match each of the confusing nonexamples. The three examples selected to match the three nondiscriminative variations of "circle" are shown in Figure 8.15.

Step 9. To select NE^S to match the E^S chosen in step 8, follow the procedure described in step 5(a), above. Figure 8.16 displays the NE selected in step 5(a). The potentially confusing ND features described in step 1: (a) a vertical, and (b) a horizontal ellipse, and (c) a square have been matched with the E^S selected in step 8. Note that the ellipses and square are similar to the circle with respect to size and area.

Step 10. Are there more D features to introduce that have a range of values or forms? If yes, return to steps 4 and 5. There are no more D features of "sector" with a range of values. If there are more D features with a fixed characteristic, return to steps 4(a) and 5(a). In step 1, the D feature, "the sector radiates from the center of the circle" was designated as a fixed feature. Therefore, return to step 4(a). In step 1, it was indicated that the potentially confusing variations of the D feature, "the sector radiates from the center of the circle," are radiations from above, below, in front of, or behind the center. The four examples illustrated in Figure 8.17 have been selected to match each of the potentially confusing variations.

Step 11. To select NE^S to match the E^S chosen in step 10, return to step 5(a). Figure 8.18 displays the NE^S selected by following the procedure described in step 5(a). When all the D features of "sector" have been introduced, proceed with step 12.

Step 12. Within each *set* of pairs of E^S and NE^S selected in steps 4 and 5, 4(a) and 5(a), randomize the order of the pairs and the position of the E and NE in each pair. In the *sets* of E^S and NE^S developed in steps 4 and 5, list last in the sequence, pairs that do not focus on the ends of the range.

Step 13. If there are disjunctive, D features to introduce, follow steps 14 to 16, inclusive. If there are no disjunctive D features, advance to step 17. The concept "sector" has no disjunctive features.

Step 14. Introduce one disjunctive feature at a time. For each alternate

Figure 8.13

Figure 8.14

Figure 8.15

IR   3L   2R

Figure 8.16

a.   b.   c.

Figure 8.17

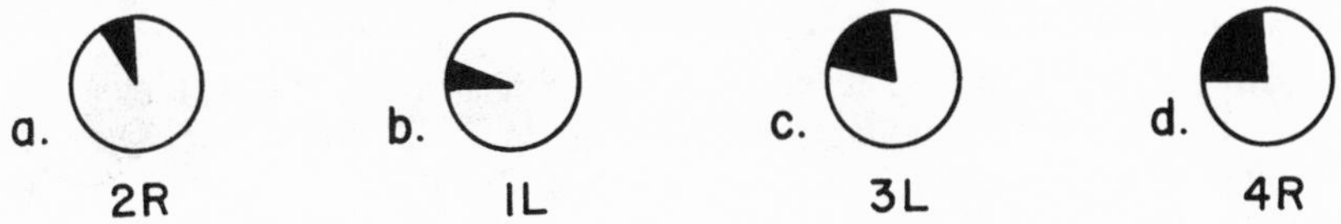

a. 2R b. 1L c. 3L d. 4R

Figure 8.18

a. b.   c. d.

value or form of the disjunctive D feature as defined in step 1, select one E. When introducing a D feature: (a) hold all untaught D features constant across successive pairs, (b) hold all previously taught D features constant within a pair, and (c) vary previously taught D features from pair to pair.

Step 15. Match each E with the alternative NE described in step 1. Put the E^S and NE^S into arrays of 1E to 3NE^S. Make each NE identical to each E except for the value of the D feature that is being taught. Make the D value or form of the NE similar to the D value or form of the E to focus attention on critical features.

Step 16. Randomize the position of the E and the NE^S in each array. Repeat steps 14-16 to introduce all disjunctive features.

Step 17. For conjunctive and disjunctive concepts introduce, one at a time, the "remaining ND features" as described in step 1. For each ND feature, select at least three E^S to sample a broad range of values of the ND feature. In steps 17 and 18, when introducing a ND feature: (a) remove all untaught ND features, or (b) hold untaught ND features constant across successive pairs; (c) vary all previously taught D features from pair to pair; and (d) where previously taught D features have a range of values, select the majority of E^S with values close to the ends of the range of the D feature. Number the E^S consecutively from 1 to 3. Figure 8.19 displays the E^S selected; the ND feature introduced is "size of the circle." For sake of brevity, the ND feature "color of the sector" is not introduced into the sequence.

Step 18. For each E selected in step 17, choose a NE with: (a) identical ND features, and (b) some identical D features. Choose a range of NE^S having all but one of the D features to only one D feature. Label the NE^S consecutively from A to C. The NE^S shown in Figure 8.20 were selected following this procedure.

Step 19. Put the E^S from step 17 with the NE^S from step 18 into the following arrays: 2, 3, 1, A; B, 2, C, 3; 3, A, C, 1; and 1, 2, 3, B.

Step 20. If there are more ND features to be introduced, retrace steps 17, 18, and 19.

Step 21. Introduce real examples of the concept in naturally occurring environmental conditions.

Step 22. For instructional purposes, list in sequence all of the pairs and arrays of E^S and NE^S selected in the previous 21 steps. For instance, return to the E^S and NE^S selected in steps 4 and 5. Match E(a) in step 4 with NE(a) from step 5; match the remaining E^S and NE^S in the same manner. Randomize the location of the E^S in each pair and randomize the order of the pairs within each step. For instance, the pairs of E^S and NE^S: a, b, c, and d, selected in steps 4 and 5, have been randomized in the order: b, a, d, and c. The order of the E^S and NE^S has been randomized within each pair in the following manner: b: NE-E; a: E-NE; d: NE-E, and c: E-NE. These pairs are then put into a training sequence as indicated below. Note that the letters b: NE-E, and the list of "features taught in each set" would not be shown in the actual training sequence.

Figure 8.19

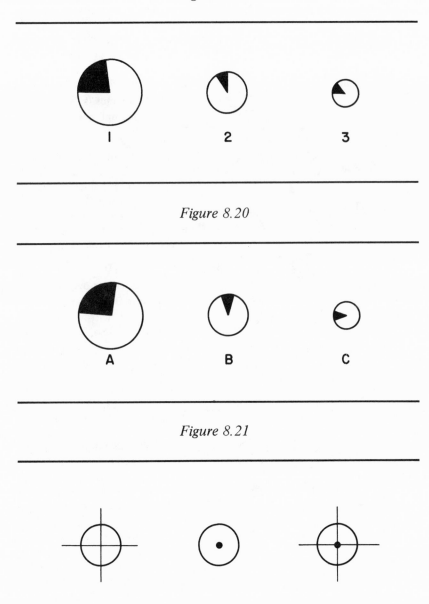

Figure 8.20

Figure 8.21

TRAINING SEQUENCE

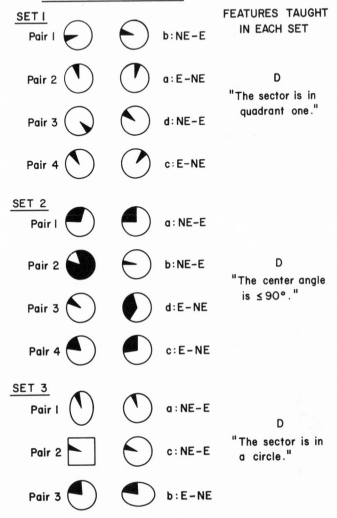

SET I

Pair I   b:NE−E

Pair 2   a:E−NE

Pair 3   d:NE−E

Pair 4   c:E−NE

SET 2

Pair I   a:NE−E

Pair 2   b:NE−E

Pair 3   d:E−NE

Pair 4   c:E−NE

SET 3

Pair I   a:NE−E

Pair 2   c:NE−E

Pair 3   b:E−NE

FEATURES TAUGHT
IN EACH SET

D
"The sector is in
quadrant one."

D
"The center angle
is ≤ 90°."

D
"The sector is in
a circle."

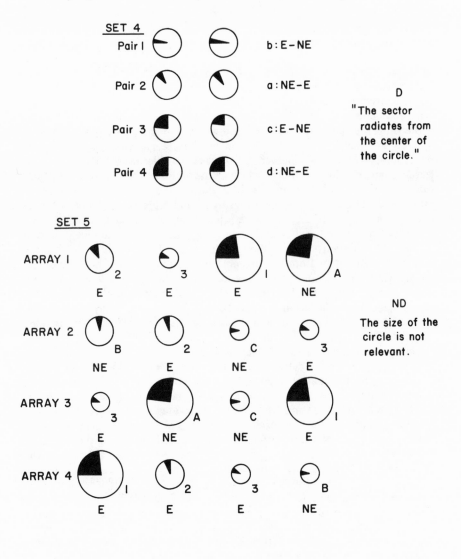

SET 4

Pair 1   b : E – NE

Pair 2   a : NE – E

Pair 3   c : E – NE

Pair 4   d : NE – E

D

"The sector radiates from the center of the circle."

SET 5

ARRAY 1   2   3   1   A
E   E   E   NE

ND

The size of the circle is not relevant.

ARRAY 2   B   2   C   3
NE   E   NE   E

ARRAY 3   3   A   C   1
E   NE   NE   E

ARRAY 4   1   2   3   B
E   E   E   NE

Step 23. Review the teaching sequence developed in step 22. If desirable in any set of E^S and NE^S, increase the stimulus value of the D features, and/or decrease the value of the ND features, and/or introduce an artificial prompt to focus attention on D features. If prompts are used in any set of E^S and NE^S, develop a parallel set in which the prompts are faded. Two prompts that might be useful in teaching the concept "sector" are: (a) quadrant lines that can be systematically faded, such as those depicted in Figure 8.21, and (b) a darkened center point that can be faded in terms of size, color, and intensity.

Step 24. Develop a "generalization test" for each set of examples and nonexamples to assess whether the learner is able to generalize his/her learning beyond the specific E^S and NE^S introduced during instruction. For each set of E^S and NE^S in which a single D or ND feature has been introduced, develop two testing arrays of E^S and NE^S; use: (a) three E^S and one NE, or (b) two E^S and two NE^S. Select examples that are parallel to, but different from, those used in the teaching sequence: (a) hold untaught D and ND features constant, (b) vary the value or form of one or more D features that have been taught from one example to the next, (c) vary the value of all taught ND features from one example to the next, and (d) for D features that have a range of values, select the majority of E^S to sample the ends of the range. Randomize the location of the E^S and NE^S in each array. Put the E^S and NE^S into an array in the manner shown in the testing sequence. Note the designations E and NE would not be shown on the actual test. The cumulative learning tests are discussed in step 25.

Step 25. Construct "cumulative learning tests." The generalization tests assess the generalization of learning from one set of E^S and NE^S. Cumulative learning tests evaluate the maintenance and generalization of learning acquired in all of the sets of E^S and NE^S that have previously been presented in the instructional sequence. For each set of E^S and NE^S in which a single discriminative and ND feature has been introduced, excluding the first set, construct a cumulative learning test. For each test, select one E for each previously taught D and ND feature. Let previously taught D and ND features vary in each E. If previously taught D features have a range of values, choose E^S with the D feature close to the ends of the range. Select a NE to match each of the E^S. The NE should be identical to the E except for one D feature on which there is a small difference. Put the E^S and NE^S into arrays of three or four as in the "Testing Sequence." The letters E and NE would not be shown in the test.

Step 26. From the last cumulative learning test, select two E^S and two NE^S to use as pretraining stimuli to focus learner attention on D and ND features before beginning instruction. See Figure 8.22.

Step 27. Validate use of the sequence with a sample of learners for whom the program was designed. Refer to Chapter Nine for methods of program evaluation.

Teaching multiple, related noun concepts. As mentioned earlier,

TESTING SEQUENCE

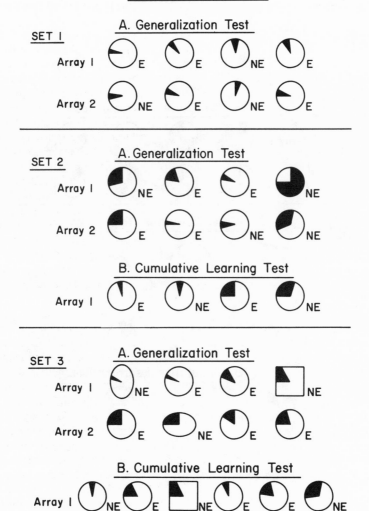

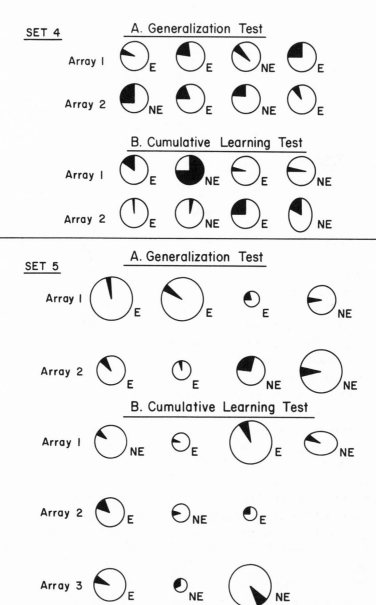

Figure 8.22

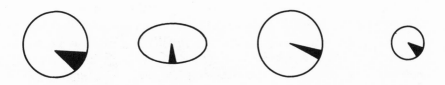

multiple, related noun concepts refer to a number of concepts such as squares, rectangles, and parallelograms within a single classification, for instance, geometric forms. Within the class, all of the concepts share common or similar discriminative features and may have identical nondiscriminative features; as a result, different concepts within the class may be confused with each other.

Becker, Engelmann, and Thomas (1975b) have discussed the relative merits of teaching related concepts in a successive or cumulative manner. If there were four concepts: A, B, C, and D, in a successive approach to instruction, a student would be taught to discriminate concept A from B, then A from C, A from D, B from C, B from D, and finally C from D. One difficulty arising from the successive approach is that the one or more discriminative features that the learner uses to discriminate A from B may not differentiate A from successive concepts. In essence, the learner may be able to discriminate A from B on the basis of incomplete learning—without having learned all of the discriminative features of A.

With a cumulative approach to instruction, the learner would be taught to discriminate A from B, then C from A and B, followed by D from C, A, and B. As each additional concept is added, the student learns to discriminate it from each of the previously introduced concepts, while s/he also practices discrimination of the concepts learned earlier. Thus, in the cumulative approach, unlike that of the successive approach, the learner does not use one set of discriminative features to differentiate A from B, and another set to discriminate A from C. Becker *et al.* concluded from their review of the topic that cumulative programming is essential for teaching sets of related concepts to naive learners. Note that in the cumulative approach, only one concept at a time is taught. Numerous researchers have concurred that where there are several concepts to be taught, they should be taught one at a time (Blake, 1976; Bourne and Jennings, 1963; Hurley, 1975).

Becker *et al.*, have suggested that when cumulative methods are being used to teach related concepts, one should: (a) initially pair concepts that are least confusing; (b) separate concepts that are highly confusing, that is, teach one concept early in the instructional sequence, and introduce later in the sequence the concept with which the former is often confused; and (c) give the learner the most practice discriminating the most confusing concepts. The authors have also described an analytical approach to establishing the relative confusability of concepts and, thus, determine how and when to introduce them into instruction and practice. The analytical procedure is relatively straightforward with objects such as geometric forms in which the discriminative features can be readily and consensually identified. For example, squares and circles having three differences in discriminative features would be taught first. Squares and rectangles having only one discriminative difference and being, therefore, potentially confusing, would be introduced at widely separated points in an instructional sequence. Considerable practice would be given to the discrimination of parallelograms and rectangles, two most confusing concepts.

The analytical analysis of the potential confusability of stimuli becomes more difficult when one must hypothesize which features of the concepts may affect their confusability and assign a weighting to each feature to reflect the magnitude of its assumed effect. Such is the case with letters of the alphabet. Becker,

Engelmann, and Thomas (1975b) hypothesize that the relative confusability of each letter of the alphabet could be determined by calculating the number and length of strokes taken to construct the letter. With this procedure, each component of a letter is given a weighting from 1-4, according to the relative length of the unit. Given the weighting assigned to each of the components of any two letters, the relative discriminability of the letters can be calculated with a formula provided by the authors. One difficulty with this type of analysis arises, as Becker *et al.*, have pointed out, when different instructional designers fail to agree as to which features of stimuli affect their discriminability and as to the amount of weighting that should be assigned to reflect the relative degree of influence of each feature. Gibson, Osser, and Pick (1963), for example, after studying the discrimination of alphabet forms by children 4-8 years of age, concluded that the following features influenced the discriminability of letters of the alphabet: (a) ascending and descending stems, as in b and p; (b) left-to-right orientation, as in d and b; (c) closure or openness, as in o and c; (d) angles, as in k, m, x, and v; (e) curves and lines, as in p, b, and g; and (f) symmetry, as in m and x. Obviously, it would be very difficult to assign an intuitive weighting to these variables to reflect their relative influence upon discrimination.

Perhaps, also, any one discriminative feature could have a differential effect upon members of various populations of performers. According to Zaporozhets (1965), for example, children at different levels of development characteristically use different scanning procedures when scanning visual stimuli. Performers with various types of perceptual abnormalities may also be affected in different ways by the same visual characteristic.

Possibly a solution to the problem would be to perform an empirical analysis of the relative confusability of particular concepts among a specific population of learners. Tennyson and Boutwell (1974) have employed such an approach. According to Tennyson, Woolley, and Merrill (1972), the relative difficulty of an example of a concept is the major cause of concept learning errors. Popp (1964) conducted a study of the relative discriminability of alphabet letters among kindergarten children aged 5.1 to

6.1 years. These children were presented with a match-to-sample format. The results of the study revealed the number of times each letter was confused with each of the others. The match-to-sample format would seem to provide a relatively quick, easy, and effective means of determining the comparative discriminability of a group of related stimuli.

Several studies have demonstrated the effectiveness of cumulative methods of instruction in which concepts that are particularly difficult to discriminate have been widely separated in their introduction during instruction. Carnine (1976b) studied the learning of phonologically similar letters of the alphabet. He found that children in the first grade made fewer errors (33% vs. 52%), and reached criterion in fewer trials (178 vs. 293) when phonologically similar letters were separated from each other in their order of introduction. Cheyne (1966) found that the cumulative method of introducing concepts resulted in higher trigram recognition scores than when noncumulative methods were used. O'Malley (1973) found that children reached criterion on more letters in a multiple discrimination task when the letters had been introduced cumulatively.

Generic Methods for Teaching and Testing Concepts

The flowchart displayed in Figure 8.23 illustrates the sequence of various methods involved in the testing and teaching of concept acquisition, generalization, and maintenance. Each step in the flowchart is discussed in the following section.

Pre-testing. The ultimate goal of any teaching program is to train a student to respond appropriately to real objects and events as they are found in the natural environment. Therefore, before beginning a concept teaching program, the teacher should assess the ability of the learner to identify a variety of common and uncommon examples of the concept in his/her natural surroundings. This assessment may be performed by having the teacher administer to the learner the final cumulative learning test in the instructional sequence in which actual examples and nonexamples of concepts are presented. If the learner reaches criterion on this test, no further instruction of the concept is required and the

Figure 8.23

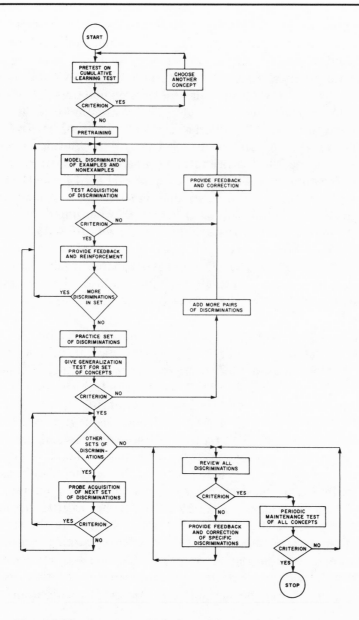

Figure 8.23. Generic methods for teaching and testing concepts.

teaching of another concept may be considered. Alternatively, if the learner fails to reach criterion, begin pretraining of the concept.

Pretraining. As discussed earlier, there are a number of advantages derived from pretraining the learner to focus attention on discriminative features of stimulus material before actual instruction begins. To achieve this goal, employ several examples and nonexamples selected from the final cumulative learning test in the instructional sequence. Also, during pretraining, review any previously learned skills that are components of, or prerequisites to, the task to be performed. For example, if instruction of the concept requires the learner to make a particular visual, motor, or verbal response that s/he may not have practiced for some time, review the response. Also, review and reinforce the performance of "learning readiness skills," such as sitting, orienting towards the teacher and/or stimulus materials, and listening to the teacher.

Modeling. After the student, during pretraining, has learned to focus attention on the discriminative features of a concept, modeling is employed to teach the learner to discriminate between examples and nonexamples of the concept. Modeling proceeds as follows:

   a. (Present a pair of examples and nonexamples to the learner.)
   b. (Model a simple verbal response.)
      Teacher: "MY TURN." (point to either the example or nonexample and ask) "IS THIS LONG?" (model the appropriate response), "YES" or "NO," (point to the remaining stimulus and ask) "IS THIS LONG?" (model the appropriate response), "YES" or "NO."
   c. Imitation phase. (*Randomize* the location of the example and the nonexample and *randomly* point to either stimulus saying) "YOUR TURN; IS THIS LONG?"

Note that if the position of the example and nonexample had not been randomized during the imitation phase, and if the teacher had not pointed randomly to either the example or the nonexample, one could not be certain if the student had acquired the discrimination between the example and the nonexample, or whether s/he had simply made the correct response on the basis of position cues or the order of the questions. Bereiter and Engelmann (1966) suggest that the teacher should initially model and request a simple response, such as nodding, pointing, or saying "yes" or "no." Nevertheless, modeling and responding should give the learner practice performing at the highest level of which s/he is capable. As either the student exhibits fatigue, or it becomes desirable to introduce variety into instruction, modeling and responding may return to a simpler level of response. However, such variation in responding may result in confusion, if the change in the response requirements is not well signaled. As Williams and Gotts (1977) suggest, the pointing response is of little functional value to the individual in the general environment. In addition, a verbal response has a facilitative effect in acquisition and retention (Lewis, 1970; Rowe, 1972). That is, if a learner makes a verbal response, rather than, or in addition to, a motor response, his/her acquisition and retention of learning will likely improve.

Some alternative verbal responses are:
   (a) "IS THIS A TRUCK?" [yes] a simple affirmative response.
   (b) "WHAT IS THIS?" [a truck] labeling response; or [this is a truck] making a complete statement.
   (c) "IS THIS TRUCK BIGGER?" [yes, this truck is bigger] statement repetition.
   (d) "TELL ME ABOUT THIS TRUCK" [this truck is bigger] statement generation.

When there is a high chance factor involved in responding in the correct manner, for example, when there are only two stimuli from which to choose, or only two response choices such as "yes" or "no," one should establish a higher criterion for judging acquisition than might be used where guessing would less likely occur. Various aspects of the modeling-responding sequence described above may be found in the DISTAR instructional programs (Engelmann and Osborne, 1976).

Rosenthal and Kellogg (1973), after reviewing several research studies, concluded that observational learning may be especially effective for people with limited verbal repertoires such as the retarded. These researchers studied the concept learning of adult mentally retarded individuals under two conditions: (a) a modeled response was followed by imitation and then a transfer task, and (b) a verbal explanation was followed by imitation and then a transfer task. The gain scores achieved in the modeling condition surpassed those obtained in the verbal explanation condition in both acquisition and transfer. Yoder and Forehand (1974) found that the mentally retarded children who received modeling of a conceptual task made fewer errors during acquisition than children did who had not received modeling. There are two types of modeling, distributed and massed. In the *distributed* approach, the learner responds after each demonstrated trial; this is called the *imitation paradigm.* In the *massed* approach, the learner does not respond until a number of trials have been demonstrated; this is called the *observational learning paradigm.* Litrownik, Franzini, and Turner (1976) studied the effects of these approaches on the conceptual learning of trainable, mentally retarded learners ($\overline{X}$ IQ = 44; $\overline{X}$ M.A. = 5.7). The group that received distributed modeling performed significantly better during the training phase than the group did that had received the massed modeling. The massed modeling group, however, performed better on the transfer tasks than the other group did. The results of this study would seem to indicate that distributed modeling should be used during acquisition, and that special steps should be taken to improve generalization.

Feedback. Figure 8.23 indicates that feedback is provided following a student's correct and incorrect responses. Several studies have demonstrated the importance of providing the learner with feedback regarding the correctness of his/her responses. In the present context, feedback is provided in the following manner. After a correct response has been made, and in conjunction with a reinforcer, the teacher points to the example of a concept, for example, a car, and says, "YES, THIS IS A CAR." The feedback confirms the child's response and again models the correct response thus strengthening the perceived relationship between the stimulus and the response. Following an error response, the teacher says, "NO," and then points to the example while saying, "THIS IS A CAR." The example and the nonexample are left in view for the learner to reexamine following the feedback. Clark (1971) suggested that after either a correct or an incorrect response, the student should be given immediate, complete, and accurate feedback. Feedback for correct and incorrect responses is more facilitating than feedback for correct responses only. Gholson and McConville (1974) found that feedback produced stimulus differentiation in the concept training of five-year-old children. Dueck (1976) found that feedback modified the manner in which elementary school children viewed stimuli. After receiving feedback only for correct responses, the children changed from a global to an analytical visual strategy. The effectiveness of the feedback may be further increased through the use of a prompt where the teacher points to the discriminative features of the examples while providing the feedback.

The learner must be given enough time to assimilate the feedback that s/he has received. Studies have indicated that a critical factor in solving a concept learning problem is the length of the post-feedback interval. The post-feedback interval is that period of time falling between the provision of feedback regarding the correctness of the learner's response and presentation by the teacher of the next step of instruction. During this period, the learner has the opportunity to reexamine the stimulus material and to determine why his/her response was either right or wrong (Travers, 1977). Providing an optimum period of time for reanalysis is crucial. Too much time may lead to distraction, as well as decreased vigilance and retention. This topic is more fully discussed by Bourne, Ekstrand, and Dominowski (1971), who discuss the notion of an optimal, suboptimal, and superoptimal length of interval. Although it has been suggested that learning takes place only after an error response and that the post-feedback interval should be extended only for error responses, this hypothesis has not been supported by a study conducted by Bourne, Dodd, Guy, and Justesen (1968). They found that an interval of optimum duration should be available following both correct and incorrect responses.

Correction. As indicated in Figure 8.23, correction procedures are instituted directly following an error response. Clark (1971) suggested that after an incorrect response, the learner should verbalize the correct response. More specifically, the learner should make the appropriate verbal and/or motor response following the teacher's response signal while attending to the stimuli that s/he is attempting to discriminate. In fact, a "positive practice" procedure may be used where the learner repeatedly makes the correct response under the conditions described above. Carnine (1975c) studied preschoolers involved in small-group instruction of arithmetic facts. He found that when the teacher corrected an error by: (a) saying the addition statement, (b) having the children say the statement, and (c) repeating the addition fact question, there was a 55 percent higher accuracy of response during training and a 48 percent increase in accuracy during the post-tests over the accuracy that was achieved when no correction was provided following an error. Carnine reported similar results in pilot studies of low performing children in the first and second grades who were being taught coding, comprehension, arithmetic, and word problem solving.

The errors that occur during concept instruction may be of several different types and each class of error requires the use of an appropriate corrective procedure.

a. Response errors: these errors involve either a failure to respond or commission of the wrong type of response.

   Correction: substitute synonymous terminology in the task command and the response signal to occasion the desired response. For example, if "touch" does not occasion the correct type of response, ask the learner to "point." Or, pretrain the desired type of response with familiar stimuli before continuing with the concept teaching program.

b. Misconception errors: in the commission of these errors, the learner classifies some examples as nonexamples while some nonexamples are classified as examples. The learner has incorrectly classified stimuli on the basis of nondiscriminative features.

Correction: use attention signals and/or prompts as required to focus the learner's attention on discriminative features. Point to, trace, or embellish discriminative features. Additional types of errors are discussed below.

Practice. Figure 8.23 indicates that practice exercises are instituted following the initial acquisition of a set of discriminations. Engelmann (1978) suggested that the longer a teacher waited between practice sessions in concept learning, the more difficult it would be for the learner to recall discriminative features. During the initial stages of concept acquisition, for instructionally naive students, practice sessions may be scheduled three times per day to reinforce newly learned discriminations. During practice and review sessions, there is frequently not sufficient time to review all previously learned concepts. Carnine (1979) suggested that priority be given to reviewing: (a) recently introduced concepts, (b) troublesome concepts, those with a high error rate, (c) any concept not recently reviewed, and (d) any concept that is similar to the recently introduced concepts.

Stimulus generalization test. The stimulus generalization test assesses the learner's response to new examples and nonexamples of concepts that had not been included during instruction. The stimulus generalization test may also include an assessment of the learner's response to examples and nonexamples that had been included in instruction. The learner's response to these items indicates maintenance of initial learning and thus provides a validation of the stimulus generalization test. The stimulus generalization test may reveal errors of over- or undergeneralization.

a. Overgeneralization: these errors occur when a learner classifies nonexamples as examples, but does not generally classify examples as nonexamples. The boundaries of the range of values of a discriminative feature have not been well established.

Correction: give the learner instruction and practice discriminating a series of pairs of examples and nonexamples selected from near the ends of the range of values of the discriminative features.

b. Undergeneralization: these errors arise when a learner fails to classify as examples stimuli that are within the range of the examples presented during instruction.

Correction: if the range of values of a discriminative feature have been represented during instruction by examples sampled only from the middle and ends of the range of values, reinstruct the learner while using a more comprehensive sampling of examples with intermediate values.

Functional generalization training. In the later stages of instruction, the skills or concepts taught should be made functional by integrating them into activities that frequently occur in the learner's life space. This step is particularly important for low functioning individuals who may not automatically generalize skills from instructional to natural settings. Students have not mastered a skill unless they can perform the skill across functional tasks that frequently occur in their life space (Williams and Gotts, 1977).

Maintenance. As previously described, maintenance trials are introduced after successively longer periods of time. Maintenance of a response is also assisted by the systematic reduction of reinforcement dispensed during training until the frequency, amount, and type of reinforcement approximates that available in the learner's life space.

Advanced Students

As was mentioned earlier, the methods described thus far have been designed for teaching concepts to low functioning, instructionally naive students. A number of modifications can be made to these methods to accommodate more advanced students. For example, for students with adequate receptive language, a deductive rather than an inductive approach to instruction may be employed. The learner may be furnished with a definition of a concept before being given examples and nonexamples to discriminate. The "definition" may simply list the discriminative features of the concept and/or describe the combinatorial rule explaining the manner in which the discriminative features are related.

Rather than simply being taught to discriminate examples and nonexamples at the classificatory level of concept acquisition (Klausmeier, Ghatala, and Frayer, 1974), students possessing the prerequisite receptive and expressive language skills may be taught to function at the formal level. According to Klausmeier *et al.,* students at the formal level of concept acquisition do not merely discriminate examples from nonexamples, but can also label the discriminative features and state the combinatorial rule describing the relationship among the discriminative features. For students capable of this level of language functioning, a simple pointing response to indicate their selection in a discrimination task is not appropriate and should be replaced by a verbal response requiring labeling and the production of verbal statements. During instruction, the learner must receive *appropriate practice* of all of the skills that s/he will eventually be expected to perform. For example, if at the end of instruction the learner is expected to label the discriminative features and state the combinatory rule defining a concept, these skills must be repeatedly practiced during instruction.

With some advanced learners, it may not be necessary during instruction to introduce the identification of a single discriminative and nondiscriminative feature, one at a time. In fact, if the learner has adequate receptive language skills, several discriminative features may be introduced and labeled at the same time.

Advanced learners may generalize and retain newly acquired skills more effectively than do low functioning students. As a result, advanced students may not require as much instruction or practice at each level of an instructional sequence, and may be able to "skip" some of the steps of instruction altogether. The inclusion of generalization and maintenance probes throughout instruction will indicate the instructional requirements for each individual. Of course, the effectiveness of any instructional sequence must be experimentally validated on the population of students for whom the program was designed.

A Further Consideration of the Nature and Teaching of Concepts

Anderson and Faust (1974) wrote that the definition of a

concept as a well defined set of discriminative features is a simplified and idealized definition. Perhaps a more realistic definition is that a concept is a group of more or less discriminative features, no single set of which allows a classification including all examples and excluding all nonexamples. Some concepts have evolved in a rather haphazard manner; their discriminative features are not well defined, there may not be a consensus as to which features are discriminative, and the boundaries with other concepts may be vague, overlapping, and inconsistent. Some concepts form very heterogeneous categories that are divided into a number of subclasses, across which it is difficult to find one or more common characteristics. In this case, it is difficult to perform a concept analysis for the purpose of identifying discriminative and nondiscriminative features and selecting examples and nonexamples for instruction. A different approach than that previously described must be employed to teach concepts of this type.

Consider, for example, the heterogeneity of objects classified as cars. Most cars have three or four wheels; the passenger car attached to a balloon does not have any wheels. Cars are fueled by diesel, alcohol, gasoline, or propane engines, or by electric motors or the wind. The majority of cars have an engine mounted in the front, while others are driven from the rear, and some have an engine in the middle. Elevator cars are propelled by a cable mounted on the roof, while street cars obtain their energy from a trolley attached to an overhead powerline. Some cars are designed to carry a single person and only during a race; limousines are used to carry up to 11 paying "fares," while station wagons carry cargo and provide enough room for sleeping bags. Cars usually travel on roads or highways; however, some travel on tracks, along cables, up vertical shafts, and across water. This list of variations is far from complete; there is a great variety of different types of objects classified as cars. Many of the characteristics of cars are common to other concepts, and it is difficult to identify one or more features that are unique to cars. Nevertheless, car is a common concept and most adults would have little difficulty classifying the vast majority of cars and discriminating them from noncars.

However, classification becomes difficult when objects are presented from the ends of the ranges of values of various discriminative features. Most adults would also probably experience considerable difficulty constructing a definition that would include all examples and exclude all nonexamples of cars.

The following steps describe a method of teaching the type of concept just described.

1. Select a number and diverse variety of examples of cars and noncars that the majority of people would readily and unequivocally classify into the appropriate categories (difficulty level I).

2. Select a number and variety of examples of cars and noncars that present a more difficult discrimination (difficulty level II). The type of examples selected here depends upon the fineness of the discrimination the learner is to be taught to make. A guideline in this respect is to choose examples and nonexamples that represent the most difficult, commonly found discriminations that the learner would ordinarily be required to make in his/her daily life. The nonexamples selected should present the learner with a number and variety of useful and common discriminations in the individual's life space.

3. Define the ambiguous region of examples and nonexamples. Ordinarily, handicapped learners would not be required to make discriminations from this category.

4. Employ a cumulative instruction technique. First, teach the concept of car giving examples and nonexamples from difficulty level I. For instance, use trucks and buses as nonexamples. Model the response of pointing to a car or labeling a car in response to the question "WHAT IS THIS?" or "IS THIS A CAR?" [yes or no]. In the second stage, introduce cars, trucks, and buses from the second level of difficulty. Again, the task is to "identify" the cars. In the third stage, the learner is taught to point to or label cars and trucks given cars, trucks, and buses from difficulty levels I and II. Finally, in the fourth stage, the learner is taught to point to or label cars, trucks, and buses

in reply to a question such as "IS THIS A TRUCK?" or a
statement such as "POINT TO A BUS."

Review of Concepts and Procedures
Covered in Chapters Six, Seven, and Eight

Before proceeding into new material, review the following
concepts and procedures discussed in the previous three chapters.
Use a paper and pencil as applicable: (1) define or explain; (2)
provide a novel example; (3) describe where, when, and how to
apply or evaluate; and (4) discuss advantages and disadvantages of
each term. As a term is being reviewed, cover all of the other terms to
avoid giving yourself clues. If you are unable to recall the
information *rapidly* and *accurately*, refer to the listed page
number(s) and review the material; page numbers with major
references have been underlined. Note troublesome terms and put
them into a maintenance schedule for repeated review after
successively longer periods of time.

Subject   Page No.

Formative and Summative Evaluation

Contents

The discussion that follows relates only to the evaluation of the types of programs described in this text. In other contexts, the concepts and procedures of formative and summative evaluation may be more broadly defined, when applied to other types of instructional programs and materials.

Formative Evaluation

Formative evaluation involves the collection of quantitative and qualitative data during the *formation* of an instructional program. The purpose of the evaluation is to identify successful and deficient instructional procedures and materials, and to correct those parts of an instructional program that impede progress of the learner towards the terminal behavioral objectives. A formative evaluation may include the evaluation, revision, and reevaluation of one or more parts of an instructional program, or a prototype of a total program. There are four stages of the evaluation: (a) consultant review, (b) one-to-one clinical tryout, (c) small-group tryout, and (d) field tryout. Each stage of evaluation and revision may be repeatedly executed until the program is ready to proceed to the next level of evaluation. Figure 9.1 illustrates the relationship between the four stages of formative evaluation and revision of the instructional methods and materials, and the summative and maintenance evaluations of the final program package.

Komoski (1974), head of the Educational Products Information Exchange Institute (EPIE), stated that only approximately one percent of the materials used in public schools in the United States has undergone formative evaluation. A survey of instructional materials used in both French and English public schools in the Province of Quebec, from kindergarten through junior college, revealed that less than two percent of the materials had been tested on learners (Pflieger, Stolovitch, and Bordeleau, 1977). Too often, students and teachers have been blamed for poor learning and inadequate teaching, when, in fact, the materials used were insufficient to support the instructional effort (Dick and Carey, 1978).

Is a formative evaluation necessary? A number of researchers have demonstrated that formative evaluation and revision of instructional materials "improve the attainment of objectives" and produce significantly better learning outcomes than were obtained from the original unrevised procedures (Baker, 1970; Kandaswamy, 1976; Nathanson and Henderson, 1976; Rosen, 1968; Sulzen, 1972). Two states, California and Florida, have passed legislation on formative evaluation. Seventeen other states have pending legislation.

Florida Senate Bill 492, section 283.25 is as follows:

> Publishers shall provide written proof of the use of the learner verification and revision process during prepublication development and postpublication revision of the materials in question. For purpose of this section, learner verification is defined as the empirical process of data gathering and analysis by which a publisher of a curriculum material has improved the instructional effectiveness of that product before it reaches the market and then continues to gather data from learners in order to improve the quality and reliability of that material during its full market life. (Cited in Stolovitch, 1978.)

Figure 9.1

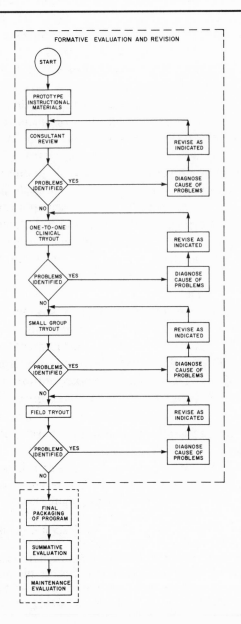

Figure 9.1. Formative, summative, and maintenance evaluations.

A study conducted at the Rocky Mountain Special Education Instructional Materials Center indicated that teachers had difficulty selecting effective instructional materials in the absence of the information provided by formative and summative evaluations. Twenty-five certified teachers of the educable mentally retarded were asked to evaluate 23 separate sets of instructional reading materials. This procedure provided 25 evaluations of each set of materials. The results indicated that there was no consistent agreement or policy among the teachers as to the value of each set of materials (Reichard, Reid, Whorten, and Reid, 1970).

Consultant review. The first step in a formative evaluation involves a consultant review. At this stage, the program developer consults the critical advice of experts with skills complementary to his/her own. The consultants may include persons with expertise in the performance area in which the knowledge and skills to be taught are included; they may have familiarity with the population of learners for whom the program is being developed; and/or the consultants may have specialized skills in the type of instructional design methods or materials that are to be used. Depending upon their areas of expertise, the consultants would be given copies of the instructional objectives, lattices, flowcharts, and/or preliminary drafts of the instructor's guides, and instructional and testing materials and equipment. The review is made *before* the program is implemented and provides a critical analysis of the following areas; the list of variables described within each area is not exhaustive.

1. *Content:* an assessment is made of: (a) the content validity of the instructional and testing materials, (b) the accuracy and currency of the content, and (c) the completeness of the performance and hierarchic learning analyses of objectives into subtasks and enabling skills.
2. *Instruction:* materials are examined to insure that the program will provide: (a) a sufficient amount and type of practice for acquisition, generalization, and maintenance of the knowledge and skills described in the terminal behavioral objectives; (b) appropriate instructional sequencing from the learner's entry level to the terminal

behavioral objective to insure that all prerequisite skills will be taught in order; and (c) suitable behavioral management and instructional techniques for the learner population and the skills being taught. An assessment is made as to whether the program will be able to adequately accommodate advanced placement of beginning students or late entry into the program, skipping of instructional units, or premature transfer of learners to other types of instruction. Instructional personnel (teachers, aides, parents, and/or instructors) are also judged as to their assumed ability to implement the program with the learner population within the constraints of instructor training and motivation, the instructional context, the methods employed, and the time, equipment, and assistance available.

3. *Learners*: the suitability to the learner population of the written, verbal, and/or graphic methods of communication employed is assessed, as is the appropriateness of the instructional activities, step size, duration of instruction, and the stimulus and response formats to the ages, grades, disabilities, and diversities of the learner population. An assessment is made as to whether the program can adequately accommodate differences in the rate and style of learning of individual learners and as to whether sufficient consideration has been given to student needs for repetition, practice, motivation, and instructional variety.

Many of the variables assessed during the consultant review are reevaluated during actual implementation of the program in subsequent phases of the formative and summative evaluations.

One-to-one clinical tryout. The one-to-one clinical tryout provides an in-depth analysis of student responses to a preliminary draft of the instructional and testing materials. The analysis involves an interaction between the program developer, a student, and the materials. The programmer presents the materials to the learner, observes the student's responses, and adjusts the methods and content of instruction in an effort to improve the instructional process. S/he also makes notes on his/her observations throughout the interaction with the student. If possible, the student is requested to express his/her perceptions and suggestions. The purpose of the analysis is to identify major problems in the preliminary draft of the materials and procedures, such as confusing instructions; inappropriate vocabulary or graphics; problems in the sequencing, omission, or redundancy of skills; or unsuitable stimulus or response formats. Often revisions can be made and reevaluated during the analysis. If an example is unclear, other examples may be tested; if an explanation is not understood, it may be elaborated; and if the learner seems bored, confused, or distracted, the presentation format may be modified (Dick and Carey, 1978). Each tentative change is noted and its effectiveness retested on other students. The one-to-one tryout is usually performed individually on three to five learners (Thiagarajan, 1978). The focus of the study is upon learners of below-average and average ability; however, students of above-average ability may also be included to determine if some sections of the instruction can be bypassed. The program developer insures that all students participating in the program evaluation have the appropriate entry level skills. No judgment is made about what the student has learned from the program, nor about the comparative effectiveness of the material with other methods or programs. The primary concern of the evaluation is with the student's response to the methods and materials used.

Smith, Smith, and Edgar (1976) conducted a formative analysis of a shoelace-tying program for severely handicapped children. They established a minimum criterion of 90 percent and considered each lesson in the program to be acceptable only if at least 90 percent of the learner responses made during the lesson were correct. In a one-to-one analysis, data were collected for each frame of each lesson allowing the programmers to determine which specific frames produced high error rates. If the error rate exceeded the criterion, the lesson was rewritten and retested. After the first lesson was written, tested, revised, and retested, the second lesson was written and subjected to the same analysis.

Small-group tryout. A small-group tryout involves an evaluation of the instruction and assessment materials in the natural environment by the instructional personnel for whom the program has been designed. In this phase of evaluation, the programmer participates as an observer and is not involved in direct implementation of the program. At least 15 students are included in the small-group tryout in which the program is administered in the same manner that it would eventually be used by teachers, aides, and/or students in self-instruction, one-to-one tutorial, or in a small- or large-group format. If possible, a random, representative selection of the students is made, or three or four students are selected from each expected level of achievement; an attempt is made to sample at least one representative from each subgroup in the population (Dick and Carey, 1978). Two or three teachers or instructors may participate in the evaluation study. The students are given a criterion-referenced entry level test, pre-test, placement test, and post-test; also, diagnostic probes are imbedded at various points throughout the program. Each test item in all of the tests is related directly to a behavioral objective describing an entry level skill, an enabling skill, a subtask, or a terminal objective.

One of the purposes of the small-group tryout is to assess individual and group learning and error patterns that indicate points at which specific types of errors occur. Where a consistent pattern of errors occurs among various learners at particular points in the program, corrective changes can be made. A second purpose of this stage of the evaluation is to determine the administrative feasibility of the materials in the environment for which they were designed. During implementation of the program, an observer assesses the *procedural reliability* or the appropriateness with which the teachers administer the program. Also, observations are recorded of the students' responses to the instructional methods and materials. The teachers and, if possible, the students are asked to describe their experience with the program and to make suggestions for its improvement. Student and teacher attitudes may be formally assessed. The need for additional inservice teacher training is also examined.

Acquisition, generalization, and maintenance of the skills taught in the program are also assessed. In addition, the time taken for each student to complete each phase of instruction and testing is recorded for the purpose of identifying areas of difficulty and improving the efficiency of the procedures used.

Smith, Smith, and Edgar (1976) suggested that a second, more extensive phase of evaluation be performed after the program and the teacher's manual have been edited. The authors recommended that approximately 50 students should participate in the second phase of the evaluation. This phase of study yields additional information about possible teacher induced error. Smith *et al.,* also emphasize the importance of obtaining direct feedback from the teachers about any program difficulties that they had observed. Student data may fail to indicate problems in the program if the teacher is making compensatory changes in administration.

Field tryout. Field or *operational testing* involves the final validation of the total program, following the revisions made during the small-group tryout. The purpose of this phase of the evaluation is to insure that the revisions made actually do reduce teacher and student error. This is the "fine-tuning" stage of program design and evaluation. From 30 (Dick and Carey, 1978) to 50 (Smith, Smith, and Edgar, 1976) students should participate in several groups under the variety of instructional conditions for which the program has been designed. All materials, tests, and teacher's manuals are employed by instructional personnel in the field; entry level and placement tests, pre-tests, diagnostic probes, post-tests, and assessments of generalization and maintenance are included in this stage.

Data analysis. The different forms of data collected in the various phases of the formative evaluation may be plotted and analyzed in several ways. Smith, Smith, and Edgar (1976) plotted the number of instructional days individual students spent on each step of the program for which there was a criterion-referenced test. A modified form of their analysis is shown in Table 9.1.

The data in Table 9.1 indicate the number of days taken by individual students and by all of the students to complete each step in the program. Steps in which progress was relatively slow should be reexamined. Several factors may influence the time

Table 9.1

STEPS IN THE PROGRAM	Students								TOTAL
	1	2	3	4	5	6	7	8	
N									
⋮									
11	1	1	1		1	1	1	1	7
10	1	2	1		3	1	1	1	10
9	1	1	1		1	2	1	1	8
8	5	2	4		7	6	1	1	26
7	1	1	1		1	1	1	1	7
6	1	1	1	3	2	1	1	1	11
5	1	1	2	5	1	1	1	1	13
4	1	2	2	6	3	1	2	5	22
3	1	1		3	1		1	1	8
2	1	1		3	1		1	1	8
1	1	1		4	1		1	1	9

Table 9.1. *The number of days taken for each student to achieve criterion on each step of the program.*

taken to complete each step. The *conditions* under which the instruction was conducted may not have been suitable; modification may have to be made to instructional materials or directions, reinforcement, feedback, and/or the correction procedures employed. Perhaps prompts should be introduced or existing prompts should be modified, or fading procedures should be conducted in a different or more gradual manner. Possibly, the *performance* requirements at a particular step of instruction were inappropriate. There may be simpler ways to perform the task. Some of the prerequisite skills may not have been taught at previous stages of the program. Alternatively, if the prerequisite skills had been taught, they may not have been rehearsed before new instruction began; and, as a result, they may not have been performed at criterion. Maybe an alternative method of performance should be adopted, or perhaps the existing method should be task analyzed into smaller steps. The *standards* or criteria of performance may have been inappropriate. They may have been too stringent and should be modified, or perhaps shaping procedures should be employed to bring the performance to successively higher levels. There is a broad variety of different aspects of the standards that could be reevaluated and perhaps modified or replaced. Additional problems may arise from invalid test items used to evaluate achievement at each step of the program. The conditions, performance, and/or standards specified in the test item may not be congruent with those taught in the program.

A final consideration is that perhaps the skills that students were relatively slow to acquire were simply more difficult to learn than skills that were taught in other parts of the program. All of the steps in the program will not necessarily be of equal difficulty. When difficult steps are identified, teacher expectations may be adjusted accordingly, adequate opportunities for practice may be scheduled, and possibly more reinforcement could be made available to learners attempting to acquire these skills.

The results of the entry level tests may also provide information about the suitability of the instructional program to the learner population. The entry level tests are examined to determine: (a) if there were learners who did not have all of the entry level skills and who succeeded in the program, and, conversely (b) if there were learners who had all of the entry level skills but who were unsuccessful in completing all of the program. An effort is made to identify the nature of the learners in each case. This information may suggest the need for addition, deletion, or modification of skills listed as prerequisite to beginning the program. Also, new skills may be incorporated or omitted from instruction.

Martin, Murrell, Nicholson, and Tallman (1975) employed a data recording system that illustrated for each student and each skill learned: (a) at which level of prompting instruction began, (b) how long each student required each level of prompting, and (c) how long it took to reach criterion on each skill taught. Averages for each of these groups of data can be calculated for a group of learners. Martin *et al.*, used a form of the *test-teach model of instruction* described earlier in this text. No prompting is involved at level 4 of instruction. At level 3, a verbal prompt is used. A verbal prompt and a gestural prompt are used at level 2. At level 1, verbal prompts are used in conjunction with physical prompts and minimal physical guidance. Level zero is the same as level 1, except that more than minimal physical guidance is employed. Testing precedes instruction. If the learner does not respond appropriately within a 30-second interval following a verbal command (level 4), level 3 prompting is introduced. Successive levels of prompting are introduced until the learner is able to respond appropriately within a 30-second time interval. Teaching proceeds in the opposite direction as each successive level of prompting is faded during instruction until the learner is able to respond at level 4. Table 9.2 displays the performance record of a hypothetical student.

Table 9.2 shows that at step 1, trial 1, instruction began at level zero of prompting. After five consecutive correct responses, instruction shifted on trial 10 to the next level of prompting. This criterion was established by the authors following experience with a particular population. On trial 12 where the learner either failed to respond, performed the wrong response, or resisted responding, a lower level of prompting was reintroduced until five consecutive correct responses were obtained. The data on the *MIMR recording forms* may be plotted in the manner shown in Figure 9.2.

The example shown in Figure 9.2 indicates that the highest level of prompting achieved on the first day of instruction of "arms up" was level 3. On the fourth day of the first week, "arms up" was put on review over a five-day period designated with the letters A-E. Trials F-I were maintenance trials. On the first day of the fourth week of instruction, "arms up" was on maintenance, "clap" was on review, and "wave" was in the early stages of acquisition.

How long should a formative evaluation continue? Dick (1977b) reported that the U.S. military used an 80/80 criterion for the development of programmed instruction. This criterion meant that when 80 percent of the learners achieved 80 percent of the objectives, the program was considered to be ready for

Table 9.2

DATE	SESSION NO.	STEP NO.	1	2	3	4	5	6	7	8	9	10	11	12	13	14	15	16	17	18	19	20	21	22	...
															TRIALS										
Dec. 1	1	1	0	0	0	X	0	0	0	0	0	1	1	X	0	0	0	0	0	1	1	1			
Dec. 2	2	1	1	1	2	2	2	2	X	1	1	1	1	1	1	2	2	2	2	2	3	3	3	3	3
Dec. 5	3	1	4	4	4	4	4																		
		2	0	0	0	0	0	0	1	X	0	0	0	0	0	0	1	1	1	1	1	2	2		
Dec. 6	4	2	2	2	2	2	3	3	3	3	3	4	4	4	4	4									
		3	0	0	0	0	0	0	1	X	0	0	0	0	0	0	1	1	1	1	1	1			
Dec. 7	5	3																							
Dec. 8	6																								

Table 9.2. MIMR recording form showing the level of prompts used on each
trial.

Figure 9.2

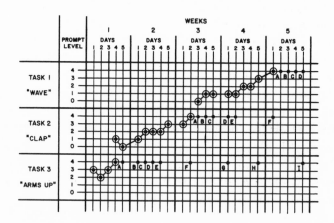

Figure 9.2.   MIMR data plot.

distribution. As Dick suggests, the criterion was arbitrary and another criterion, such as 95/100, could have been established for different types of students and tasks. According to Baker (1975), if a program must be adapted to meet the needs of subgroups of students within the learner population that differ on entry level skills, motivation, or learning styles, then the program will have to be retested until "satisfactory" performance within each subgroup is obtained. Tennyson and Tennyson (1978) state that one cannot afford to wait for empirical testing of every aspect of instructional technology; one must begin with his/her best guesses and continue to evaluate and revise materials or techniques as new information is acquired. Tennyson and Tennyson also suggest that after the release of a program for general distribution, *maintenance evaluation* should continue. Maintenance evaluation is concerned with the continuing effectiveness of instructional material following general implementation, and with the updating of goals, objectives, content, and procedures in accord with increased information and/or changing conditions.

Essentially, the decision to terminate formative evaluation and distribute a program must be based upon cost-effectiveness estimates of the alternatives that are available. Answers to the following questions must be sought. What percentage of the students receiving the program did not achieve a satisfactory criterion; how far from criterion were they? What percentage of the students did not achieve criterion with other programs that were available? What are the consequences of not fully achieving criterion? What are the time and labor costs and the potential advantages of further formative testing and improvement of the developing program? Are there other performance areas where the time and effort of program development could be spent more beneficially? Is a maintenance method of evaluation and improvement a viable option to continuing formative evaluation? The answer to these and other questions will help determine whether to terminate formative evaluation.

Summative Evaluation

A summative evaluation (or experimental control study) is

executed following the development of the final form of an instructional program. The study is conducted in the variety of environments for which the program was designed. The material is administered by regular teachers or other instructional personnel for whom the program was developed. The results of the evaluation are subjected to a rigorous statistical analysis. The number of students who participate in the study is determined by the requirements necessary to achieve statistically significant results. The number of students required is influenced by the homogeneity of the population, the number of subgroups in the study, and the type of statistical analyses that are to be used. A summative evaluation has two principal purposes: (a) to demonstrate the effectiveness of a program to train a particular group of learners to achieve specific objectives, and (b) to compare a newly developed program with alternative, existing programs. The focus of evaluation is upon the analysis of group rather than individual scores. Three types of studies may be conducted. In the first study, pre- and post-tests may be given to two groups of learners selected from the same population. These groups are *matched* on any variables that may influence the outcome of the study, such as pre-test scores, entry level skills, general aptitude, and experience with the type of materials and techniques that are to be employed. After the pre-test has been administered, one group, the *treatment group,* is administered the new program. The other group, the *control group,* is not given a program but receives an equal amount of stimulation and attention. Both groups are then given the post-test; the *gain scores* from pre-test to post-test for both groups are compared. If the new program is successful, the treatment group will have significantly greater gain scores.

A second type of summative evaluation also involves two matched groups of students. One group receives the new program, the other group receives an existing program teaching the same knowledge and skills. The gain scores achieved by these two groups are compared. If the new treatment program is more effective than the existing program, then the treatment group will have statistically greater gain scores than those obtained by the other group.

Alternatively, a summative evaluation might be conducted concurrently on three matched groups. One group would receive the new program, the second group would be given the existing program, while the third group would receive an equivalent amount of stimulation, but no instructional program. This research design produces the same results as achieved by the combination of the first two research designs previously described. Once again, the gain scores obtained by each group would be compared.

When one is comparing the results of one program to those obtained by another, there are a number of variables to examine. One obvious consideration concerns the number and type of skills taught in each program. The more component skills a task is analyzed into, the more it will appear that a learner has achieved (Williams and Gotts, 1977). Another difficulty in attempting to make a comparison is that the skills taught in different programs may also vary in terms of their relative difficulty and/or importance. Generalization and maintenance of the skills learned must also be evaluated across persons, places, instructional materials, and language cues (Williams, Brown, and Certo, 1975). These authors note that difficulty in comparison often arises when one program teaches many skills with little generalization, while another program teaches few skills with extensive generalization.

Other factors influencing the comparison are: (a) the rate and style of learning students exhibited on the programs being compared; (b) the types of learners accommodated by the program; (c) materials costs (initial and maintenance costs); (d) personnel costs (teachers, instructors, and/or aides); (e) inservice requirements; and (f) instructor satisfaction—an index of the likelihood that the program will continue to be administered in an effective manner.

The instructional program selection and evaluation checklist described on the following pages assists program consumers in the selection of suitable programs for teaching specific skills to particular learners. The checklist also functions as a guide to program developers regarding the type of information consumers require to make critical selection and use of programs. Notes explaining technical terms are provided at the end of the checklist.

An Instructional Program Selection and Evaluation Checklist

	Yes	No	N/A
1. LEARNER POPULATION CLEARLY DESCRIBED:			
a. age			
b. grade			
c. functional level (e.g., TMR; social, recreational, and/or occupational)			
d. special population (e.g., cerebral palsied)			
e. entry level skills[1]			
2. INSTRUCTIONAL MODEL:			
a. transfer-based or diagnostic-prescriptive teaching model[2]			
b. direct instruction model[3]			
c. other teaching models; specify:			
d. the structure of the program and the techniques employed are selected on the basis of:			
i. tradition			
ii. experimental determination			
iii. logic			
iv. theory			
v. other; specify			
3. INSTRUCTIONAL GOALS AND OBJECTIVES:			
a. describe the scope and sequence of the program content			
b. describe teacher instructional activities			
c. describe anticipated changes in learner's:			
i. cognitive, perceptual, or affective states or processes, or			
ii. observable, measurable behavior			
d. are congruent with the principles of normalization[4]			

	Yes	No	N/A
e. describe methods or skills that may be in conflict with other past, future, or contemporary programs of instruction			
f. Is the rationale for selecting the goals and objectives described (e.g., the functional value of the skills, or the coordination with other areas of skill development)			
g. Is the program part of a larger, coordinated curriculum			
4. INSTRUCTIONAL SEQUENCE:			
a. linear (all students follow the same instructional sequence)			
b. branching (students may follow alternate sequences)[5]			
c. special instructional aids or prompts (e.g., DISTAR alphabet) are faded from use at the end of the program			
d. amount of material presented at each step is appropriate to student's learning abilities[6]			
e. an appropriate amount of practice is provided to facilitate acquisition and maintenance while avoiding boredom and fatigue			
f. generalization of learning is adequately facilitated[7]			
g. maintenance of learning is adequately facilitated[8]			
5. TESTING:			
a. pre-test of ability to perform terminal behavioral objective			
b. entry level skills test: test of skills, prerequisite to beginning the program			
c. placement test: indicates where to start each learner in the program; facilitates homogeneous grouping			

	Yes	No	N/A
d. diagnostic tests: these tests are embedded in each lesson and indicate particular learner problems and diagnostic measures			
e. probes: assess incidental acquisition and generalization of skills; permit skipping of selected steps in the program			
f. post-tests (mastery): tests of terminal behavioral objectives			
g. generalization and maintenance tests			
6. ADMINISTRATION AND SCORING:			
a. prerequisite teacher skills are specified			
b. special training is required to administer the program			
c. the special training is readily available			
d. the program can be administered by:			
i. the learner			
ii. a teacher			
iii. a teacher's aide			
iv. a parent or volunteer			
v. other; specify			
e. if the program is learner administered, is there a systematic method to teach the child how to use the materials independently			
f. are there ways to determine the competency of instructional personnel			
g. are specific directions given for:			
i. teaching each skill or concept			
ii. correcting particular types of errors			
iii. selecting and administering reinforcement			
iv. managing behavior problems			
v. supplemental activities			
vi. enrichment exercises			

		Yes	No	N/A
h.	the program may be administered to:			
	i. individuals			
	ii. groups, if yes, specify size			
i.	new students may be incorporated after other students have begun the program			
j.	students can transfer at the end of the program to other commonly used instructional programs[9]			
k.	separate parts of the program may be selectively administered			
l.	features of the program may be used to complement other programs			
m.	special considerations are required in terms of:			
	i. space			
	ii. equipment			
	iii. scheduling			
n.	daily preparation time is considerable			
o.	the program is scheduled:			
	i. daily, specify			
	ii. weekly, specify			
	iii. other, specify			

7. INDIVIDUALIZATION:

		Yes	No	N/A
a.	the rate of progress (pacing) can be slowed or accelerated as required			
b.	program steps can be omitted by capable learners			
c.	remedial exercises are included			
d.	the instructional presentation mode can be modified			
e.	the manner of student response to materials can be adapted			
f.	directions, instructional format, materials, and the style of learner response are suitable to age, grade, sex, functional level, and diagnostic category; if no, specify			

	Yes	No	N/A
8. MOTIVATIONAL CHARACTERISTICS:			
a. there is sufficient variety in presentation and response to stimulate and hold interest and attention			
b. provides students with a high rate of success			
c. feedback, reinforcement, and remedial assistance are provided as required after each instructional unit			
9. ECONOMIC CONSIDERATIONS:			
a. there are high costs for:			
i. initial program purchase			
ii. replacement material costs			
iii. instructional aids			
b. the program is time-consuming for:			
i. teachers			
ii. learners			
c. the cost-effectiveness of the program has been demonstrated			
10. EXPERIMENTAL VALIDATION:			
a. the program has been tested in controlled studies on the population for which it was designed			
b. the experimental procedures, sample, control group, and teachers are described			
c. the reliability and validity of the tests are reported			
d. generalization and maintenance have been evaluated			
e. objective evidence is provided to document the advantages of this program over other programs			

Notes

1. Entry level skills describe the minimum, prerequisite, observable,

measurable behaviors a learner must be able to perform before beginning an instructional program. These skills should be described in terms of behavioral objectives that describe the *conditions* under which the *performance* is to be made to specified *standards*.

2. In the transfer-based or diagnostic-prescriptive teaching model, instruction focuses on cognitive or perceptual skills (for example, visual sequential memory). Improvement in these skills is expected to transfer to improvement in reading or writing. Examples: the Frostig-Horne remedial program and instructional procedures based on the Illinois Test of Psycholinguistic Abilities and the Purdue Perceptual Motor Survey.

3. In the direct instruction model, skills that the learner will ultimately be expected to employ are taught directly (for example, in a reading program, a learner would be taught to discriminate letters of the alphabet rather than geometric figures). Examples: the DISTAR programs in reading, language, and arithmetic.

4. In accord with the principles of normalization, exceptional individuals are taught in the most normative manner possible to perform under the most normative conditions in which they are capable: thus, unnecessary stigmatization and dependency are avoided while maximum self-actualization is achieved.

5. Branching programs accommodate individual differences between various learners. In a branching program, tests are incorporated at various points throughout instruction: a learner's response to these tests may indicate which instructional branch s/he should follow to receive remedial programming, to receive different styles of instruction, or to skip various parts of the program.

6. Ideally, an instructional program should be divided into "test-teach units." In each of these units, the learner is presented with a unit of information or a particular skill, following which s/he is given a test to assess his/her understanding of the knowledge or his/her ability to perform the skill. Then, depending upon the accuracy of his/her response, s/he should receive appropriate remedial instruction, feedback, and reinforcement. The appropriate size of each test-teach unit is determined by the capability of the learner: more capable students can manage larger units of instruction.

7. Generalization, or transfer of learning, is one of the major problems associated with instruction. Generalization refers to the ability of a learner to apply a skill learned in one situation to another situation, which although different in many respects, possesses the same essential characteristics. Generalization is facilitated by changing the non-essential features of instruction after initial learning has become well established under one set of conditions. Changes in non-essential features may be introduced, for example, by changing the time or place of instruction, the teacher, and/or the directions used. These changes must, of course, be made in a

progressive and systematic manner to insure that the learner's newly-acquired skills are maintained in spite of the changes made in the non-essential features of the instruction.

8. Like generalization, maintenance of learning is a basic concern in all types of instruction. Maintenance of learning refers to the ability of a learner to recall information or perform a skill some time after it was initially learned. Maintenance of learning is facilitated through the use of massed and distributed practice. Massed practice gives a learner frequent opportunities to practice a new response in a short period of time, and facilitates rapid acquisition of that response. Distributed practice, giving successively fewer opportunities to practice (review) a newly-acquired response after successively longer periods of time, facilitates maintenance of the response.

9. Some instructional programs introduce prompts (instructional aids), such as a modified alphabet, to assist learning. If these aids are not progressively and systematically faded from use, a learner may experience undue difficulty when introduced to programs that do not employ the same aids.

Review of Concepts and Procedures
Covered in Chapter Nine

Review the following concepts and procedures discussed in Chapter Nine. Use a paper and pencil as applicable: (1) define or explain; (2) provide a novel example; (3) describe where, when, and how to apply or evaluate; and (4) discuss advantages and disadvantages of each term. As a term is being reviewed, cover all of the other terms to avoid giving yourself clues. If you are unable to recall the information *rapidly* and *accurately*, refer to the listed page number(s) and review the material; page numbers with major references have been underlined. Note troublesome terms and put them into a maintenance schedule for repeated review after successively longer periods of time.

Subject   Page No.

References

Abramson, T., and Kagan, E. Familiarization of content and differential response modes in programmed instruction. *Journal of Educational Psychology,* 1975, *67,* 83-88.

Adelson, E., and Fraiberg, S. Gross motor development in infants blind from birth. *Child Development,* 1974, *45,* 114-126.

Alberto, P.A., and Schofield, P.A. An instructional interaction pattern for the severely handicapped. *Teaching Exceptional Children,* 1979, *12,* 16-19.

Allyon, T. Intensive treatment of psychotic behavior by stimulus satiation and food reinforcement. *Behavior Research and Therapy,* 1963, *1,* 53-61.

Anderson, R.C., and Faust, G. *Educational psychology: The science of instruction and learning.* New York: Dodd, Mead & Co., 1974.

Baer, D.M., and Wolf, M.M. The entry into natural communities of reinforcement. In R. Ulrich, T. Stachnik, and J. Mabry (Eds.), *Control of human behavior: Volume II.* Glenview, Ill.: Scott, Foresman & Co., 1970.

Baine, D. An instructional program selection checklist. *Teaching Atypical Students in Alberta,* 1979, *8,* 23-26.

Baker, E.L. Generalizability of rules for an empirical revision. *AV Communication Review,* 1970, *18,* 300-305.

Baker, E.L. Formative evaluation of instruction. In W.J. Popham (Ed.), *Educational evaluation.* Englewood Cliffs, N.J.: Prentice-Hall, Inc., 1975.

Bandura, A. Vicarious processes: A case of no-trial learning. In L. Berkowitz (Ed.), *Advances in experimental social psychology,* Vol. 2. New York: Academic Press, 1965.

Becker, J.A., Rosner, S.R., and Nelson, K. Stimulus mode and concept formation in preschool children. *Developmental Psychology,* 1979, *15*(2), 218-220.

Becker, W.C., Engelmann, S., and Thomas, D.R. *Teaching: A course in applied psychology.* Toronto: Science Research Associates, 1971.

Becker, W.C., Engelmann, S., and Thomas, D.R. *Teaching 1: Classroom management.* Toronto: Science Research Associates, 1975(a).

Becker, W.C., Engelmann, S., and Thomas, D.R. *Teaching 2: Cognitive learning and instruction.* Chicago: Science Research Associates, 1975(b).

Bereiter, C., and Engelmann, S. *Teaching disadvantaged children in the preschool.* Englewood Cliffs, N.J.: Prentice-Hall, Inc., 1966.

Berlyne, D.E. Attention as a problem in behavior. In D.I. Mostofsky (Ed.), *Attention: Contemporary theory and analysis.* New York: Appleton-Century-Crofts, 1970.

Bigge, J.L., and O'Donnell, P.A. *Teaching individuals with physical and multiple disabilities.* Columbus: Charles E. Merrill Publishing Co., 1976.

Bilsky, L., and Heal, L.W. Cue novelty and training level in the discrimination shift performance of retardates. *Journal of Experimental Child Psychology,* 1969, *8,* 503-511.

Blake, K. *The mentally retarded: An educational psychology.* Englewood Cliffs, N.J.: Prentice-Hall, Inc., 1976.

Bloom, B.S., Engelhart, M.D., Furst, E.J., Hill, W.H., and Krathwohl, D.R. *Taxonomy of educational objectives: The classification of educational goals: Handbook I: Cognitive domain.* New York: Longman, Inc., 1956.

Bourne, L.E. Knowing and using concepts. *Psychological Review,* 1970, *77,* 546-556.

Bourne, L.E., Dodd, D., Guy, D.E., and Justesen, D.R. Response-contingent intertrial intervals in concept identification. *Journal of Experimental Psychology,* 1968, *76,* 601-608.

Bourne, L.E., and Dominowski, R.L. Thinking. *Annual Review of Psychology,* 1972, *23,* 105-130.

Bourne, L.E., Ekstrand, B.R., and Dominowski, R.L. *The psychology of thinking.* Englewood Cliffs, N.J.: Prentice-Hall, Inc., 1971.

Bourne, L.E., and Guy, D.E. Learning conceptual rules II: The role of positive and negative instances. *Journal of Experimental Psychology,* 1968, *77,* 488-494.

Bourne, L.E., and Jennings, P.C. The relationship between contiguity and classification learning. *Journal of General Psychology,* 1963, *69,* 335-338.

Bourne, L.E., and O'Banion, K. Conceptual rule learning and chronological age. *Developmental Psychology,* 1971, *5,* 525-534.

Brown, A.L. The role of strategic behavior in retardate memory. In N.R. Ellis (Ed.), *International review of research in mental retardation,* Vol. 7. New York: Academic Press, 1975.

Brown, A.L., and Scott, M.S. Recognition memory for pictures in preschool children. *Journal of Experimental Child Psychology,* 1971, *11,* 401-412.

Brown, L. Instructional programs for trainable-level retarded students. In L. Mann and D. Sabatino (Eds.), *The first review of special education,* Vol. 2. Philadelphia: Journal of Special Education Press, 1973.

Brown, L. *et al. The design and implementation of an empirically based instructional program for young severely handicapped students: Toward the rejection of the exclusion principle, Part 3.* Madison, Wis.: Madison Public Schools, 1973(a) (ERIC Document Reproduction Service No. ED 100 100).

Bruner, J.S., Goodnow, J.J., and Austin, G.A. *A study of thinking.* New York: John Wiley and Sons, Inc., 1956.

Carnine, D.W. Discriminating stimuli that appear between two discriminating stimuli along a numerosity continuum from stimuli that appear beyond one of the discriminative stimuli. An unpublished paper received from the author. Eugene, Oregon: University of Oregon, 1975(a).

Carnine, D.W. Emphasizer effects on children's and adults' acquisition rate and transfer scores on simple and complex tasks. An unpublished paper received from the author. Eugene, Oregon: University of Oregon, 1975(b).

Carnine, D.W. Correction effects on academic performance during small-group instruction. An unpublished paper received from the author. Eugene, Oregon: University of Oregon, 1975(c).

Carnine, D.W. Effects of two teacher-presentation rates on off-task behavior, answering correctly, and participation. *Journal of Applied Behavior Analysis*, 1976(a), *9*, 199-206.

Carnine, D.W. Similar sound separation and cumulative introduction in learning letter-sound correspondences. *Journal of Educational Research,* 1976(b), *69,* 368-372.

Carnine, D.W. Direct instruction—DISTAR. In N.G. Haring and B. Bateman (Eds.), *Teaching the learning disabled child.* Englewood Cliffs, N.J.: Prentice-Hall, Inc., 1977.

Carnine, D.W. Direct instruction: A successful system for educationally high-risk children. *Journal of Curriculum Studies,* 1979, *11*(1), 29-45.

Carnine, D., and Fink, W. Increasing the rate of presentation and use of signals in elementary classroom teachers. *Journal of Applied Behavior Analysis,* 1978, *11,* 35-46.

Carnine, D., and Silbert, J. *Direct instruction reading.* Unpublished manuscript. Eugene, Oregon: University of Oregon, 1975.

Caron, A.J. Conceptual transfer in preverbal children as a consequence of dimensional training. *Journal of Experimental Child Psychology,* 1968, *6,* 522-542.

Caron, A.J. Discrimination shifts in three-year-olds as a function of dimensional salience. *Developmental Psychology,* 1969, *1,* 333-339.

Certo, N., Schwartz, R., and Brown, L. Community transportation: Teaching severely handicapped students to ride a public bus system. In N.G. Haring and L.J. Brown (Eds.), *Teaching the severely handicapped.* New York: Grune and Stratton, 1977.

Cheyne, W.M. Vanishing cues in paired-associate learning. *British Journal of Psychology,* 1966, *57,* 351-359.

Clark, D.C. Teaching concepts in the classroom: A set of teaching prescriptions derived from experimental research. *Journal of Educational Psychology,* 1971, *62,* 253-278.

Clark, H., Boyd, S., and Macrae, J. A classroom program teaching disadvantaged youths to write biographical information. *Journal of Applied Behavior Analysis*, 1975, *8*, 67-76.

Clymer, T. The utility of phonic generalizations. *Reading Teacher,* 1963, *16*(4), 252-258.

Cole, R.E., Dent, H.E., Eguchi, P.E., Fujii, K.K., and Johnson, R.C. Transposition with minimum errors during training trials. *Journal of Experimental Child Psychology*, 1964, *1*, 355-359.

Conway, J.B., and Bucher, B.D. Transfer and maintenance of behavior change in children: A review and suggestions. In E.J. Mash, L.A. Hamerlynck, and L.C. Handy (Eds.), *Behavior modification and families.* New York: Brunner/Mazel, 1974.

Cooke, S., Cooke, T.P., and Apolloni, T. Generalization of language training with the mentally retarded. *The Journal of Special Education*, 1976, *10*, 299-303.

Cuvo, A., Leaf, R., and Borakove, L. Teaching janitorial skills to the mentally retarded: Acquisition, generalization, and maintenance. *Journal of Applied Behavior Analysis*, 1978, *11*, 345-355.

Davies, I.K. *Competency-based learning: Technology, management, and design.* New York: McGraw-Hill Book Co., 1973.

DeCecco, J.P. *The psychology of learning and instruction.* Englewood Cliffs, N.J.: Prentice-Hall, Inc., 1974.

DeGraaf, C.A. *Teaching action concept usage to institutionalized retardates with systematic instructions and still pictorial illustrations.* Unpublished doctoral dissertation, Southern Illinois University, 1972.

Denny, M.R. Research in learning and performance. In H.A. Stevens and R. Heber (Ed.), *Mental retardation.* Chicago: University of Chicago Press, 1964.

Devore, G.M., and Stern, C. Real objects versus pictures in the instruction of young children. *Journal of School Psychology*, 1970, *8*, 77-81.

Dick, W. Summative evaluation. In L.J. Briggs (Ed.), *Instructional design.* Englewood Cliffs, N.J.: Educational Technology Publications, 1977(a).

Dick, W. Formative evaluation. In L.J. Briggs (Ed.), *Instructional design.* Englewood Cliffs, N.J.: Educational Technology Publications, 1977(b).

Dick, W., and Carey, L. *The systematic design of instruction.* Glenview, Ill.: Scott, Foresman & Co., 1978.

Dickerson, D.J. Effects of naming relevant and irrelevant stimuli on the discrimination learning of children. *Child Development,* 1970, *41,* 639-650.

Dueck, K.G. Mathemagenic mechanisms in inductive learning. *Canadian Journal of Behavioral Science,* 1976, *8*(1), 78-87.

Durling, R., and Schick, C. Concept attainment by pairs and individuals as a function of vocalization. *Journal of Educational Psychology,* 1976, *68,* 83-91.

Dykman, R., Ackerman, P., Clements, S., and Peters, J. Specific learning disabilities: An attentional deficit syndrome. In H. Myklebust (Ed.), *Progress in learning disabilities,* Vol. II. New York: Grune and Stratton, 1971.

Egeland, B. Effects of errorless training on teaching children to discriminate letters of the alphabet. *Journal of Applied Psychology,* 1975, *60,* 533-536.

Engelmann, S. Information cited was obtained from an untitled manuscript received at a Direct Instruction Workshop held at the University of Oregon, Eugene, Oregon, August, 1978.

Engelmann, S., and Bruner, E. *DISTAR Reading, Level I.* Chicago: Science Research Associates, 1969.

Engelmann, S., and Bruner, E. *DISTAR Reading, Level I. Revised.* Chicago: Science Research Associates, 1974.

Engelmann, S., and Carnine, D. *DISTAR Arithmetic I, Second Edition.* Chicago: Science Research Associates, 1975.

Engelmann, S., and Osborne, J. *DISTAR Language 1, Second Edition.* Chicago: Science Research Associates, 1976.

Etaugh, C.F., and Averill, B.E. Effects of type and source of labels on children's perceptual judgments and discrimination learning. *Child Development,* 1971, *42,* 1619-1623.

Ferster, C.B. Clinical reinforcement. *Seminar in Psychiatry,* 1972, *4,* 101-111.

Fink, W.T. *Effects of a pre-correction procedure on the decoding errors of two low-performing first grade girls.* Unpublished manuscript. Eugene, Oregon: University of Oregon, 1976.

Fisher, M.A., and Zeaman, D. An attention-retention theory of retardate discrimination learning. In N.R. Ellis (Ed.), *The international review of research in mental retardation, 6.* New York: Academic Press, 1973.

Foxx, R.M., and Azrin, N.H. Restitution: A method of eliminating aggressive-disruptive behavior of retarded and brain damaged patients. *Behavior Research and Therapy,* 1972, *10,* 15-27.

Frase, L., and Schwartz, B. Effect of question production and answering on prose recall. *Journal of Educational Psychology,* 1975, *67,* 628-635.

Frayer, D.A. *Effects of number of instances and emphasis of relevant attribute values on mastery of fourth and sixth grade children.* Madison, Wis.: Research and Development Center for Cognitive Learning. Technical Report #16, 1970.

French, J.E. Children's preferences for pictures of varied complexity of pictorial pattern. *Elementary School Journal,* 1952, *91.*

Gagné, R.M. *The conditions of learning, third edition.* New York: Holt, Rinehart & Winston, 1977.

Gagné, R.M., and Briggs, L.J. *Principles of instructional design.* New York: Holt, Rinehart & Winston, 1974.

Garcia, E.E. The training and generalization of conversational speech form in nonverbal retarded. *Journal of Applied Behavior Analysis,* 1974, *7,* 137-149.

Garcia, E.E., and DeHaven, E.D. Use of operant techniques in the establishment and generalization of language: A review and analysis. *American Journal of Mental Deficiency,* 1974, *79,* 169-178.

Gholson, B., and McConville, K. Effects of stimulus differentiation training upon hypotheses, strategies, and stereotypes in discrimination learning among kindergarten children. *Journal of Experimental Psychology,* 1974, *18,* 81-97.

Gibson, E.J. *Principles of perceptual learning and development.* New York: Appleton-Century-Crofts, 1969.

Gibson, E.J., Osser, H., and Pick, A.D. A study in the development of grapheme-phoneme correspondence. *Journal of Verbal Learning & Verbal Behavior,* 1963, *2,* 142-146.

Gold, M.W. Stimulus factors in skill training of the mentally retarded on a complex assembly task: Acquisition, transfer, and retention. *American Journal of Mental Deficiency,* 1972, *76,* 517-526.

Gold, M.W., and Barclay, C. The effects of verbal labels on the acquisition and retention of a complex assembly task. *The Training School Bulletin,* 1973, *70,* 38-42.

Granzin, A.C. Child performance on discrimination tasks: Effects of amount of stimulus variation. *Journal of Experimental Child Psychology,* 1972, *24,* 332-342.

Granzin, A.C., and Carnine, D.W. Child performance on discrimination tasks: Effects of amount of stimulus generalization. *Journal of Experimental Child Psychology,* 1977, *24,* 332-342.

Greer, J.G., Anderson, R.M., and Davis, T.B. Developing functional language in the severely retarded using a standardized vocabulary. *Educating the severely and profoundly retarded.* Baltimore: University Park Press, 1976.

Griffiths, H., and Craighead, W.E. Generalization in operant speech therapy for misarticulation. *Journal of Speech and Hearing Disorders,* 1972, *37,* 485-494.

Handleman, J.S. Generalization of autistic-type children of verbal responses across settings. *Journal of Applied Behavior Analysis,* 1979, *12,* 273-282.

Haring, N.G. *Field initiated research study: An investigation of phases of learning and facilitating instructional events for the severely handicapped, annual progress report, 1977-1978.* Seattle: College of Education, University of Washington.

Harrow, A.J. *A taxonomy of the psychomotor domain.* New York: Longman, Inc., 1972.

Hillyard, A.L. *Stimulus complexity during original learning and generalization.* Unpublished doctoral dissertation, University of Alberta, Edmonton, Alberta, 1979.

Hofmeister, A.M., and Gallery, M. *Training for independence: A program for teaching the independent use of zippers, buttons, shoes, and socks.* Niles, Illinois: Developmental Learning Materials, 1977.

Hughson, E.A., and Brown, R.I. III—A bus training program for mentally retarded adults. *British Journal of Mental Subnormality,* 1975, *21,* 79-83.

Hull, M.E., Barry, O.J., and Clark, D.L. *Procedures for teaching vocational concepts to special needs students: Final report.* Austin, Texas: Texas A and M University, College Station,

1976 (ERIC Document Reproduction Service No. ED 133 599).

Hurley, O. Learning concepts: Positive to negative instances. *Journal of Research and Development in Education,* 1973, *6,* Monograph Supplement, 131-137.

Hurley, O. Learning concepts: Ratio of positive to negative instances. *Journal of Research and Development in Education,* 1975, *8,* 62-63.

Iscoe, I., and Semler, I.J. Paired-associated learning in normal and mentally retarded children as a function of four experimental conditions. *Journal of Comparative and Physiological Psychology,* 1964, *57,* 387-392.

Johnson, S.M. Self-reinforcement versus external reinforcement in behavior modification with children. *Developmental Psychology,* 1970, *3,* 147-148.

Johnson, S.M., and Martin, S. Developing self-evaluation as a conditioned reinforcer. In B. Ashem and E.G. Poser (Eds.), *Behavior modification with children.* New York: Pergamon, 1973, 69-78.

Kandaswamy, S. *Learner verification and revision.* Unpublished doctoral dissertation, Indiana University, 1976.

Kazdin, A. *Behavior modification in applied settings.* Homewood, Ill.: The Dorsey Press, 1975.

Kennedy, J.M. *A psychology of picture perception: Images and information.* San Francisco: Jossey-Bass, 1974.

Klausmeier, H.J., Ghatala, E.S., and Frayer, D.A. *Conceptual learning and development.* New York: Academic Press, 1974.

Komoski, K.P. An imbalance of product quantity and instructional quality: The imperative of empiricism. *AV Communication Review,* 1974, *22,* 357-386.

Krathwohl, D.R., Bloom, B.S., and Masia, B.B. *Taxonomy of educational objectives: The classification of educational goals: Handbook II: Affective domain.* New York: Longman, Inc., 1964.

Kraynak, A., and Raskin, L. The influence of age and stimulus dimensionality on form perception by preschool children. *Developmental Psychology,* 1971, *4,* 389-393.

Kysela, G.M., Daly, K., Hillyard, A., McDonald, L., Butt, B., Ahlsten, J., McDonald, S., and Smith, N. *The early education project: I.* Centre for the Study of Mental Retardation, University of Alberta, Edmonton, Alberta, 1976.

Langone, J., and Westling, D.L. Generalization of prevocational and vocational skills: Some practical tactics. *Education and Training of the Mentally Retarded,* 1979, *14,* 216-221.

Levy, S.M., Pomerantz, D.J., and Gold, M.W. Work skills development. In N.G. Haring and L.J. Brown (Eds.), *Teaching the severely handicapped,* Vol. II. New York: Grune and Stratton, 1977.

Lewis, A. Concept formation. *Education,* 1970, *70,* 270-273.

Litrownik, A.J., Franzini, L.R., and Turner, G.L. Acquisition of concepts by TMR children as a function of type of modeling, rule verbalization, and observer gender. *American Journal of Mental Deficiency,* 1976, *80,* 620-628.

Lovaas, O.I., Koegel, R., Simmons, J.Q., and Long, J.S. Some generalization and follow-up measures on autistic children in behavior therapy. *Journal of Applied Behavior Analysis,* 1973, *6,* 131-166.

Lovaas, O.I., Schreibman, L., Koegel, R., and Rehm, R. Selective responding by autistic children to multiple sensory input. *Journal of Abnormal Psychology,* 1971, *77,* 211-222.

Lubker, B.J. Irrelevant stimulus dimensions and children's performance on simultaneous discrimination problems. *Child Development,* 1967, *38,* 119-125.

Lubker, B.J. The role of between and within setting irrelevant dimensions in children's simultaneous discrimination learning. *Child Development,* 1969, *40,* 957-964.

Lupei, J.D. Riding a public bus. In D.R. Anderson, G.D. Hodson, and W.G. Jones (Eds.), *Instructional programming for the handicapped student.* Springfield, Ill.: Charles C. Thomas Publisher, 1975.

Madsen, C.H., Becker, W.C., Thomas, D.R., Koser, L., and Plager, E. An analysis of the reinforcement function of "sit down" commands. In R.K. Parker (Ed.), *Readings in Educational Psychology.* Boston: Allyn and Bacon, 1968.

Markle, S.M., and Tiemann, P.W. *Really understanding concepts.* Champaign, Ill.: Stipes, 1969.

Marks, M.R., and Raymond, C.K. A new technique for observing concept evocation. *Journal of Experimental Psychology*, 1951, *42*, 424-429.

Martin, G., Murrell, M., Nicholson, C., and Tallman, B. *Teaching basic skills to the severely and profoundly retarded: The MIMR basic behavior test curriculum guide programming strategy.* Portage La Prairie, Manitoba: Manitoba Institute on Mental Retardation, 1975.

Martin, G., and Pear, J. *Behavior modification: What it is and how to do it.* Englewood Cliffs, N.J.: Prentice-Hall, Inc., 1978.

McCandless, B.R. *Children: Behavior and development.* Hinsdale, Ill.: Dryden, 1967.

McCormack, J. *et al. Systematic instruction of the severely handicapped: Teaching sequences.* Medford, Mass.: Massachusetts Center for Program Development and Evaluation, 1976 (ERIC Document Reproduction Service No. ED 126 667).

McCormick, L.P., and Elder, P.S. Instructional strategies for severely language deficient children. *Education and Training of the Mentally Retarded,* 1978, *13,* 29-36.

McDaniels, G.L. The evaluation of Follow Through. *Educational Researcher,* 1975, *4*(11), 7-11.

Melton, A., and Irwin, J. The influence of degree of interpolated learning on retroactive inhibition and the overt transfer of specific responses. *American Journal of Psychology,* 1940, *53,* 173-203.

Mercer, C., and Snell, M. *Learning theory research in mental retardation: Implications for teaching.* Columbus: Charles E. Merrill Publishing Co., 1977.

Merrill, M., and Tennyson, R. *Teaching concepts: An instructional design guide.* Englewood Cliffs, N.J.: Educational Technology Publications, 1977.

Miller, W.A. What children see in pictures. *Elementary School Journal,* 1938, *39,* 280-288.

Modigliani, V. On the conservation of simple concepts: Generality of the affirmation rule. *Journal of Experimental Psychology,* 1971, *87,* 234-240.

Murdock, J.Y., Garcia, E.E., and Hardman, M.L. Generalizing articulation training with trainable mentally retarded subjects. *Journal of Applied Behavior Analysis,* 1977, *10,* 717-733.

Nathanson, M.B., and Henderson, E.S. *Developmental testing really works.* Paper presented at the 16th Annual Conference on the National Society of Performance and Instruction, Chicago, April, 1976.

Neef, N.A., Iwata, B.A., and Page, T.J. Public transportation training: In vivo versus classroom instruction. *Journal of Applied Behavior Analysis,* 1978, *11,* 331-344.

Noonan, J.R., and Barry, J.R. Performance of retarded children. *Science,* 1967, *156,* p. 171.

O'Connor, N., and Hermelin, B. Recognition of shapes by normal and subnormal children. *British Journal of Psychology,* 1961, *52,* 281-284.

O'Malley, J.M. Stimulus dimension pretraining and set size in learning multiple discriminations with letters of the alphabet. *Journal of Educational Research,* 1973, *67,* 41-45.

Page, T.J., Iwata, B.A., and Neef, N.A. Teaching pedestrians skills to retarded persons: Generalization from the classroom to the natural environment. *Journal of Applied Behavior Analysis,* 1976, *9,* 433-444.

Paivio, A. *Imagery and verbal processes.* New York: Holt, Rinehart & Winston, 1971.

Panyan, M., and Hall, R. Effects of serial versus concurrent task sequencing on acquisition, maintenance, and generalization. *Journal of Applied Behavior Analysis,* 1978, *11,* 67-74.

Parton, D.A. Learning to imitate in infancy. *Child Development,* 1976, *47,* 14-31.

Pflieger, J.L., Stolovitch, H.D., and Bordeleau, P. *Preenquete sur le materiel educatif audio-visuel utilise dans les ecoles du Quebec.* Unpublished manuscript. Universite de Montreal, 1977.

Popp, H.M. Visual discrimination of alphabet letters. *The Reading Teacher,* 1964, *17,* 221-225.

Premack, D. Toward empirical behavior laws: I. Positive reinforcement. *Psychological Review,* 1959, *66,* 219-233.

Reese, H.W., and Lipsitt, L.P. *Experimental child psychology.* New York: Academic Press, 1970.

Reichard, C.L., Reid, W.R., Whorten, J.E., and Reid, B.A. Evaluative procedures for instructional materials. *Academic Therapy*, 1970, *6*, 171-175.

Risley, T.R., and Reynolds, N.J. Emphasis as a prompt for verbal imitation. *Journal of Applied Behavior Analysis*, 1970, *3*, 185-190.

Rosen, M.J. *An experimental design for comparing the effects of instructional media programming procedures: Subjective versus objective procedures. Final report.* Palo Alto: American Institutes for Research, 1968.

Rosenthal, T.D., Alford, G.S., and Rasp, L.M. Concept attainment, generalization, and retention through observation and verbal coding. *Journal of Experimental Child Psychology, 13*, 183-194.

Rosenthal, T.D., and Kellogg, J.S. Demonstration versus instructions in concept attainment by mental retardates. *Behavior Research and Therapy*, 1973, *11*, 299-302.

Ross, A.O. *Psychological aspects of learning disabilities and reading disorders.* New York: McGraw-Hill, 1975.

Rowe, E.J. Discrimination learning of pictures and words: A replication of picture superiority. *Journal of Experimental Child Psychology*, 1972, *14*, 323-328.

Schreibman, L. Effects of within-stimulus and extra-stimulus prompting on discrimination learning in autistic children. *Journal of Applied Behavior Analysis*, 1975, *8*, 91-112.

Schworm, R.W., and Abelseth, J.L. Teaching the individual with severe learning problems: Strategies which point to success. *Education and Training of the Mentally Retarded*, 1978, *13*, 146-153.

Seymour, F.W., and Stokes, T.F. Self-recording in training girls to increase work and evoke staff praise in an institution for offenders. *Journal of Applied Behavior Analysis*, 1976, *9*, 41-54.

Siegel, M. Teacher behaviors and curriculum packages: Implications for research and teacher education. In L.J. Rubin (Ed.), *Handbook of curriculum.* Boston: Allyn and Bacon, 1976.

Siegler, R.S., and Liebert, R.M. Effects of presenting relevant rules and complete feedback on the conservation of a liquid quantity task. *Developmental Psychology,* 1973, *7,* 133-138.

Skinner, B.F., and Krakower, S.A. *Handwriting with write and see.* Chicago: Lyons and Carnahan, 1968.

Smith, D., Smith, J., and Edgar, E. A prototypic model for developing instructional materials for the severely handicapped. In N.G. Haring and L.J. Brown (Eds.), *Teaching the severely handicapped.* New York: Grune and Stratton, 1976.

Smith, R.M., and Neisworth, J.T. *The exceptional child: A functional approach.* New York: McGraw-Hill, 1975.

Snell, M.E. *Systematic instruction of the moderately and severely handicapped.* Columbus: Charles E. Merrill Publishing Co., 1978.

Stainback, S., Healy, H., Stainback, W., and Healy, J. Teaching basic eating skills. *American Association for Severe and Profound Handicap Review,* 1976, *1*(7), 26-35.

Stephens, W.A., and Ludy, I.E. Action-concept learning in retarded children using photographic slides, motion picture sequences, and live demonstration. *American Journal of Mental Deficiency,* 1975, *80,* 277-280.

Stevenson, H.W. *Children's learning.* New York: Appleton-Century-Crofts, 1972.

Stokes, T.F., and Baer, D.M. An implicit technology of generalization. *Journal of Applied Behavior Analysis,* 1977, *10,* 349-367.

Stokes, T.F., Baer, D.M., and Jackson, R.L. Programming the generalization of a greeting response in four retarded children. *Journal of Applied Behavior Analysis,* 1974, *7,* 599-610.

Stolovitch, H.D. The intermediate technology of learner verification and revision (LVR). *Educational Technology,* 1978, *18,* 13-15.

Striefel, S., and Wetherby, B. Instruction following behavior of a retarded child and its controlling stimuli. *Journal of Applied Behavior Analysis,* 1973, *6,* 663-670.

Sulzen, R.H. *The effects of empirical revision and the presentation of specific objectives to learners prior to programmed instruction upon the criterion behavior of military subjects.* Unpublished doctoral dissertation, University of California, Los Angeles, 1972.

Sulzer-Azaroff, B., and Mayer, G.R. *Applying behavior analysis procedures with children and youth.* Toronto: Holt, Rinehart & Winston, 1977.

Swanson, H.L. Response strategies and stimulus salience with learning disabled and mentally retarded children on a short-term memory task. *Journal of Learning Disabilities,* 1977, *10,* 635-642.

Swanson, H.L., and Watson, B. Dimensional salience and short-term memory recognition in mentally retarded children. *Perception and Motor Skills,* 1976, *42,* 1163-1166.

Swanson, J.E. *The effects of number of positive and negative instances, concept definition, and emphasis of relevant attributes on the attainment of environmental concepts by sixth grade children.* Madison, Wis.: Research and Development Center for Cognitive Learning, Technical Report #244, 1972.

Tawney, J.W., and Hipsher, L.W. *Systematic instruction for retarded children: The Illinois program. Part II, Systematic Language Instruction.* Danville, Ill.: Interstate Printers, 1972.

Tennyson, C.L., and Tennyson, R.D. Evaluation in curriculum development. *Educational Technology,* 1978, *18,* 52-55.

Tennyson, R.D. Pictorial support and specific instructions as design variables for children's concept and rule learning. *Educational Communication and Technology,* 1978, *26,* 291-299.

Tennyson, R.D., and Boutwell, R.C. Methodology for defining instance difficulty in concept teaching. *Educational Technology,* 1974, *14,* 19-24.

Tennyson, R.D., and Rothen, W. Pretask and on-task adaptive design strategies for selecting number of instances in concept acquisition. *Journal of Educational Psychology,* 1977, *69,* 586-592.

Tennyson, R.D., Woolley, F.R., and Merrill, M.D. Exemplar and nonexemplar variables which produce correct concept classification errors. *Journal of Educational Psychology,* 1972, *63,* 144-152.

Terrace, H.S. Discriminative learning with and without errors. *Journal of Experimental Analysis of Behavior,* 1963, *6,* 1-27.

Thiagarajan, S. Instructional product verification and revision. *Educational Communication and Technology Journal,* 1978, *26,* 133-141.

Thomas, C., Sulzer-Azaroff, B., Lukeris, S., and Palmer, M. Teaching daily self-help skills for long-term maintenance. In B. Etzel, J. LeBlanc, and D. Baer (Eds.), *New developments in behavioral research: Theory, method, and application.* Hillsdale, N.J.: Erlbaum, 1976.

Tighe, T.J., and Tighe, L.S. Facilitation of transposition and reversal learning in children by prior perceptual training. *Journal of Experimental Child Psychology,* 1969, *8,* 366-374.

Travers, R.M.W. *A study of the advantages and disadvantages of using simplified visual presentations in instructional materials.* Final report on grant no. OEG-1-7-070144-5235, U.S. Office of Education, 1969.

Travers, R.M.W. *Essentials of learning: Fourth edition.* New York: Macmillan, 1977.

Travers, R.M.W., and Alvarado, V. The design of pictures for children in elementary school. *AV Communication Review,* 1970, *18,* 47-64.

Travers, R.M.W., McCormick, M.C., Van Mondfrans, A.P., and Williams, F.E. *Research and theory related to audio-visual information transmission.* Salt Lake City: University of Utah, Bureau of Educational Research, 1964.

Tucker, D.J., and Berry, G.W. Teaching severely multihandicapped students to put on their own hearing aids. *Journal of Applied Behavior Analysis,* 1980, *13,* 65-75.

Turrisi, F.D., and Shepp, B.E. Some effects of novelty and over-learning on the reversal learning of retardates. *Journal of Experimental Child Psychology,* 1969, *8,* 389-401.

Twardosz, S., and Baer, D. Training two severely retarded adolescents to ask questions. *Journal of Applied Behavior Analysis,* 1973, *6,* 655-661.

Underwood, B.J. Interference and forgetting. *Psychological Review,* 1957, *64,* 49-60.

Vargas, J.S. *Behavioral psychology for teachers.* New York: Harper and Row, 1977.

Walker, H.M., and Buckley, N.K. Programming generalization and maintenance of treatment effects across time and across settings. *Journal of Applied Behavior Analysis,* 1972, *5,* 209-224.

Walls, R.J., Ellis, W.D., Zane, T., and Vanderpoel, S.J. Tactile, auditory, and visual prompting in teaching complex assembly tasks. *Education and Training of the Mentally Retarded,* 1979, *14,* 120-129.

Wang, M.C. *Diagnostic tests for the quantification curriculum, units 1-8.* Pittsburgh: Learning Research and Development Center, University of Pittsburgh, 1973.

Warren, S.F. A useful ecobehavioral perspective for applied behavior analysis. In A. Rogers-Warren and S.F. Warren (Eds.), *Ecological perspectives in behavior analysis.* Baltimore: University Park Press, 1977.

Webster's third new international dictionary. Springfield, Mass.: Merriam, 1964.

Wehman, P. Vocational training of the severely retarded: Expectations and potential. In O. Karen, P. Wehman, A. Renzaglis, and R. Schutz (Eds.), *Habilitation practices with the severely developmentally disabled,* Vol. 1. Madison, Wis.: University of Wisconsin, 1976.

Wehman, P., Abramson, M., and Norman, C. Transfer of training in behavior modification programs: An evaluative review. *The Journal of Special Education,* 1977, *11,* 217-231.

Westling, D.L., and Koorland, M.K. Some considerations and tactics for improving discrimination learning. *Teaching Exceptional Children,* 1979, *11,* 97-100.

Wilhelm, H., and Lovaas, O.I. Stimulus overselectivity: A common feature in autism and mental retardation. *American Journal of Mental Deficiency,* 1976, *81,* 26-31.

Williams, W. Procedures of task analysis as related to developing instructional programs for the severely handicapped. In L. Brown, T. Crowner, W. Williams, and R. York (Eds.), *Madison's alternative for zero exclusion: A book of readings.* Madison, Wis.: University of Wisconsin, 1975.

Williams, W., Brown, L., and Certo, N. Basic components of

instructional programs. *Theory into Practice,* 1975, *14(2),* 123-136.

Williams, W., Coyne, P., DeSpain, C., Johnson, F., Scheverman, N., Stengert, J., Swetlik, B., and York, B. Teaching math skills using longitudinal sequences. In M.E. Snell (Ed.), *Systematic instruction of the moderately and severely handicapped.* Columbus: Charles E. Merrill Publishing Co., 1978.

Williams, W., and Gotts, E. Selected considerations on developing curriculum for severely handicapped students. In E. Sontag, J. Smith, and N. Certo (Eds.), *Educational programming for the severely and profoundly handicapped.* Reston, Va.: Division of Mental Retardation of the Council for Exceptional Children, 1977.

Williams, W., and York, R. Developing instructional programs for severely handicapped students. In E. Haring and D. Bricker (Eds.), *Teaching the severely handicapped,* Vol. III. Seattle: American Association for the Education of the Severely/Profoundly Handicapped, 1978.

Wolfe, V.F., and Cuvo, A.J. Effects of within-stimulus and extra-stimulus prompting on letter discrimination by mentally retarded persons. *American Journal of Mental Deficiency,* 1978, *83,* 297-303.

Yoder, P., and Forehand, R. The effects of modeling and verbal cues upon concept acquisition of normal and retarded children. *American Journal of Mental Deficiency,* 1974, *78,* 566-570.

York, R., and Williams, W. Curricula and ongoing assessment for individualized programming in the classroom. In R. York, P. Thorpe, and R. Minisi (Eds.), *Education of severely/profoundly handicapped people.* Heightstown, N.J.: Northeast Regional Resource Center, 1977.

Zaporozhets, A.V. The development of perception in the preschool child. *Society for Research in Child Development: Monograph,* 1965, *30*(2), 82-101.

Zeaman, D., and House, B.J. The role of attention in retardate discrimination learning. In N.R. Ellis (Ed.), *Handbook of mental deficiency.* New York: McGraw-Hill, 1963.

Zimmerman, B.J., and Jaffe, A. Teaching through demonstration:

The effects of structuring, imitation, and age. *Journal of Educational Psychology,* 1977, *69,* 773-778.

Zimmerman, B.J., and Rosenthal, T.L. Observational learning of rule-governed behavior by children. *Psychological Bulletin,* 1974, *81,* 29-42.

Index